NAZI

TERRORIST

THE STORY OF NATIONAL ACTION

MATTHEW COLLINS

GW00601044

First published by HOPE not hate in Great Britain in 2019.

This edition printed and published in Great Britain by HOPE not hate LTD, PO Box 61382, London N19 9EQ

ISBN: 978-1-9993205-2-2

About the author:

Matthew Collins is widely regarded as one of Britain's leading experts on the far-right. Matthew is a regular contributor on television, radio and in newspaper.

The BBC has produced two documentaries about Matthew's life. 'Life Etc' in 2002 and 'Dead Man Walking' in 2004. He is also the author of the book 'Hate: My Life in The British Far Right' published by Biteback in 2011.

"There is nobody else who could or should tell this extraordinary story. With considerable wit and aplomb, Matthew Collins exposes the sheer madness and hatred of National Action's obsession with death and violence."

Kevin Maguire, *Daily Mirror*

"A startling insight into the Nazi death cult that was National Action."

Lizzie Dearden, *The Independent*

"Told in captivating, granular detail, Collins brilliantly draws the moronic, hate-filled figures who wanted to derail democracy. Anyone keen to understand the drivers of the modern far right should get this. A riveting, rollicking read."

Mark Townsend, *The Observer*

"An MP and a cop are still alive because of HOPE not hate. This extraordinary book tells how they infiltrated National Action and stopped the murder of an MP. It›s an astonishing and disturbing read that explores and exposes the wanton sickness of the new breed of Britain's neo-Nazi terrorists."

Steve Moore, *Sunday World*

"*Nazi Terrorist* is a work of painstaking patience, nerves and bravery. Society owes Matthew Collins and Robbie Mullen a huge debt of gratitude. Without them National Action would have enacted its unthinkable sickness on innocent members of society."

John Ward, *Daily Star on Sunday*

"Once more Collins delivers a timely warning that fascists and Nazis will stop at nothing. Be grateful that he and Nick Lowles met Robbie Mullen when they did."

Brian Whelan, *Joe.co.uk*

CONTENTS

ACKNOWLEDGEMENTS

This book was written quickly and urgently over long days and nights once the trial of three more suspected National Action members had ended in April 2019. Some occurrences, information, names and characters have been omitted due to ongoing investigations and prosecutions of other alleged National Action members.

Any spelling or grammar errors will be my own, but somebody else will get the blame for not spotting them.

Writing and publication would not have been possible without the expert planning, encouragement and patience of Nick Lowles, Jemma Levene, and Matthew McGregor at HOPE not hate.

A debt of gratitude for his patience must also go to its editor, Tim Lezard, and to Nick Ryan.

As always the case with a book that relies heavily on the bravery of a number of people in difficult environments and circumstances, it isn't possible to thank publicly many people who provided help and information from within the far right.

In particular I would like to personally thank the 'A' & 'B' teams, 'bagmen' and 'bagwomen' who work and volunteer diligently for HOPE not hate, ensuring we are constantly abreast of the ongoing machinations of the far-right and able and competent to react to them.

Individually I would like to thank Titus, Fid, Brenda, Maurice, Little Bear, John Goldstein, Duncan Cahill and Daniel De Simone for finding and researching the almost impossible.

To Billy Bragg for simple words of encouragement and the image of him clutching an Ivor Novello award whilst writing me kind words and to Horace Heaton Jnr, for the hours of necessary insanity.

I am also personally indebted to TUFAC for the hours of encouragement from Hamburg to Pisa via Genoa, Glasgow, Tolpuddle and back.

Robbie and I are hugely indebted to the extraordinary brilliance of Thompsons Solicitors. In particular to Steve Cavalier, Tom Jones and Vicky Phillips for their advice and generosity.

Finally, I would like to thank Robbie Mullen, personally. His bravery and his sense of decency, literally, saved people's lives. May he be blessed with a happy and rewarding future life.

FOREWORD: **KEVIN MAGUIRE**
ASSOCIATE EDITOR, DAILY MIRROR

L ate in 2017 a story broke about British neo-Nazis plotting to murder a Labour MP. The plan was thwarted when one of those present blew the whistle.

Experience told me that somewhere down the line would be HOPE not hate. For theirs is an impressive, if dangerous, operation. They don't brag (enough) about what they do. They do promise though, that no matter who or where it is, whichever dingy meeting of hatred or shuffling march of the moronic – no matter how big or small – someone, somewhere will be working among the racists and haters for HOPE not hate.

Throughout their court cases and appearances, Matthew Collins, Nick Lowles and Robbie Mullen remained calm under considerable pressure to ensure justice was served.

Life is rarely ordinary and neither must it be said are Collins and Lowles. Mullen had been a member of a terrorist organisation, after all. Under extraordinary stress and risk of prosecution, they refused to hand their man over until he was guaranteed immunity from prosecution. His actions saved the life of an MP.

For Collins and Lowles, it began a game of cat and mouse, holidays abandoned, secret flights out of the country, safe houses and secret codenames and words to protect their source. Names were changed, addresses were altered and even though the police had their man, Jack Renshaw, Collins and Lowles stuck to their principles and to the promise made to Mullen and everyone else who risks their lives helping them: "We will protect your identity, even if we face jail ourselves" In hectic, dangerous and unimaginable circumstances, Collins and Lowles functioned as if nothing at all was happening Even their colleagues at HOPE not hate knew nothing. I now realise just why and how they greyed so quickly.

It's only right this story should be told by Matthew Collins, but it's not just about Robbie Mullen and the murder plot. *Nazi Terrorist* tells the whole story of National Action. And nobody in this country, from the halls of academia to the crusty old pubs where Britain's fascists still meet to hatch their evil plots, has spent more time and energy investigating and humiliating them. His dedication to exposing violent Nazis and fascists has been spectacular, and personal.

His first book, '*Hate*', was published in 2011. It rather brazenly and candidly told his own story of similar scenarios and sadness, which Robbie Mullen now faces some twenty- five years later. Collins is the archetypal poacher turned gamekeeper and a writer of some expertise, wit and aplomb. In *Nazi Terrorist*, he's captured the sheer depths of madness, depravity and terror of the British far right as no other writer could. Now, in his life and work, Collins guards the fortunes, secrets and lives of men and women like Robbie Mullen every day.

I often imagine them all hunched in a dark room somewhere puffing on cigars and turning over another page in a ledger filled with spectacular success stories that, unlike the one laid out here, never see the light of day. Should you find them in a bar, anywhere from Budapest to Havana smoking a cigar, buy them a drink. They're doing more every day than you will (hopefully) ever need to know about.

London, 2019

PREFACE: WHY DO YOU COME HERE?

"The court heard that Renshaw has admitted plotting to attack a police officer because she was investigating him in relation to possible child grooming offences."

Warrington Guardian, 28th June 2018

A very posh lawyer and I would argue when, exactly, I received the message that something big was happening.

By the time I was being cross-examined in the Old Bailey, a year later, I wasn't sure it mattered any more. It was fact. A British neo-Nazi had admitted planning to murder his MP. Indeed, he was only days away from doing it.

Someone who was in the room when the killing plan was announced, texted me. I was on holiday. My break was ruined. I'd spend the remaining days abroad hanging by the telephone making hushed calls, answering questions and offering reassurances.

I no longer made phone calls without encryption. Even we, the old dogs of HOPE not hate, were being taught new tricks by the modern breed of Nazis we were monitoring. They were also hunting us and were sophisticated at hiding themselves. They bragged they were impenetrable. Only an act of gross stupidity on their own part could catch them out.

We were in the very guts of National Action, an outlawed organisation concerned with terrorism. If members were caught, they faced up to ten years' imprisonment.

We discovered not only had National Action members ignored a government ban; they'd upped their game, changing leaders and opening a gym exclusively for training members and supporters. They not only wanted a race war, they were preparing for one.

We blogged on our website, exposing titbits of information we'd uncovered about the group, making little hints and digs at them, letting them know we were still watching them.

But it wasn't until one of their most senior members came to us that we had our eyes fully opened to the scale of their operation and just how – no matter how experienced we were with dealing with the most hardline of neo-Nazis – these kids were deadly serious about terrorism.

They idolised terrorism for the sake of it. Academics had focused on their aesthetics, trying to find ideological justifications for their nonsense, playing into the hands of a small but sinister clique desperate to be feared as brilliant minds. They churned out dross after dross until even they tired of themselves. They became vulgar and 'brutes'.

Across the political spectrum from Timothy McVeigh and Anders Breivik to Jihadi John via the Provisional IRA and Khmer Rouge, National Action abandoned its own ideology to admire others, seeking to mimic the very best at doing the very worst.

Their degeneration terrified us. National Action members existed inside their own cult world, cut off from the rest of society, communicating only with each other where possible. They, themselves, often didn't know who they were talking to; only by their individual quirks and perversions would they learn the identities of people in their new, secret chat groups.

Like any group, National Action had its schisms and obtuse personalities, but more than any far-right organisation we'd come across, this motley crew of sad individuals egged each other on, driving their racial hatred and perversions to new levels. They were fascinated by pornography, beheadings and violence.

National Action operated under intense pressure and paranoia because members knew they faced up to ten years in prison if they were they caught still active, still recruiting. They no longer wanted simply to shock and offend little old ladies and *Daily Mail* readers. Left to their own devices, packaged away in darkness, racism, fascism and Nazism were no longer enough for them.

Although National Action attracted many young men through its bright graphics and a sense of danger, it explored ideas and ideals that went as far as embracing Satanism. Throughout NA's existence, both publicly and privately, rape and paedophilia were often seen as weapons to use on or against their enemies.

In Robbie Mullen we found an individual who was bright and fiercely independent but unable to extricate himself from National Action through fear and habit. Seeing inside NA through his eyes, we understood how difficult it was for him to leave.

From the moment we received his unsolicited email begging for help, he impressed upon us how urgent it was, how imminently National Action was preparing to unleash terrorism and violence. Mullen warned us that although we'd been close to understanding the real nature and truth about NA, we'd no idea how ready and desperate this group was to kill people. The clock was ticking down to murder.

Their outbreak of terror was to be the 'White Jihad'. More than fascism, or the usual drunkard's admiration of Hitler and the smashing of a few shop windows and spraying swastikas on walls, by the time Mullen came to us National Action was at the point of no return. It felt defeated, there was nothing left for its members to do but destroy themselves and those around them in the desperate hope others would follow suit and there'd be an almost apocalyptic ending of society.

The national outpouring of grief after Jo Cox was murdered in June 2016 excited National Action. A vile tweet, glorifying in her killing, led to the group being proscribed by the government.

The following year, like ghouls, National Action members travelled to Manchester Arena to watch people grieving after a jihadi suicide attack.

Death and terror had become their only obsessions. They wanted others to suffer in similar sadistic acts of their own doing. Their new leader wrote copiously about how he was a medieval king destined to rule a dystopian society.

Mullen contacted us because he'd wanted us to break them up, where the government and the police had failed. National Action obsessed over every sentence we wrote about them, so it seemed only natural that we should be the ones to bring them down. Mullen had realised all the violent things he'd heard from NA members were more than just words. He'd realised the bloody training they undertook in their gym and elsewhere was to prepare his comrades for murder.

It came to a head one evening in a Warrington pub in July 2017, when National Action's leader was told by one of their supporters he was going to kill the MP Rosie Cooper and, if he could, a woman police officer investigating him for grooming boys.

Mullen panicked, leaving the pub and texting me, alerting me to the impending bloodbath. I heard my phone beep, but I was in bed and ignored it.

I rang him back first thing the following morning. Armed with HOPE not hate's assurances and our personal fledgling friendship, our rescue plan swung into action. Nick Lowles made the relevant phone call to the authorities while I calmed down Mullen who was to say the least, anxious, terrified and confused.

But first things first, I asked. Who even was Rosie Cooper?

CHAPTER 1: **MORE IN COMMON**

"Batley and Spen is a gathering of typically independent, no-nonsense and proud Yorkshire towns and villages. Our communities have been deeply enhanced by immigration, be it of Irish Catholics across the constituency or of Muslims from Gujarat in India or from Pakistan, principally from Kashmir. While we celebrate our diversity, what surprises me time and time again as I travel around the constituency is that we are far more united and have far more in common with each other than things that divide us."

Jo Cox in her maiden speech to Parliament, June 3 2015

Thursday, June 16, 2016. The news broke with numbing shock. Gasps broke out in the halls of Westminster. Popular MP and mother of two young children, Jo Cox, had been shot in broad daylight.

Details were initially fuzzy – it wasn't clear if Cox would live or who her assailant was, but all too soon it was confirmed the MP for Batley and Spen, in West Yorkshire, a passionate advocate for refugee rights, had died.

***

Jo Cox died on the spot an hour after the attack, shot three times and stabbed a further 15 times by a man who screamed "Britain first!".

News of the attacker's words spread even before Cox's death was officially confirmed. Those words echoed the name of a far-right anti-Muslim organisation. They threw fuel on an already-raging fire of anger and venom drummed up during the country's increasingly bitter referendum debate, as the nation prepared to vote over whether to leave the European Union.

It wasn't long until the attacker's name was available. Locals identified him as Thomas 'Tommy' Mair, a 52-year-old from Birstall, a village six miles outside Leeds. Some even suggested that Mair, a loner, was most likely a Muslim convert.

An elderly man, Bernard Kenny, 77, was stabbed in the stomach as he tried to protect the MP. A year later he was awarded the George Cross, the UK's highest civilian medal, for his extraordinary bravery. Cox had pleaded with Kenny and her office staff to flee the attacker for their own safety.

"Get away you two! Let him hurt me. Don't let them hurt you!" she managed to cry out as she was being murdered.

Two months after being awarded the George Cross, Mr Kenny passed away at home aged 79.

Jo Cox was a bright and fiercely intelligent woman and, at 41, a young and enthusiastic MP. She was also the mother of two young children. Only the year before her murder she had entered Britain's most ethnically-diverse Parliament with its highest-ever number of female members. Her maiden speech on June 3 2015 has become one of the most famous of its kind.

Cox was an MP who cherished the modern, multicultural Britain. She revelled in and celebrated its diversity. She was described by Nick Lowles, the head of antifascist group HOPE not hate, in striking terms:

> *"A brilliant, vivacious woman.... a fierce and passionate campaigner for the dispossessed, the poor, and her constituents. She took a deep interest in issues such as Syria and its refugee crisis, forged by her long experience with Oxfam. A new Parliamentarian, she had so much to give."*

This made her, of course, everything the far right hated. Surely though, no-one from the depleted British fascist scene would kill a female MP in cold blood? But it was becoming clearer, as the story changed, that Thomas Mair – who had shouted "Britain first!" – had disturbing far-right sympathies.

And as those of us monitoring Britain's fascists had already begun to notice, there were those on the extreme right who were desperate to embark on a course of terror.

***

Arrested close to the scene of the Cox murder, Thomas Mair would describe himself as a "political activist". Appearing before magistrates in London two days after he murdered Cox, he shouted: "Death to traitors, freedom for Britain!" when asked to state his name. Some of the media claimed Cox's murder was evidence of a growing far-right movement in Britain. The EU referendum vote was due to take place in just over a week's time and although it was close, the Remain campaign appeared to be in the lead.

The campaigning was mired by deeply toxic anti-immigration sentiments and sniping by rival groups. Remainers, those who wanted Britain to stay in the European Union, were portrayed as an unpatriotic, cosmopolitan elite. Leavers were caricatured as ageing, right wing and, most damning of all, racist. Neither misrepresentation was particularly true. As the campaign became more and more poisonous, it was obvious – perhaps convenient for some – to believe much of the 'leave' sentiment was being controlled by people even further to the right of Britain's largest radical-right party, the United Kingdom Independence Party (UKIP), which had long campaigned for the country to leave the EU. It was during the campaign that UKIP had swung further right and increasingly championed anti-immigrant rhetoric.

Ramping up this rhetoric, its leader Nigel Farage infamously posed in front of a highly-inflammatory and controversial 'Breaking Point' poster, using an image of refugees taken nowhere near the UK to suggest the country was full up.

At times the hatred and the language felt so sinister it was as if politics in Britain was returning to a darker European age. The extreme far right had, in places, tagged themselves onto the mainstream leave campaigns, but in no way dominated it. And Farage himself had made clear that although in many people's eyes he may echo much of the far right's sentiments, he wanted them nowhere near the campaign or, apparently, needed them.

***

The far right's rhetoric has always held murderous intent. But the idea the increasing racism and hatred people were witnessing in 2016 was driven by existing British far-right groups, such as the moribund British National Party (BNP), the anti-Muslim thugs of Britain First, or the drug- and drink-fuelled louts from the English Defence League (EDL), was wholly wrong. All these were 'nasty' movements but the reality was that, numerically at least, the organised British far right was in massive decline by the time Jo Cox was so savagely killed.

The far right was in fact moving to a post-organisational state: there was nowhere for it to call home, and those with what might have once been termed "far-right views" didn't necessarily belong to a notable extremist party or movement. Empowered by social media, anti-Muslim bigotry and anti-immigrant prejudice were becoming increasingly mainstream and no longer the preserve of fringe parties. Certainly, there were plenty of well-known fascists and neo-Nazis on the streets campaigning for a Leave vote, but the racist sentiments and scaremongering pushed through the pages and websites of some mainstream media often came from the same outlets which had been so steadfast in their disapproval of the organised extreme right.

At the 2015 General Election when Jo Cox took her seat in Parliament, long-time British far-right parties such as veteran of the fascist scene, the National Front (NF), as well as the BNP, only managed to stand 15 candidates. A smattering of smaller race-hate groups also fronted a few candidates (including three loosely linked to the EDL). Yet the largest and most confrontational of the far-right organisations at the time, Britain First – which would rise to close to two million Facebook followers but had little more than 1,000 registered members – didn't even stand in the election. The BNP, which mixed anti-immigration, anti-Muslim and anti-EU sentiments with vociferous racism and conspiracy theories, had managed to muster 600 candidates at the 2010 General Election, and had won two European Parliamentary seats the year before.

All these groups had now been outflanked by the mainstream anti-EU (and increasingly anti-immigrant and anti-Muslim) UKIP, which was shortly to reach its zenith with the country's Brexit vote. The demise of the traditional far right was best exemplified in the example of the BNP's crushing decline and self-destruction following its 2010 electoral defeat, where it lost some 60 local council seats and failed to get anywhere near the two Parliamentary seats it had set its eyes on. Few of the near 15,000 members who would begin deserting the BNP as it imploded moved to other extreme far-right parties or groups. The BNP, the greatest far-right electoral party Britain ever had, simply fell into paralysis and disrepair and with it, so did the rest of the far right.

The majority of those who'd joined the BNP's ranks fell back into mainstream political discourse in a society that had notably shifted to the right on the issues that concerned them. The major beneficiary of their votes and support (around one million people based on the BNP's 2009 electoral returns) was UKIP who'd done a fine job in driving the more palatable language of the neo-Nazi BNP into the mainstream.

With the BNP's collapse, an active hardcore band of fascists and neo-Nazis was left ideologically and politically homeless. The electoral process had proven, in their eyes, to be 'corrupt'. The rise of the violent and lawless anti-Muslim street gang, the EDL, which formed under the BNP's nose in 2009, had also eaten into the party's moral and ideological discipline. The post-2010 collapse was swift, and the overall impression of what remained of Britain's far right was a drunken, racist, drug-fuelled, shambolic mess.

Although the noisy and social media savvy Britain First was to emerge from this mess, along with what was to become a tiny hardline neo-Nazi group, National Action, neither were serious exponents of the electoral path. The National Front – which did stand at elections – was immersed in drug and criminal culture, an obscure and disorganised shadow of its former self.

Conspiratorial and emasculated, British fascism was in retreat awaiting for what its adherents believed would be an inevitable race/civil war. The electoral experiment had proved fruitless and in vain. There was no evidence the far right was growing in electoral popularity, merely evidence it was angry.

By the time Griffin lost his seat in the 2014 European elections he'd already begun advocating British fascists who were serious should leave Britain and join him and others in central and eastern Europe where the conditions – racial, religious and political – offered a more preferable climate. Further electioneering in Britain was pointless. Agitation was the only way forward.

Griffin himself had one foot out of the UK by the time Jo Cox was murdered, and was active inside Hungary along with Britain First's founder, Jim Dowson, until they were both humiliatingly expelled in 2017. It was these shrinking electoral opportunities and the overall far-right movement's shrinking size, as well as changes taking place in modern Britain, that made fascists more dangerous by June 2016.

The difficulty, however, was engaging with others to help them understand fascists were more dangerous due to their growing electoral and cultural irrelevance and not because, as they were perceived by some, to be growing in hugely organised numbers.

Deeply suspicious and ideologically-driven people, fascists preferred their lives and views to have a more cult and fringe-of-society appeal than they did any electoral respectabilities. They took very little delight in the growth of UKIP or the mainstreaming of some of their own language and actions. They never envisaged or wished to take power in Britain lawfully by the use of the ballot box. As history dictated, they predicted their assent to power coming in the bloody ruins of a war-torn Britain and not behind the overbite of Nigel Farage and his smattering of brown- or black-faced collaborators.

As the Brexit referendum proved, and the British far right already knew, fascists in Britain First no longer held the sole domain on outright racism. The racism of eugenics and the faux science and conspiracy that drove and gave them purpose were still a mad affront to people panicked into the arms of UKIP by economic and cultural insecurity.

Britain First, which was being run by former BNP members, reacted angrily to the suggestion that murderer Thomas Mair was one of its number because he had shouted "Britain First!". In a video posted on the group's Facebook page its combative leader Paul Golding stated:

"We had nothing to do with it [Cox's murder], we would not condone actions like that. We carry out protests and we stand in elections – I recently stood in a London election and received over 100,000 votes – so that's the kind of political activities that we carry out.

"Yes we do direct actions sometimes, we invaded a Halal slaughterhouse because we disagree with halal slaughter, but this kind of thing is disgusting. it's an outrage.

"I hope the person who carried out this heinous crime will get what he deserves."

The problem for Golding, as HOPE not hate pointed out, was the weekend before Cox's murder his group held a training camp in Wales where members practised using fake knives. And only a month before the murder Golding issued a statement claiming Britain First was going to target elected Muslim officials. The language he used was anything but that of a political party:

"Our intelligence led operations will focus on every aspect of their day to day lives and official functions, including where they live, work and pray and so on."

***

As far as many in the far right were concerned, Jo Cox may as well have been a Muslim. Pictures spread very quickly of her on her 2015 election night standing with Muslim members of her campaign team, with her head covered: crime enough for the Muslim-haters who already viewed the Labour Party as hand-in-hand with a plot enabling Muslims to Islamicise the UK.

The upwardly-mobile Jo Cox, with her houseboat in London, was a prime hate figure for the likes of Britain First, with its anti-Muslim, anti-Labour agenda.

But was Mair a member of Britain First? In an age when memberships of far right political parties were low but viewership of their wider social media groups and pages was high, all Britain First had to do was throw its membership lists open to prove he wasn't a paid-up member. They refused. There was little else to signify he'd belonged to an extremist organisation.

Wading through scores of old, tea-stained membership lists was also fruitless. The National Front's West Yorkshire membership lists were rumoured to have been sold to a national newspaper on the hunt for a paedophile in 2015, but there wasn't anything of use coming out from Fleet Street either. The national and international news media camped out in Birstall, outstaying their welcome, while journalists door-knocked old hands from the far right. One Fleet Street reporter even found herself sitting in the living room of an ageing neo-Nazi from West Yorkshire, surrounded by piles of old membership lists at his feet, drinking tea and admiring the hundreds of watercolours he had painted of Adolf Hitler. He was profusely apologetic, but said he had nothing with Mair's name on it. It was as if he felt ashamed.

Trophy hunters and 'slacktivists' trawled the internet looking for photographs of Mair taking part in any far right demonstrations. One image that immediately did the rounds was of a man looking not too dissimilar to Mair holding a Britain First banner at a demo in Dewsbury, West Yorkshire, earlier that year. In fact, it wasn't Mair, but the picture still persists and the man in the photo has never come forward to clear himself.

US civil rights group the Southern Poverty Law Centre (SPLC) was the first to give a concrete insight and evidence into Mair's political history and beliefs. In 1999 Mair had purchased a booklet from the National Alliance, the world's leading neo-Nazi organisation at that time. He also bought a manual that included instructions on how to build a pistol, sending just over $620 to the National Alliance. According to invoices for goods purchased from National Vanguard Books, the Alliance's publishing imprint, Mair also bought works that instructed readers on the *Chemistry of Powder & Explosives, Incendiaries,* and a work called *Improvised Munitions Handbook.* Under "Section III, No. 9" (page 125) of that handbook, there were detailed instructions for constructing a "Pipe Pistol For .38 Caliber Ammunition" from components that could be purchased from nearly any hardware store.

In the pre-internet era, the National Alliance cornered the market in international race-hate, conspiracy theory and far-right terrorism, delivering large brown envelopes full of its materials around the world. The far right in Britain were, and still are, massive admirers of National Alliance's work, much of which was (and is) illegal in Britain and much of which appeared on the BNP's reading lists and bookshelves. National Alliance leader Professor William Pierce was a poor but prolific writer who penned the seminal (for the far-right world) white supremacist novel, *The Turner Diaries*, in 1978. The novel told the story of an American blue-collar worker, Earl Turner, who joined a band of terrorists and assassins to 'take back' America. The book is full of what have become modern conspiracy theories about government control and secret ruling societies. Absolutely everyone the far right hates is put to the sword in the novel: gays, blacks and Jews.

This message has withstood the test of time in its importance to race haters. The reader is given a series of instructions about the apparent inevitability of a worldwide race war later this century and, rather helpfully, how to fight it. The book has inspired far-right terrorists and murderers around the world, most notably, Timothy McVeigh, the Oklahoma City bomber in the United States, whose bomb outside a federal building in 1995 killed 168 people, including 19 children. McVeigh's bombing mirrored almost exactly a similar atrocity described in the book.

As well as graphic passages depicting the torture and violence used by white supremacists, the book (and its follow up, *Hunter*) is disturbingly misogynistic, reducing and encouraging women to be viewed as little more than worthless, silent, sexual objects. In particular, the idea of the sexually liberated or confident 'liberal' woman is scorned and dehumanised. Some parts of Pierce's writing actually question whether women are deserving of sexual pleasure. His writing dehumanises women to such an extent that such parables as "never hurt a woman" don't appear to apply any more.

During the 1990s, groups in the UK attached to the BNP and a terror-aligned offspring, Combat 18, as well as the National Alliance-inspired National Socialist Alliance (NSA) – that acted as an umbrella for Combat 18 – set up book clubs to distribute Pierce's materials. David Copeland, a British neo-Nazi who murdered three people (including a pregnant woman) and injured scores more in three race-inspired nail-bomb attacks in London in 1999, had also read the book. Copeland was linked to both the NSA and the BNP. In his statement to police, he said:

> *"If you've read the Turner Diaries, you know there'll be an uprising, racial violence on the streets. My aim was political – to cause a racial war in this country."*

In Germany, a murderous neo-Nazi outfit called the National Socialist Underground (NSU) – which murdered 10 people, carried out two bombings and several robberies during the 2000s – used the book and took inspiration from the US neo-Nazi idea of 'leaderless resistance' (forming autonomous cells rather than hierarchical groups) – to format a cell structure. The German translation of Pierce's book, *Turner Tagebücher*, has been banned in Germany since 2006. Here in the UK, *The Turner Diaries* was also extensively read by members of an emerging British neo-Nazi group, National Action.

***

Jo Cox's death led to a national outpouring of grief. She was lauded with platitudes from across the mainstream political spectrum. For just a brief moment, Britain began to question whether the incredibly toxic and inflammatory nature of the Brexit debate had contributed to her death. It felt as if the confirmation Mair was driven by the obscene hatred of the far right and not the growing mainstream discourse of anti-Muslim hatred, xenophobia and conspiracy theory, was also, for some, a relief. To the far right, news that one of their own limited numbers – someone driven by their ideology and not the 'vulgarities' of something so simple as fiscal and economic insecurity – had been a rather pleasant surprise.

The murder of Cox also allowed a brief examination of the lives of other women MPs in Britain targeted daily by hatred. Black Labour MP Diane Abbott pointed to years of horrendous racist abuse delivered to her offices daily both by post and social media. Much of it focused on her colour but never without mention of her gender. Scottish National Party (SNP) MP Mhairi Black who, like Jo Cox, was elected in 2015, received thousands of hate messages. The Jewish Labour MP for Wavertree in Liverpool, Luciana Berger, had also been one of the most high profile targets of misogynistic, racist and anti-Semitic abuse since entering Parliament in 2010.

In October 2014, Berger received more than 400 abusive messages on Twitter during a single week. Many carried hashtags and images created by an American website with more than 10,000 UK visitors per day, urging trolls to join "Operation: Filthy Jew Bitch".

Even in death, Cox wouldn't be spared by the far right who felt and showed no apparent shame or remorse for her death. Nick Griffin, former MEP and former leader of the BNP, endorsed a statement that Cox had been the victim of her love for multiculturalism. He would go even further, describing Cox as having "blood on her hands" for her support of humanitarian work in Syria, a country that reportedly funded Griffin to carry out propaganda on the regime's behalf.

The South East Alliance (SEA), a violent splinter of the EDL, which sat in coalition with the National Front, described Cox as a "dirty bitch" and wished it had been a Muslim that killed her. "Now, that would be ironic," they wrote.

The EDL leadership claimed Cox had been stabbed in a domestic dispute and that people campaigning for a Remain vote in the referendum were simply using it as an excuse to build support.

Aside from the dehumanising of Cox, the far right convinced itself there was an inevitability and justification to her murder. Race war was both inevitable, desirable and imminent. For the far right in Britain, it has been so since the Empire Windrush, bringing Caribbean workers to the UK, docked in Essex in June 1948, beginning (as they saw it) mass and irreversible immigration.

Cox was denigrated in their terms and language, becoming a simple collaborator to a process constructed by 'Zionists' [Jews] to extinguish the white race and replace it with further collaborators or converts to Islam.

And straight after her murder, National Action took a step into infamy by celebrating Cox's murder, using Mair's statement "Death to Traitors, Freedom for Britain" as a recruitment tool. Although that drew swift condemnation from even seasoned British fascists, the campaign to dehumanise and vilify Cox began almost immediately it was clear 'one of their own' had murdered her.

The media satisfied itself Thomas Mair was a mentally ill loner living in his grandmother's old house, surrounded by obscure books, thoughts and ornaments. Sad, mad, lonely Thomas Mair was a ticking bomb waiting to go off, anyway. So the stories inevitably went. That and the reported story he faced homelessness because his home was earmarked to be given over to asylum seekers.

The media also satisfied itself Mair's actions were part of a rise of the far right in Britain but not that embedded in the same British far right were dark desires inspired long before Brexit. Mair wasn't the first or even the most murderous far-right terrorist Britain had produced.

West Yorkshire, where he lived, was pivotal to the 1990s book clubs set up by Combat 18 and its adherents, who believed the politicising of the BNP at the time was an affront to their revolutionary beliefs.

It's also where the Redwatch website is still administered, targeting those the British far right didn't approve of, publishing their photos and addresses. It's where manuals of American white supremacist Louis Beam's writings on terrorism and 'leaderless resistance' were copied and posted out along with copies of *The Turner Diaries*, and where people met to discuss and plan race war.

Mair had lived all of his life in a house only a few streets away from Terence Gavan, a BNP member who spent a decade building up a cache of weapons in a bedroom hideaway. Gavan began his collection the same year Mair wrote to the National Alliance in the United States to order manuals on homemade bombs and weapons. Gavan was jailed for 11 years in 2010. A bus driver, he manufactured highly dangerous firearms and explosives at the home where he lived with his mother in Batley. These included 54 improvised bombs including nail bombs and a booby-trapped cigarette packet, as well as 12 homemade firearms.

In 2008, Martyn Gilleard, part of the gang behind Redwatch, was jailed at Leeds Crown Court. Gilleard, then 31, intended to cause "havoc" with explosive devices he'd made at home and hid under his five-year-old son's bed. Gilleard intended to target Muslims, black and Jewish people with the bombs. He was found guilty of terrorist offences and of possessing some of the most extreme child pornography police had ever witnessed. He made four nail bombs each capable of causing an explosion similar to that of a hand grenade. In their investigations, police also found an armoury of gun powder, fuses, live bullets, swords, axes, knives and a bayonet along with internet material on how to poison people. He had kept notes, including one in which he wrote: "Be under no illusion, we are at war. And it is a war we are losing badly."

As long ago as 2009, then-Assistant Commissioner in the Metropolitan Police, John Yates, said there'd been an increase in right-wing activity drawing resources away from the threat from Islamic terrorism:

> "Mostly they tend to be less organised, you tend to see the concept of the lone wolf. There have been several manifestations of that in past months and several arrests. That is something we take extremely seriously and we make sure we balance our resources to deal with that threat."

In raids in West Yorkshire, according to the *Daily Telegraph* in 2009, police found rocket launchers, pipe bombs and dozens of firearms said to be prepared for a right-wing campaign of violence.

Mair was sentenced to a whole life sentence at the Old Bailey in November 2016, refusing to speak or to either justify or defend himself. A final statement was denied to him by a judge frustrated by his silence.

It's doubtful any words would have offered any comfort to anybody. Far right terrorism was now upon us.

CHAPTER 2: THE BIRTH OF A TERRORIST

"National Action is a racist, anti-Semitic and homophobic organisation which stirs up hatred, glorifies violence and promotes a vile ideology, and I will not stand for it."

Home Secretary Amber Rudd, in announcing the ban on National Action, December 2016

On December 12 2016, Home Secretary Amber Rudd laid an order in Parliament banning an already notorious neo-Nazi youth group called National Action (NA).

It would be the first far-right organisation to be proscribed in the UK since the Second World War. The group would have five days – until December 16 – to desist and disband.

The announcement didn't come as a shock to those who had their ear to the ground in Westminster. Since the murder of the Yorkshire MP Jo Cox earlier that year, it was inevitable at least one far-right extremist group would be banned. Interested parties in the media received a couple of hours' notice of the official announcement.

The Home Office had toyed with the idea of banning the group in the immediate aftermath of the murder of Jo Cox but held off acting then. The decision was ratified before Cox's murderer, Thomas Mair, was sentenced to a full life sentence in November.

Mair wasn't a member of National Action, a tiny organisation of neo-Nazis making headlines for holding training camps where its members trained in preparation of a race war. NA had a strong vein of anti-Semitism and viewed itself as the "elite" of the fractured and increasingly internecine neo-Nazi world in Britain. It had no connections to the murderer Mair. Investigations into which organisations he associated or engaged with had drawn a relative blank. Indeed, so obscure and isolated was Mair that although he accessed the internet at his local library, he's believed to have not once sent a simple text message. A handful of neatly-written letters he sent to obscure pro-apartheid groups in the 1990s, and the purchase of bomb-making instructions and other literature from the United States during the same period, offered no real clues or help.

National Action was notified of its impending ban the week before the Home Secretary's announcement, receiving a formal but polite email instructing it of the best way to comply with the order and avoid criminal proceedings. Despite intense pressure and suggestion, another active far-right group in the UK, Britain First, survived a similar proscription order by the skin of its teeth. It was NA, though, that would pay the price not just for Cox's murder, but for the horrendous way in which it celebrated it.

In her statement to Parliament, Rudd said National Action was "a racist, anti-Semitic and homophobic organisation", making it a criminal offence to join or support it. The Home Secretary used a provision made under the Terrorism Act 2000 that allows the proscription of an organisation if it's believed to be "concerned in terrorism". Ms Rudd said the group had "no place" in Britain.

Penalties for proscription offences carried up to a maximum of ten years in prison and an unlimited fine. National Action was already unlike any other far-right group in Britain. It delighted in deliberately unsettling and offending people, revelling in the very idea of infamy from its inception in February 2013. Some, even on the far right, found it a moronic group, surmising that due to its often ridiculous behaviour it was either set up by, or at least infiltrated by, the security services.

It was at times so childishly cruel and crude that it *had* to be a design of the state, conjured up in a dark room somewhere to put people off engaging in the otherwise serious business of Nazism and fascism. Time and evidence would prove this was woefully not the truth behind the organisation and though it suffered the indignity at times of being treated like a public order nuisance, its descent into terrorism went almost completely unchecked.

Whether this descent was something its leaders had actually planned, desired or anticipated is unclear, and so probably unanswerable. For those of us tasked with monitoring the group from the first moment it burst into view, it seemed brilliantly choreographed and inevitable that National Action would fulfil what some inside the organisation thought was a merely accidental or coincidental prophecy. It had bragged about being neo-Nazi, carrying out "demonstrations, publicity stunts and other activities" to promote National Socialism. It would eventually grow from a rather noisy but pathetic protest group demonstrating outside an Indian restaurant in Coventry to study, encourage and champion terrorism and terrorists.

In its three years National Action gradually widened its parameters of homage to just about every knife-wielding, bomb-planting terror group, secret cell, genocidal dictator or murderous lone individual around the world. Most notoriously, as it would play out for them and the British public, it had championed Thomas Mair and adopted him as a "mascot" after his murder of Jo Cox. It also venerated 'Jihadi John', the London-born Islamist who joined Islamic State and found worldwide infamy by beheading prisoners and hostages. Such veneration even inspired National Action unlike any other far right group to cross more than one Rubicon. The more they were barbaric,

Marxist, Maoist, anarchist and Islamist terrorists were venerated by the group, and members were actively encouraged to learn more about their actions. By the time NA was banned, it had even advanced and expanded a bastardised version of jihad which the group named 'White Jihad'.

***

National Action had wanted to turn everything people knew, feared and hated about the far right on its head. The 'movement', the collective groups and individuals who shared similar ideology, was exhausted. In the case of groups such as the EDL and Britain First, dominated by UKIP types, it also looked shabby, disorganised and ideologically weak. In their early planning discussions, NA's founders believed – and planned – they could simply impose their will and methodology over the entire British far right. They recorded themselves picking and choosing who in the far right they could find and use, as well as those they liked (or didn't) and who'd failed to live up to their own as-yet-unexecuted expectations.

In listening back to the podcasts and Skype conversations of National Action's very early days it was obvious there was something very juvenile about the group's two founders, Ben Raymond and Alex Davies. They were vulgar and self-important boys, immature, and full of impatient and desperate vanity, wanting the world to change at their command.

From a bedsit in Bognor Regis, on the south coast of England, former student Raymond was a self-obsessed pseudo-intellectual, infatuated with ideology and obscure ideas. He'd never been a member of a proper political party or even a serious far-right grouping. He had a social awkwardness that he'd convinced himself was the result of undiagnosed autism, a condition throughout his time in National Action he'd refer to and encourage others to suspect he suffered from. Rather than engaging with others away from his computer, Raymond spent years of isolation on the internet. He'd spent a short time in the New British Union (NBU), a rabidly unpleasant and but comical dressing-up group established in appreciation of war-time British fascist leader Oswald Mosley. The NBU was a tiny organisation pretending to be active offline, when in reality it did little more than convince others that its leader, former BNP and Britain First member Garry Raikes, had suffered a very serious nervous breakdown.

During one particular period of loneliness Raymond set up his own political party, the Integralist Party, based on nineteenth Century French far right movement Action Française. Established in 1899, Action Française was a nationalist reaction to the influence of left-wing intellectuals and opposed the secularist, republican legacy of the French Revolution. Raymond also produced a magazine, *Attack*, at his own expense, where he pontificated about all that was wrong with a movement he played no part in and had as yet paid no notice to him:

"Integralists therefore operate on two fronts; to wage a war of intellectual counter terror against the political class, and to promote cultural vitalism to strengthen the population. It marks a historic turning point in the politics of the radical right, breaking from the failed traditions of the contemporary radical right, we are resolved to found our new creed of Integralism, offering not only a new form of ideological strength, vigour, and identity, but a new form of organisation."

From the outset of his time both on the outside and then on the inside of the far right, Raymond wrote and talked about dismantling everything and everyone before him. He believed a new man and a new movement could become apparent. He wrote in *Attack*:

"What we need is a fresh start with a new movement, one that knows what it is and is conscious of its mission and the ideals on which it is based. What we need is a movement that is young and ambitious, that is actively thinking about Britain's national revival and working in the now for that end, that has genuine ambitions of power."

Raymond was at least consistent in being comically immature. Issue after issue of *Attack* went unread as he reproduced the same demands. In 2012 he took himself off on a short trip to the United States. It was a period that persuaded him he had to redress his friendless, orphaned hours online arguing in internet forums with extremists from across the political spectrum. Addicted to the internet late at night and sleeping through most days, the self-declared double-glazing salesman (who in reality had only ever had a very short career working in a Job Centre) seemed to favour arguing with anarchists in the US and South America.

Raymond was obsessed by far left anti-Semitism and radicalism, studiously recording passages and phrases, as he had with fascists, to bastardise into texts he could use in his own work. Often these new wordings would contradict themselves, but Raymond consoled himself that at least he was making an intellectual effort at a time when the British far right was led by the moronic street thugs of the EDL and Britain First and, worse still, the horrendous UKIP. He was also a dab hand at graphics and design, a talent like writing that had deserted the movement.

Having finally made the bold decision to involve himself with others, he hoped, when his time eventually came, his new gang of intellectual hooligans – when it materialised – would mimic leftism and appear fashionable to younger people. He was smart enough to realise he also needed lots of lofty pictures and images to appeal to this demographic. Aged 23 at the time, Raymond wanted to be leader of a youth movement that would hold his intellect in high regard.

During 2012, Raymond was joined by another young man, Alex Davies, then by a former British National Party (BNP) youth leader, Daniel Lake (they 'comically' used the name of the rock band, Emerson, Lake and Palmer). The three were united by a demand for a rapid return to radicalism inside the British far right, to replace the debilitating and humiliating electoral ambitions of the fascists in the BNP and set the far right back on a radical path of believing in the confrontational and intellectual approach towards a new era of fascism.

Lake and Davies had both been members of the BNP and both had quit in impatience and frustration at what they saw as its stifling abandonment of radicalism. Davies had first engaged with Raymond during one of his late night fishing trips on the web for enemies and soulmates. Raymond was attracted to Davies in turn because he seemed bright and outgoing. He particularly liked that Davies was argumentative and bolshy, though he also confided in others he felt Davies could be intellectually lazy.

While in the BNP, Davies ran aground with a reputation for argumentativeness. Maybe it was living in Swansea, maybe it was something out of his control, but he was frustrated that he'd never favourably caught the eye of the party's scouts or been brought to the attention of the leadership. Older hands in his local branch compared him most unfavourably to the argumentative and childish character 'Rick' from the cult 1980s comedy about student life, *The Young Ones*.

Even the moderators of the BNP's Facebook page mocked Davies for his puritanical petulance and for trying to inflame debates with members already struggling with the party's collapse, its struggles with the EDL and its debilitating exodus of members. Davies tried to argue to counter both the EDL and the rise of Britain's radical-right anti-EU and anti-immigrant political party, UKIP, the BNP and its then-leader Nick Griffin had to return to its radical roots. But Griffin, now in his fifties as the party's fortunes began to nosedive, had moderated his life-defining radicalism and extremism to make the BNP *almost* respectable. He showed little interest in budging from a profitable and louche life as an MEP in Brussels. He knew the party's time was almost up from the moment he was elected to the European Parliament in 2009. He detected the entire British establishment throwing every facet of its weight against him. One of those facets Griffin was certain was being used against him and the party was UKIP.

Davies, like Raymond, also admired and looked for help to the self-defined and marginalised "intellectuals" of the British far right, many of whom had gathered for years in London pubs to pontificate the future direction of their movement. The focal point for these discussions was the New Right group, once led by former BNP officer Jonathan Bowden and Troy Southgate, a man who had been deeply influenced by Nick Griffin's radicalism during the National Front's self-destructive period in the 1980s (when Griffin had been one of the NF's leading figures). Southgate convened the New Right in 2005, having trawled through various far-right fringe groups for his inspiration, including the International Third Position, Brown Anarchism and National Bolshevism. They were joined in organising their meetings by Jeremy Bedford-Turner, a former violent National Front activist who went on to be an officer in the Royal Corps of Signals, becoming fluent in Pashtun and other tribal Afghan languages. Southgate and Bedford-Turner were eventually to fall out and Bowden was to die a short time later after being found naked outside his home reciting poetry and swinging a samurai sword. Bedford-Turner then turned to a man called Larry Nunn to help with running forums. A Northamptonshire-based financial adviser and former BNP organiser, Nunn launched an online discussion group, Western Springs, and various other forums. Together with one of the far right's most prominent 'intellectual' groups, the Traditional Britain Group, they together became a cultural hothouse for race-haters, fantasists, political adventurists and other fascist riff-raff that felt intellectually and culturally superior to Nick Griffin and the 'moderate' BNP.

Raymond and Davies hoped one day they'd find their seats among these men, the intellectual powerhouses (as they saw it) of the British far-right scene. Raymond wrote flowery descriptions of his political desires:

"Only a movement of strength lives in appreciation for the task of survival and the victory that will come. "Only when you establish a power relationship with your enemies do you exist in a state of struggle and have any bargaining power…Our people don't think emotionally or spiritually in that way, for us, strategy is a matter of constitution, of numbers, opportunities, and most of all strength, in relation to the adversary – what I propose is coming to the game with agame [sic] plan to inspire the confidence we need."

Raymond would also bemoan the lack of an officer class, to lead his proposed army. Not one for fighting – he shied away from the readiness of fists – Raymond looked to enter the fray at the very top. He and Davies looked in particular to the London Forum because it was seeking a new direction for British fascism. The London Forum was an outlet for the frustrated intellectual who was finding their intelligence smothered by a search for respectability at the ballot box and the mind-numbing island mentality that had so attracted white van man and UKIP types into the BNP.

Unlike so many other bodies the two saw thrashing around pointlessly and at the point of death, the London Forum and its tiny collection of bespectacled Holocaust-deniers and thoroughbred Nazis were the only certainty for inspiration and possible funding for a new group that shared their disillusionment and horror at the condition of Britain's fascists and neo-Nazis.

Raymond and Davies agreed that for a new movement to succeed, the old nationalist establishment had to be destroyed together with the horrendous UKIP types that dominated far-right street movements. The two divided the fractured British far right into 'good' and 'bad' camps. Davies breathlessly chirped of Nunn: "He's got the money, he's got the vision, he's got the ideas."

By the time Raymond and Davies decided to form National Action late in the year, Raymond's idealism would switch to draw heavily on the National Renaissance Party, a fascist party in the US that enjoyed 30 turbulent and violent years until 1980. It also leaned heavily on another of Raymond's obsessions, a Canadian called Sebastian Ernst Ronin, uncharitably described by one detractor as "a Canadian who advocates a hybrid peak oil/white nationalism philosophy that seems to always attract interest from angry people, but never do much of anything."

***

From the beginning, the young men that were to become National Action's leaders demanded they be the centre of attention in terms of content, activity and style, beginning with NA but then across the entire far right in Britain. NA was to encompass all of their prejudices and to espouse not just their hatreds of the modern world and society, but also their frustration that even in marginalised politics their early contributions, that seemed so vast to themselves in their bedrooms, had been ignored.

Being ignored and belittled by the sort of trash Davies felt had filled the ranks of the BNP in Swansea and Carmarthen hurt him the most. His mother had always referred to him as her "darling boy" and saw him as some kind of genius. His siblings, too, looked up to and after him, but it appears his parents' divorce had hit him hard. His mother was now working at a motorway services and it's possible there had been some kind of fall from comfortable middle class, social grace.

Davies desperately wanted National Action to be an all-out assault on the left. Davies in particular had flirted with leftism as a source of radicalism at Queen Elizabeth School and later Gower College in Swansea. People recall him having a rather squeaky voice, always on the fringe of conversations or social groups.

A former schoolmate told me: "I think Alex's home life may have been hectic. If I recall, he seemed to live with both his mother and step father and I think, his grandparents. He seemed to always be in search of excitement. He was desperately needy."

Like Raymond, Davies had developed an almost divine confidence in his own brilliance. Like many others that fall into the right, he would view the left as some kind of competing social club he'd bitterly been denied membership of.

In an interview with an American Holocaust denial website in 2014, Davies spoke of the need for witty cartoons, humour and a distinctive style and clothing to attract everyone from "goths, skins and punks".

But in the early days their main desire was to sweep away the likes of Nick Griffin and Andrew Brons, the BNP's two warring MEPs and veterans of the British far-right scene, who had almost come to blows during an argument in the European Parliament as their party collapsed around them.

Griffin was their number one target. The downward trajectory of the BNP had been a traumatic experience for many young people, like Davies, who'd joined an exciting organisation that uttered loudly politically incorrect thoughts. His relative youth and the fact he'd missed the BNP boat in terms of the relatively popular support and revulsion that symbolised the growth of the modern party under Griffin, was a further frustration for Davies. Like many other young members, Griffin's apparent surrender to the inevitability of the party's collapse and his failure to radicalise its remnant was a bitter disappointment. The party's youth wing, The Young BNP (YBNP), had been promised they'd inherit the party from Griffin. By 2012 it was apparent there'd be little left for them to take over whenever Griffin would eventually relinquish control of the party to them.

Just reforming and building the BNP into an electoral concern had been Nick Griffin's life-defining and Herculean masterstroke. His previous political efforts in the 1980s, as leader of a 'radical' faction of the National Front, once our most prominent far-right movement, had led it from obscurity into oblivion. After destroying much of the NF, Griffin decided to try his luck in the BNP during the early 1990s. The party, steeped in Nazis and filled with former NF members, was understandably wary of him. He was viewed as too intellectual, almost too cosmopolitan, for a party that was formed in 1982 to be even more openly Nazi, even more thuggish and confrontational than the NF.

The BNP had also already created a tremor of its own without Griffin with the election of one of its activists, Derek Beackon, to Tower Hamlets Council in 1993. The party's leadership viewed it as proof that a campaign of violence – literally grabbing voters by the scruff of the neck – worked. Griffin had gone to the BNP believing it was misreading the signs of a wind of change.

Yet, as he infamously wrote while ingratiating himself to the party:

"The electors of Millwall did not back a postmodernist Rightist Party, but what they perceived to be a strong, disciplined organisation with the ability to back up its slogan "Defend Rights for Whites' with well-directed boots and fists. When the crunch comes, power is the product of force and will, not of rational debate."

But Griffin was master of political camouflage. He believed the modern British fascist should be all things, especially racist and anti-Semitic, but also radically respectable when necessary.

His arguments worked and Griffin took over the BNP in 1999, turning it into a far-right party the likes of which had never been seen, even during the National Front's heyday in the 1970s.

As he later led the BNP into decline, Griffin would complain everything precious about nationalism was gradually being swallowed up and spat out by the wild and unhindered degeneracy of the EDL.

After a few false starts, the EDL was founded as a reaction to Islamist extremists protesting against returning British soldiers from Afghanistan, and was led by a former football hooligan and BNP member, Stephen Yaxley-Lennon (who liked to style himself 'Tommy Robinson'). The EDL rejected the politicising, politics and relative discipline of the BNP and at times even violently turned on the party and the rest of the traditional far right.

Although the EDL did eat into the periphery of the BNP, many within the party rejected its boozing and brawling and the incestuous fallouts over money, drugs and women that so defined its rise (and eventual decline). The sheer size and scale of the EDL's early outings bothered and excited the traditional far right. Time and time again, as the BNP collapsed around the country, Griffin would try and address the problem from his office in Brussels by both attacking and attempting to cultivate the EDL's support. Often he embarrassed and humiliated both himself and the party while failing to do so.

The seeds of that failure and the rise of National Action lie in the BNP and the EDL. After national campaigns and humiliations, the BNP's electoral support, which had begun to increase dramatically once Griffin took over the party in 1999, went into terminal decline in 2010 just as the EDL picked up in notoriety and public focus. Where the EDL had first filled the numerical and radical street-based void in the BNP so lamented by NA's founders, its predilection for rough-housing, drugs and debauchery wasn't the kind of 'pure' Aryan movement NA's founders eulogised.

And although the Griffin was far more extreme than most in the far right, his failure in the eyes of the hardcore was an unwillingness to jettison electoral ambitions early enough. It was easy for youngsters, such as those who formed the nucleus of the early National Action, to disregard and write off the years Griffin and the BNP had spent radicalising them.

According to a story Alex Davies would later tell members of National Action, he and Ben Raymond joked they'd be the biggest double act on the far right since John Tyndall (who would later lead the BNP) and Martin Webster (who came out as gay) led the National Front during the 1970s. Davies, warming to the idea of being a major player on the far right like Tyndall and Webster, retorted that Raymond would be "the queer one," reducing Raymond to tears.

As for early National Action founder Danny Lake, his part in a February 2013 Skype conversation that laid the public foundations for all and everything NA wanted to be, was almost his only contribution to the group. He either switched off or was turned off by the preposterous expectations of Raymond and Davies. He'd been there and done it all already. He flitted in and out of the BNP for years, even leading the BNP's militant youth group 'Resistance', but grew tired and bored with its limitations.

Lake had for a short time watched others throw themselves into a radical group, English National Resistance (ENR), numbering no more than a dozen members that fell out of step with the BNP between 2009 and 2011. As part of his journey, like Raymond and Davies, he travelled through and around all of the discussion groups in search of a new radicalism but, unlike Raymond and Davies, exhausted his tolerance of fascism at the same time.

Despite fizzling out and leaving little trace, ENR was a quick lesson into what was to come from National Action in its early days. As well as a nod to mainstream youth culture, it specialised in using social media and producing poorly made but 'arty'-looking videos of its members engaged in low-level political agitation. ENR set the groundwork for the better use of social media and art, but was ridiculed into submission by the left for its impetuous and "radical" political statements. Similar to NA was its dark and deep obsession with women and what they did with their bodies. In particular, the group had an obsession with those who cheated on their partners, and women who slept with black men (though never, of course, where white men slept with black women).

Such was this obsession that the notable blog 'Harry's Place' paid far less attention to its anti-Semitism and attempts to use cutting-edge technology and 'lefty-youth' persona, instead finding its overt sexual obsessions more intriguing.

> "Seeking to model themselves on European 'Black Bloc' and 'autonomous nationalist' groups (essentially neo-Nazis posing as Anarchists), the ENR favour 'direct action' tactics – currently in the form of spray painting slogans and illegal fly posting...
>
> "...looking at their promotional video, it seems the ENR website has lots of drivel attempting to merge leftist rhetoric with racial nationalism and claims to not support neo-Nazism while at the same time posting music by openly Nazi 'hate rock' and 'RAC' bands and offering links to sites including the Combat 18 affiliated 'Racial Volunteer Force'.
>
> "People are attracted to extreme political movements for a variety of reasons, but one that often pops up is an issue with sexuality: for example, London nailbomber David Copeland was a rabidly homophobic loner who dreamt of being an SS commander with female sex slaves; would-be neo-Nazi bomber Martyn Gilleard hated 'race-mixing sluts' and had a large child porn collection ..."

Similarly disturbing attitudes towards women and sex would also set National Action, its friends and even much later, a newer generation of adherents, apart.

CHAPTER 3: BUILDING A MOVEMENT

"Our goal is to discredit the frauds and cheats of the right wing who have held us back, and build a solid ground for a new politics on the body of the old right wing, we will make way for National Socialism to enter British politics, and finally begin its fight."

Ben Raymond, joint founder of National Action

One month after they broadcast their discussions as Emerson, Lake and Palmer, Danny Lake took leave of Ben Raymond and found himself in the forests and bedsits of the squatting movement. This suited Raymond because, although he felt confident he could work with Alex Davies, Lake's age, experience and maturity unnerved him.

Under the username 'Goyles', Raymond declared on the American Nazi website Iron March he'd been instructed by the Renaissance Party of North America (RPN) to head a committee "for the possibilities of that organisation in Britain". It's unlikely there'd ever been an official instruction issued to Raymond, but the downward state and condition of the far right in Britain showed no signs of abating or improving suitably enough for rather middle class, eclectic tastes. Although the English Defence League (EDL) was itself now splitting into violent gangs that displayed signs of outright Nazism, Raymond pushed their podcast out as far and wide as the internet would allow. He claimed it, their new group, would be the "next big thing", baying for the destruction, in particular, of the EDL, the British National Party (BNP) and its leadership.

BNP leader Nick Griffin paid little attention initially to the threats emanating from a tiny, dark corner of the internet (he was almost computer illiterate anyway). His beef was primarily still with the EDL. Earlier in 2012 he'd called together a selection of his finest thugs at a meeting in Stoke-on-Trent to sound out whether a night of the long knives could be carried out against a whole host of dissenters in both the BNP and the EDL. He was taken aback to be told, bluntly, not only was it numerically impossible to win such a war, but few, if any, had the heart to undertake it. Although abandoning electioneering and returning the BNP to its roots of street violence and ultra extremism held some personal appeal to him, Griffin was reminded that having sent his followers on a not dissimilar trajectory of during his time leading a faction of the National Front in the late 1980s, he was left bankrupt and sitting in the ruins of a French farmyard surrounded by nobody.

The BNP was in tatters; little old ladies no longer sent their life savings to the party on the back of the endless begging letters and emails for which it had become infamous. The party's Belfast call centre had collapsed in acrimony ending in a kidnapping the year before and Loyalist paramilitaries were among those now chasing Griffin and his family over unpaid debts. With two more years left in the European Parliament, Griffin decided to spend as much time as possible in Brussels and not at home where the party he had initially modernised and rebuilt was dying a painful death.

By early 2013, the BNP was made aware of the early rumblings of National Action. The party's Midlands organiser, Paul Hickman, a dour and relatively immature but committed neo-Nazi, had broken party rules by promoting NA and hosting its early Skype discussion on his *Voice of Albion* internet radio site. An earlier blog of his making, *Birmingham Nationalist*, had been deleted by the site's host for promoting violent extremism.

Although the BNP had relaxed some of its strict rules about paying homage to National Socialism and Nazism, Hickman was way overstepping the mark. After flirting with the BNP's youth wing in his early twenties, Hickman became an active member in 2005, rising through the ranks. But it was his first stint around the Young BNP that had been the happiest period of his life. As a schoolchild growing up in mid-1990s Birmingham, he felt he was part of a white minority. He also claimed he was bullied at school by Muslims. As the BNP went into electoral and numerical decline after 2010, Hickman found himself elevated to the position of organiser as reward for his continued activism during a period of inactivity and defections. With a shrunken local membership, he became more and more open about his Nazism and was increasingly disillusioned with life and the BNP's insistence on continuing the electoral path. Hickman felt his local branch, indeed the whole party, was allowed to fill up with "UKIP types" who had no nationalist ideology or interest in preserving the white race; the party had even accepted Jewish members, he complained. In one branch meeting he was chastised for displaying the Celtic Cross flag on the wall of the pub.

His personal life was even less fulfilling. Despite study and being employed in nursing for a while, a subsequent prison sentence left him working in a low-paid and dead-end job well below what he felt his intellect and endeavours deserved. He was depressed. A month after broadcasting Raymond, Lake and Davies discussing the formation of a new group, Hickman quit the BNP in April 2013. In particular, he wanted to break an infamous Nick Griffin putdown that "the BNP is the only show in town."

The thought of helping National Action somehow recreated those happy YBNP days of his early life and lifted some of the endless gloom around him Now conscripted to help build NA, Hickman appeared on an American internet radio show in June 2013 to promote the group to a wider audience. He complained that white British youth were becoming "niggerised".

The BNP, he complained, was "only telling half the truth" and Griffin, most shamelessly, had abandoned Holocaust denial during a disastrous appearance on the BBC's flagship political *Question Time* programme in 2009. Further to that, the modernisation of the BNP had gone too far, the attempts at mainstreaming the party had gone too far and, worst of all, it had abandoned National Socialist principles and gone chasing after the wrong sort of people. Hickman, impoverished and bordering on desperate, bemoaned the salaries that Griffin and Andrew Brons were taking as MEPs. He lauded instead the selfless MEPs of the violent Greek Nazi party Golden Dawn.

***

In August 2013, Ben Raymond launched National Action on a WordPress site, declaring the organisation to be an exciting new project "which has promising foundation, backing, and willing organisers". His flair for nonsense was foremost in the foreword: "We are the leaders of the Class Struggle," the site shouted.

A month later National Action moved to a new dedicated site that offered advice on how to dress and how to behave if you wanted to join the group. It was both stark and colourful, with the group's symbol looking like a bastardised anarchist 'A' with a 1930s blackshirt-era Mosleyite thunderbolt though it. In fact it was modelled on the symbol of the 'Sturmabteilung' the terrorist forerunner of the Nazi Brownshirts in Germany. Managing to encapsulate all three meanings in one symbol was a measure of the breadth of influence Raymond was looking for in the new group.

In a section on joining National Action there were a whole host of do's and don'ts. Raymond issued a mantra he appears to have followed throughout his time in NA, advising: "The Policeman isn't your enemy." Followers and adherents were advised not to say anything in front of the police and to always be mindful of entrapment, ensuring they remained highly secretive.

As one future National Action member, Robbie Mullen, noted not long after joining, no matter how bold and revolutionary Raymond's words, he immediately issued a caveat suggesting no laws were to be broken.

Raymond also encouraged a lawful sense of paranoia inside the group. If only they could act like terrorists without breaking the law. On September 5 2013, he wrote:

"Why is it that the people have yet to rise against their masters?
"To be more blunt: why have we not started to fight back in a war against our race that started when the Empire Windrush first docked in Tilbury?...
Never has Nationalism come close to permanently halting the tide of degeneracy and filth.

"The debacle that has brought us to our knees as a movement – the collapse of the BNP – had its roots, not in the smooth talking salesmanship of Nick Griffin but in our own psychological weakness. We, the Nationalists, those with the truth on our side and a people to save were too concerned with how it might 'look' if we were a bit too honest about those who were peddling the crap about a multiracial society.

"This why we have formed National Action, to show our people that there is an alternative to the prevailing current. To show that there are men and women left who still believe in this country – our country."

Former BNP Midlands organiser Paul Hickman had acted as the conduit for Alex Davies into the New Right and the London Forum, introducing him to Larry Nunn, host of the Western Springs group. There was much excitement: Nunn had apparently approved of the group and its startling, dynamic and youthful look.

National Action's founding document, *Strategy and Promotion*, was written by Raymond and Davies in the early part of 2013, before being passed to Nunn. Hickman was drafted in to referee arguments over policy and wording and, most of all, correct Raymond's grammar. From that process, Hickman developed a deep dislike and skepticism of Raymond's intellect and intentions. The feeling was apparently mutual. When Hickman later took his own life in 2017 and NA was collapsing in acrimony, accusation and arrests, Raymond failed to acknowledge his contribution to the group's formation until long after the event and ostensibly only in defence of his own tarnished reputation.

Davies had long considered himself an expert on economics and the left. Raymond was the self-declared expert on strategy, sedition, youth culture and revolutionary movements. Conscious not to undermine his sense of self-importance as the group's technical founder, Davies never openly subscribed to the idea that he was a "youth". Each undertook their own petty fancies in formulating *Strategy and Promotion* but as Raymond had already spent years writing aimless documents in his bedroom, the majority of the content was ready. Between the three, Hickman was the only one ever to hold a proper job or a position inside the far right. While waiting for National Action to take off, Hickman temporarily joined the National Front.

The final document was an impressive-looking PDF but it didn't stand up to proper scrutiny. The idea of taking the document to be professionally printed was floated, but deemed too expensive to be mass produced. The internet was where National Action would take up its recruitment drive and distribution of ideas. It would also become crucial to the gang's operation in the future. The eleven-page *Strategy and Promotion* was a thorough portrayal of the group's early idealism and prejudices. Yet though it looked good, the content and language was severely underdeveloped and not too dissimilar to what Raymond had written in his magazine *Attack*. It was meant to be their revolutionary document for change, but it was also a lot of words for words' sake.

Nearly 30 years previously, Derek Holland of the National Front had alarmed thousands of British fascists and fascist-watchers with his document *The Political Soldier*, which helped set the course for intellectual and radical rise and decline in the British far right. If *Strategy and Promotion* was meant to ignite similar excitement and controversy whilst radicalising hundreds of British youths, particularly at universities, it fell somewhat short of the task.

The document offered a simple two-step programme for a revolution and the ideology and theory it would take to put into practice.

"Building is difficult without the right tools – as it stands today we cannot fight if there are those who are limiting our supply of ammunition because it suits some vague long term agenda. By openly pointing to the root cause with is the race issue and the Jew we can gain a superior and complete understanding where beore [sic] there was only miasma. Our goal is to discredit the frauds and cheats of the right wing who have held us back, and build a solid ground for a new politics on the body of the old right wing, we will make way for National Socialism to enter British politics, and finally begin its fight." – National Action: Strategy and Promotion, September 2013

On economics, the document pointed to "social credit", favoured by irrelevant anti-Jewish cranks. Its exponent Clifford Douglas wasn't even an economist. The group deliberately ignored every radical Nazi's favourite and flawed economist, Hilaire Belloc. Having failed to determine exactly what the benefit of social credit is or was, the short few paragraphs on economic theory boiled down to the view that Jews held all the money and must therefore be denied all access to it.

"There isn't anything honest or benevolent about the motives of these Jews who openly declared their motivation to be the destruction of all nations and bonds – but it is more docile and liberal which does not reflect Jewish tyranny. Despite the economic science of the right being a thousand times superior and credible to that of the left, the right wingers are regularly beaten by modern adherents of (rebranded) Marxism. It is a powerful and angry outlook on the world that remains dominant, despite what the right says, the upper class political world remains essentially Marxist."

As for actual economics itself? Well, once the Jews have no money left, all the rest of it flows, apparently.

"Let's get something clear, there is no such thing as a 'good economist' economics is a deflective topic that detracts from the real issue – an

argument with any opposing charlatan demands that you defeat his whole position step by step in a way he understands, a futile and pointless effort beyond human endurance. In the real world people need to buttress their arguments with a world view. To win (for our meme to succeed) requires bringing it all back to the central issue race angle to deliver the knockout blow. Our race is our brick hammer."

***

In November 2013 Hickman and Davies stayed over in London to meet Young BNP and future National Action activists both at the National Front's annual Remembrance Day parade, and a demonstration in support of Greek neo-Nazi party Golden Dawn outside the Greek Embassy.

The pair saw the Golden Dawn demonstration as the perfect opportunity for them to impress the YBNP and other Nazis in attendance but, despite their best efforts to appear invincible and impressive to other fascists at the embassy, they were forced to drop their banners and run when confronted by antifascists. They fared no better at the NF's Remembrance Day march where, horribly disorganised and split into two violently warring factions, the National Action and YBNP contingent was shoved between the two groups. Hickman quit the NF soon after.

A week later, on November 23, in what is believed to be National Action's first action, Hickman videoed himself late in the evening hanging a banner over the bridge of a motorway near his home. It read: "Anti racist is a code word for anti white".

Raymond's concern that Davies was "intellectually lazy" soon became apparent. Ensconced at Warwick University, a well-known hotbed of 'Reds', apparently, it wasn't long before Davies stopped attending lectures, egged on by Hickman to focus instead on building National Action. "You can do both," Raymond complained, but Davies was beginning to see the early signs of growth and interest in the group.

Before the end of the year National Action had begun to reap the benefits of constant internet attacks on the BNP and the EDL. Two people applied to join the group from the north west of England, as did a few others in Yorkshire and the Midlands. Christopher Lythgoe, a 27-year-old unemployed loner from Warrington who had stalked updates about NA on the Iron March forum, was quickly installed as North West organiser. Lythgoe had previously had minor interactions with the EDL. Joining as his deputy was Matthew Hankinson, an 18-year-old business student from a wealthy family in Newton-le-Willows in Merseyside, who also came aboard via Iron March. Ashley Bell from Leeds, who would go on to temporarily lead the group, jumped ship from the National Front, having previously been a member of the EDL. The NF was in such a state of infighting that Bell (who used the pseudonym Tommy Johnson until the

NF revealed his identity) allegedly helped himself to £400 from the party's coffers when he left.

Raymond kept the group's online followers updated with exaggerated reports of their stunning early progress. In Thurrock, Essex, members of the YBNP handed out National Action leaflets to shoppers, with Raymond claiming shoppers were "highly receptive to our radical message". Meanwhile in Coventry, Davies and Hickman delivered leaflets to disinterested shoppers before being forced to flee. Retreating didn't bother them as long as news of their activities went reported on the left-wing forums that Raymond trawled for hours on end.

In Wakefield later that month, four National Action supporters unfurled a banner in front of EDL and Unite Against Fascism (UAF) supporters who were facing off against each other. Raymond described both groups as "the footsoldiers of Zion." Again, NA was forced to retreat when each group took offence to their Nazi saluting, but such delicate feelings didn't stop the EDL also attacking the Bishop of Pontefract physically on the day.

For the student Davies, this outbreak of early activism was some relief. Raymond had convinced Davies a radical right-wing group with all the hallmarks of anti-capitalism and anti-Semitic sentiment in its founding document could replace a diminishing left presence on campus. With Davies as leader, obviously. Time and time again, despite his hours trawling the internet to borrow words and sentiment from the radical left, Raymond would misread things.

The introduction of his political beliefs and the plastering of National Action stickers around campus hadn't made Davies a popular student. His studies were suffering and instead of instant and refreshing popularity, he found himself being threatened and ridiculed as a "spotty Nazi" by other students. The university also made it clear to him that they wanted him gone.

Although he went home to Wales at the Christmas break bitterly disappointed with the results on campus, he was buoyed by what he viewed as the quality of his new recruits. Hankinson was over six feet tall, fiercely intelligent, cultured and an accomplished club boxer. Almost morose, Lythgoe, about whom he knew very little, would turn out to be a serious revolutionary who said little about himself but a lot about violence and terrorism. Bell was a fitness fanatic who practised 'straight edge' – a movement that emerged from the early-1980s US hardcore punk scene and encouraged its followers to disavow meat, alcohol, drugs, tobacco, coffee and promiscuous sexual activity. They were like nobody the fledgling leadership had ever encountered in the BNP. This was the new breed of neo-Nazi they'd dreamed of.

***

By the end of 2013, Raymond and the others were blogging and agitating across the internet. The more offensive and dismissive they were against others in the far right, the better. Raymond's writings became more and more bizarre, antagonistic, extreme and prolific:

"It is an unwritten rule that nationalists must refrain from attacking other nationalists – we must fight together – on this I agree, but this requires that the parameters of 'Nationalist' be set for the phrase to have meaning. To ensure we are on the right path I propose instituting the following litmus test; to be on 'our side' a nationalist must be openly racist and openly antisemitic – This isn't a hard standard to meet. Any true Nationalist meets this, all it really tests is team spirit and practical politeness."

Where the English Defence League was the first far-right group to be built and administered on social media; and Britain First became the masters at exploiting it, growing their Facebook page to two million 'likes'; National Action became the immediate masters of hiding inside and exploiting the powers of the internet and modern communications. To protect themselves, followers used the anonymous web browser Tor to encrypt internal communications and hide on other forums where they littered the competition with abuse and threats. Raymond contributed under a series of different names wherever he could on the Iron March forum, which was where neo-Nazis from Britain and the US exchanged ideas and tactics. An entire thread, running into thousands of postings about and by the group, was soon up and running.

Raymond enjoyed tapping into the American Nazi movement's obsession with the British Nazi scene. In this obsessive and inwardly-focused world, Britain was a tiny island where whites were forced to live cheek-by-jowl with blacks and Asians by a government controlled by Jews. And that wasn't just an assumption by American followers; it was the picture also wholly painted by British members of the forum too. Our cities were no-go areas for white people and, as the entire British far right obsessed, young white girls were being raped by Muslim men. On and on it went: the internet continually opened endless new doors and opportunities to spread National Action's message. Of course, the untruthful obsessions about 'no-go areas' for whites in the UK reflected a theme also taken up by the right-wing press in the US itself. And American Anglophiles ranging from culturally-conservative old ladies obsessed with *Downtown Abbey,* to gun-toting anti-government conspiracy theorists of the sort eulogised by William Pierce's neo-Nazi race war novel, *The Turner Diaries,* lapped it up.

America's white supremacist obsession with arming the "unarmed British" stretched as far back as George Lincoln Rockwell, the former head of the American Nazi Party, and his ill-fated visit to veteran British neo-Nazis John Tyndall and Colin Jordan in 1962. From there it encompassed a host of bearded weirdos who flocked to ex-BNP leader Nick Griffin's 'Political Soldier' movement inside the NF during the 1980s and the serious advocates of terrorism who inspired Combat 18, London nail bomber David Copeland in the 1990s and eventually Jo Cox's murderer, Thomas Mair.

Just before midnight on New Year's Eve, as most other young men his age were doing something infinitely more enjoyable, Raymond advertised National Action on Stormfront, the world's most widely-read white supremacist site:

"Wanted: white youths between 15-29 who are looking to become racial activists. Our group is about carrying out direct actions nationwide, and we would love to hear from you. Flyers, stickers, and activities will be provided to you free of charge to willing volunteers.

"If you're interested please contact us.

"National Action is a bold new nationalist initiative formed by experienced youth activists, anybody who is interested in activism and entering our community should get in contact with us because what we have put together is a very thought out plan which we are all really excited about – and we would like YOU to help us. We are currently working to a timetable, about a year or so – we have some very set and clear aims and hope that all the things we have been wanting to put into practice for years.

"Write to National Action by contacting us at the following address: contact@national-action.info

"State your enquiry and we WILL get back to you.

"The document featured below is an 11 page PDF that concisely summarises exactly what our strategy is, and what we are all about . It is a really thought out document that really explains a lot of the new ideas we have. Read our program here:

"What do we do? We engage in all manner of activities, with the aim of raising awareness to the myriad of problems that threaten the very existence of our nation. The final aim being to ferment a social revolution in Britain, returning ownership of this country to its legitimate sons and daughters.

"To achieve this we will need young men and women of calibre in our ranks. Previous generations have failed to break the chains that constrain this nation – it will be the task of this generation to smash what weighs us down, otherwise we will sink. As it stands, ours will be the last in a position capable of freeing our people. If this generation fails, we are finished. That is the reality of our predicament."

CHAPTER 4: OPERATION GET JEW BITCH

"This weekend saw the first of a planned schedule of inspirational events designed to promote White pride, personal development, health and fitness among young White people, through a collaboration between three organisations: Sigurd, the newly emergent British based, Odinist, physical culture group; White-Rex, the longer established Russian based mixed martial arts, music and physical culture group; and Western Spring."

Larry Nunn, writing as Max Musson, 'Culture Camp', 2014

2014 was to be the year National Action planned to make international headlines.

This was the year the group's plans to unsettle mainstream society and sweep away the rest of the far right in a tide of revolutionary purity would come to fruition. 2013 had gone almost exactly to plan. Not only had Ben Raymond and Alex Davies got new recruits who shared their frustrated visions, people were actually donating to the group's PayPal account. Not just the odd £5 here and there, but at least one American donor had given $1,000 before the end of 2013.

The political conditions for another successful far-right political party may have been actually ripening given UKIP's success, however, the wider British far right could not have been less interested – or capable of delivering. The British National Party (BNP) was dying. The National Front (NF) was (politically) dead and infected by former English Defence League (EDL) drunkards, trudging around the country on anti-Muslim witch hunts. Britain First, with its mass of publicity and physical confrontations outside mosques and the doorsteps of those it deemed jihadis, wasn't even considered competition. It was considered soft on 'The Jewish question', tired, corrupt and washed-up. Its members were overweight, wore cheap uniforms and were afflicted with the same vices (drink and drugs) as much of the rest of the far right.

UKIP, or "Jewkip" as it was disparagingly referred to by many far-right extremists, held court on immigration in the mainstream media and would soon be riding high as pressure grew to hold a referendum on Britain's continued membership of the European Union. Well, riding high in comparison with the rest of that whole bad bunch. But there'd be no political party regrouping for the far right and as far as National Action and the rest of the movement was concerned, there'd be no revolution at the ballot box.

Ashley Bell, the fitness and straight edge fanatic from Leeds, was seen as the perfect example of the sort of 'new man' National Action wanted. He was aloof and condescending, adventurous and quick with his fists. He held no sentimentality to anything or anyone. More importantly, he'd crossed over to fascism via a period on the fringes of a host of righteous and progressive groups, including the fringe of the animal liberation movement. A puritanical believer in the Aryan body beautiful, Bell had been attracted to the EDL's anti-Muslim message around halal food and, in his own words, "the flags." From there he moved to the NF whose sharper sense of racism, anti-Semitism and supposed organised ideology drew him in. Once in the NF, he found pretty much the same level of drug dealing, criminality, alcohol abuse and stupidity he had witnessed in the EDL.

His attempts to persuade other activists in his previous far-right groups to take up his puritanical views came to a frustrating dead end: they were simply not interested. The failure to recruit people with a similar faith in the body beautiful aside, Bell brought others who'd been attracted to the EDL's anti-Muslim message but were tired of the disorganised way it went about its business of arguments and inter-gang rivalries.

In October 2013, the EDL's founder Stephen Lennon (aka 'Tommy Robinson') had held a press conference with controversial counter-extremism group, Quilliam, claiming to have quit the movement he helped found. Some thought it was a stunt. Indeed, it later turned out Lennon was receiving payment from Quilliam for claiming he'd rejected extremism totally.

To get his hands on the money, he had to claim the EDL was a far-right extremist group (not forgetting it was something he had founded and led). The EDL had cost British taxpayers more than £10m in policing costs by 2013, and Lennon himself had led a mini-riot on the streets of Woolwich, south London, after British soldier Lee Rigby was murdered there earlier that year. He'd also said in 2011 that British Muslims would "feel the full force of the EDL" if any more Islamist atrocities occurred. Now he claimed to be concerned about the "dangers of far-right extremism" and was joining Quilliam in a crusade focused on the dangers of both this and Islamist extremism. The parameters of Lennon's role with Quilliam were never fully explained, but it put Lennon, Quilliam and the EDL under a sharp spotlight.

It was, of course, in every sense a great con and it wasn't long before Lennon would be leading a new far right, anti-Muslim group. Lennon may have always pleaded he wasn't a racist, and neither were any of the groups or protests he organised (his increasingly strident obsessions with Muslims notwithstanding), but his main problem was he and the EDL weren't demonstrably "anti-racist" either, despite his own fierce criticism of the

BNP, a party he'd previously been a member of. In its early days the EDL had drawn its members and supporters from the football terraces, men with very tabloid tastes and prejudices who liked to fight with the police and counter-demonstrators in city centres. In the main, the dreaded "UKIP types" National Action hated so much. Whether Lennon liked it or not, the EDL acted as a conduit and lightning rod to greater and further political extremism and extremists. Every time the "not racist" EDL fractured, the factions lurched further and deeper into the cesspit of Nazism.

During Lennon's various periods in prison the football lads melted away from the English Defence League and all that was left were groups of drunken, conspiracy theory-obsessed thugs whose behaviour in public and private was shambolic and chaotic.

By the time he'd officially 'quit', the rumours were that Lennon had left prison earlier in 2013 and upon attending an EDL march realised he'd lost his moral authority over the group – there were Nazi salutes and 'dodgy' flags and banners that would hurt his reputation. The EDL had been splintering violently from 2010 onwards and most of these splinters entered a world cohabited by minuscule groupings of older far-right extremists, such as the National Front, the British Movement and renegade BNP members, who all shared pretty much the same dislike of the EDL leader as the BNP. Before Lennon could do any of his Quilliam-inspired anti-extremist work he was sent back to prison, sentenced to serve 18 months in 2014 for mortgage fraud.

With the EDL on the brink of collapse there was a sigh of relief inside the BNP's headquarters. Without Lennon, the EDL was nothing. What many were witnessing was actually the early inclinations and desires that would fuel National Action.

***

To survive, the BNP *had* to start pushing a new generation of activists to the forefront of the party. Nick Griffin was already aware he had little chance of keeping his seat in Brussels and there were rumours surfacing inside the party that once his louche lifestyle expectations were once more the sole responsibility of the BNP, members of the party's executive would move to push him out. In May 2014, and with the party haemorrhaging money to a number of professionals it had employed, Griffin took the precaution of filing for bankruptcy. This would, it was alleged, further burden the party with his personal debts. This decision was met with incredulous fury inside the party.

No sooner had the EDL threat subsided, BNP organisers in London and the Midlands were warning about another new threat to the party – from the new group called National Action. It was described as "lice in the heads" of some young BNP members, with an abundance of stickers to give away and a seditious and flash website of its own.

The party's youth wing was something Griffin had always encouraged and cherished. His daughter Jennifer had once even led the group, prompting accusations of nepotism. The YBNP had proudly churned out a successful amount of ideological extremists, all of whom (except Jennifer) had gone on to hate Griffin with a passion. One was even arrested on the eve of the 2010 General Election for an alleged plot to murder him.

In January 2014, after the public announcement, ridicule and discord surrounding what was his second bankruptcy went into full swing, Griffin summoned the YBNP's leadership to join him (at taxpayers' expense) for a two-day summit at the European Parliament. Among those taking part were some who would go on to take leading roles in National Action: primarily Kevin Layzell from Essex, Person B from East London and Jack Renshaw, an already-infamous young party member from Blackpool. Like most young BNP members, they joined the party only after it went into decline. Their opportunities to enjoy electoral successes, political respectability and packed and lively local branch meetings were gone. Instead, they were in a party of diminishing importance and increasing friction, but were all bound together in the belief and adulation that Nick Griffin had *almost* saved their country. Griffin now needed these young idealists, the proper ideologues of the party, to stand up and defend him.

Layzell and Person B were relatively close. They lived near each other and attended the same London meetings. Person B was an independent, outgoing and aloof character with a taste for nice clothes and confrontation. He had a flair for art and graphics and keeping fit ... and absolutely no desire to progress in the BNP. Layzell was something of a "mummy's boy", often ridiculed and the butt of jokes for his dress sense and awkward, cardboard personality. But he was dependable. Come rain, wind and shine, Layzell would turn up to activities. The other key personality, Jack Renshaw, had a self-assuredness that made Layzell feel awkward. Layzell and Renshaw were both hoping the BNP would take them on as full-time organisers now the interlopers who had worked for the party were on their way out. Cocky and self-assured, Renshaw had come to the attention of antifascists for a number of reasons. While studying at Manchester Metropolitan University he was very open about his political affiliations – something unimaginable, even suicidal, years before.

Renshaw had taken to swanning around with BNP heavies trying to engage "lefties" in confrontation, often offering himself up for bait. Adorned in a blazer and looking like a schoolboy, Renshaw would wander up to groups of students in pubs, opening up with lines such as "Have you given much thought to the Jewish question?" In his lectures he preferred arguments and issuing dark threats to other students to doing coursework. Just being at university and away from home seemed to be purpose enough for him. He craved infamy and violence, but his cherub-like, almost polished-plastic looks and diminutive size and frame seemed to ensure he didn't get in too much trouble. He did complain, however, that he was spat at a lot.

Back in Blackpool Renshaw had flitted between homes, staying with his mother (the two played golf together), his father and his uncle. There appears to have been antagonism between the parents, but his father very publicly worried about his son's slide into extremism and the eventual wasted opportunity university was turning out to be. Excessively cocky and flash, Renshaw even caught taxis to university lectures despite living in nearby student accommodation.

The old women in the BNP loved hearing "Jack" speak. He could turn on his cherubic charm, being polite and forthright in a way so rarely found in young people. He had no interest in relationships with girls, much to the disappointment of one woman who excitedly set her daughter up with him for her prom night. He took the opportunity to spend the entire evening ranting about Jews to other students and didn't even compliment his date on her dress. Because it was Jack, he was instantly forgiven. He seemed confident he'd one day replace Nick Griffin as leader of the BNP, a job that Layzell had also set his sights on. In Brussels, while Layzell carefully prepared a dour discussion document on improving the BNP's image and building the BNP locally via better community engagement, Renshaw took the opportunity to further impress Griffin with a rant about paedophiles, Marxists and Jews. He bragged how he'd single-handedly taken the war to the "reds" in Manchester and demanded the party spend more of its efforts confronting the "red menace" lurking everywhere.

Paedophilia was something of an obsession for Renshaw throughout his time in the BNP and National Action. He'd take a particular interest in the case of Andrew Gregson, a hotelier in Blackpool who had targeted young boys to whom he'd sold class A drugs. In 2014 Gregson was convicted of six offences against young men the previous year. After Gregson's conviction, Renshaw made three Freedom of Information requests demanding to know the details, including the address, of the judge responsible for sentencing him.

There's strong evidence to suggest there was even a paedophile ring among fascists in Blackpool. Two active BNP supporters, Robert Ewing and Gareth Dewhurst, were convicted in 2015 over the murder of missing Blackpool schoolgirl Paige Chivers years before. Her father, with no known links to the BNP or the far right, was murdered at his home in 2013. Ewing and Dewhurst had joined BNP demonstrations in Blackpool with Renshaw and Nick Griffin, accusing the Muslim community of not just murdering the missing Paige Chivers, but also the missing daughter of another BNP member, Charlene Downes.

Whilst the YBNP were being wined and dined by Griffin, there were uncomfortable moments. Some of the young members had tired of the party, had even tired of Griffin. Griffin admitted he was expecting to lose his seat at the next European elections, but he wanted the YBNP to be at the forefront of a re-election campaign he envisaged being confrontational and aggressive. The YBNP, hardly a toughened street army, asked for greater roles in the party and wanted Griffin to meet with the leadership of National Action. There was even a suggestion of a merger between the two.

Having seen enough of the sort of outright Nazism and extremism, black face-masks and online anonymity of National Action, as well as the horrendous writings from the pen of NA founder Ben Raymond, Griffin steadfastly refused. He'd already made some inroads with the North West Infidels (NWI), a violent EDL splinter group with a knack of violence and stunts. He pleaded that the BNP was a radical party and promised he'd encourage greater protest actions by party members in conjunction with groups such as the NWI and even some National Front members on the ground. But in National Action itself, he saw trouble.

Surprisingly, it was Renshaw who came to Griffin's aid, agreeing the party should continue with the electoral pretence right up until Griffin was voted out.

National Action pressed ahead on campuses. In January 2014 a speech at Warwick University by Socialist Workers Party (SWP) international Secretary Alex Callinicos was disrupted not just by women's groups campaigning against a mounting rape scandal in the SWP, but also by NA members. It was Davies' own campus, but for some reason NA failed to report the demonstration.

Later in the month Raymond made his way to Coventry for another demonstration, this time against halal food. The protest was outside an Indian restaurant. He reported on the group's website that 11 supporters took part, but it was actually eight. Another new member who would also go on to have significant impact on NA joined that day. Wayne Bell from Castleford in Yorkshire had impressed Ashley Bell (no relation) during his time in the EDL. Sporting an enormous and gruesome-looking scar down his face, he flashed his cash around and had a penchant for violence. So threatening did his new group now look – along with Hankinson and Lythgoe – that Raymond was almost beside himself with excitement. He was still nervous and terrified the group would be attacked; Wayne Bell claimed Raymond clung to him and demanded he be his bodyguard for the day.

Further evidence they were winning over BNP radicals was the decision by former YBNP member Sam Mayhew to join them in Coventry. Mayhew had also tired of the constraints of life inside the BNP and having delivered National Action leaflets in Essex the year before, decided to join NA before he was pushed out of the BNP.

The protest in Coventry was meant to be a gentle way of easing former EDL members into the group. The morose Hickman videoed the action for National Action's website. The lead-in graphics to the video were stunning, but the footage of the day was poorly shot and blurred. According to leaflets the group handed out, the restaurant wasn't warning its customers that it sold halal meat and as a result wasn't "fit for human consumption."

Raymond was meant to be the focus of the resultant video, but so embarrassed was he by his poor mimicking both of Oswald Moseley's tone and style, that he cut his contribution to just a few seconds. Only a two-minute film of the demonstration went on the group's website.

Although Raymond was horrified by how he looked and sounded on camera, a National Action video with professional-looking graphics was now available for everyone to see. Davies hid his face throughout the demonstration behind a NA placard.

National Action may not have been recruiting the university intellectuals Raymond had dreamed of, but it was recruiting equally serious and disturbed, angry young men; the sort of young man Raymond warmly referred to, while squeezing the heavily-scarred thug Wayne Bell's arms, as "brutes." Neither need he have worried about easing members into his desired all-out assault on Judaism, either. Every single one of them hated Jews. Now all Raymond had to do was generate a few shock stories from compliant journalists to cast his group of brutes into the headlines of the 'Jewish-controlled' media.

Ashley Bell took his straight edge message to Leeds University where he and Wayne Bell put up posters calling for drug dealers to be murdered. Across England, Wales and Scotland, the idea they could recruit a disciplined mass of students started, instead, to become an operation to intimidate those same students.

In the first quarter of 2014, National Action stickers and posters were reported at Cambridge, Coventry, Chester, Aberdeen, Nottingham, Newcastle, Sunderland and Stirling universities. This wasn't the work of students, but groups of activists determined to confront left-wing students or, at least, scare them into thinking NA was everywhere.

Student writer Colin Cortbus was the first to bite in March 2014, writing a sensationalist article for the *Huffington Post* which asked if National Action members could be your classmates:

"...a new race-hate group, led by university students, has held what is believed to be the first action by an overtly Neo-Nazi group on a British university campus for many years."

Although Raymond was meant to be working, he showed little interest in anything other than driving National Action full time. He'd later claim to be a double glazing salesman, but aside from an unsuccessful stint working at the Job Centre, there's little other evidence of him having ever worked. He'd later claim he'd subsequently assert to NA members he lived off a substantial inheritance from his dead parents.

Working through the night Raymond filled forums with recruitment materials and dazzled American white supremacists with tales of National Action's extraordinary bravery, simultaneously filling newspaper comment sections with horror stories of its activities.

Cortbus wasn't alone in falling for National Action's bait. Three days after his piece appeared, the *Huffington Post* stepped up its coverage, asking its readers to meet the group that just wanted to "piss people off." An interviewee, most likely Davies, dumbed down the group's revolutionary spill in favour of a more rudimentary approach to its actions. He also asked if the *Huffington Post* would pay for his travel and lunch to do the interview. Davies was feeling the heat for his actions at Warwick University. The student newspaper *The Boar* had taken to recording his late night trips to the pub to meet Hickman and come home plastering the streets with National Action stickers.

***

By April 2014 the group had broken 200 'likes' on Facebook. Given much of what remained of the far right operated online and even the BNP had more than 100,000 such likes, it didn't seem National Action was breaking any records. But the intensity with which the group operated offline, out of sight of regular internet users, was also increasing. Its carefree approach – sticking right-armed salutes in the air the moment a camera was out – both titillated and infuriated the rest of the UK's far-right movement. NA activists even bragged they'd been in conversation with the (police's) Counter Terrorist Unit in the West Midlands, and were delighted in reporting they were being monitored as extremists. It actually ran much further and deeper than this; in subsequent reports into the group that would be divulged during 2018's court trials, almost every member of the group had some kind of interaction with the authorities during their time in NA.

National Action leader Alex Davies is even alleged to have been on the government's anti-extremist 'Prevent' programme the whole time he led NA. While he was out recruiting young neo-Nazis, the government appeared worried he was in danger of being radicalised!

In June 2014, Colin Cortbus took his story to the *Sunday Mirror*, which duly obliged with a front-page headline: "Exposed: Rise of Hitler-loving National Action group who want to 'ethnically cleanse' the UK." This was more like the sort of publicity National Action wanted. The day before, *The Mirror* photographed 20 NA activists handing out leaflets at Liverpool's Lime Street station. According to Cortbus, Raymond and Davies were "dangerous fanatics" who admitted they were ready to use extreme means to "rid the UK of Jews and non-whites". Davies excitedly told the paper NA was "more radical" than the BNP.

The group's 'progress' would make Raymond very excited, if not entirely coherent:

"Our strategy to promote ourselves and drag politically correct sentiment through the mud has been very effective. The extent to which we have been able to incite the media to print the most ridiculous drivel has been an

unequalled conquest. Not only has National Action punched well above its weight, but it has secured a reputation for being utterly based."

The people of Liverpool, however, had taken offence at National Action's leaflets (which read: "Cleanse Britain of parasites. The white man is on the march – white power"). Small scuffles broke out during NA's leafleting operation and the police were called.

As the day broke up one young man stood out from the rest of the NA crew Garron Helm, a new recruit also on the government's 'Prevent' programme had previously flirted with EDL splinter group NWI, as well as the NF before following Ashley Bell into National Action. Helm began shouting threats and abuse at the public. He followed this up with Nazi salutes and running his finger across his throat at those opposing NA. In the pub afterwards, Helm regaled his new friends with tales of his fighting prowess, his hatred of Jews and his links to the Liverpool underworld.

The 21-year-old was from a large Irish family that spread across Bootle and Seaforth. One of 11 children, his father had, according to Helm, died in an industrial incident in Ireland and the family had received (according to Helm) a large pay-out from the Irish government. His mother and stepfather played in an Irish republican flute band.

Having someone from an Irish or even Irish republican background wasn't particularly unusual in the British far right, though the majority of the scene was violently anti-Irish republican and could, at times, be more than a bit antagonistic to Irish or Anglo-Irish members. To the National Action recruits who'd grown up in a period of peace in Northern Ireland, Helm's spouting of pro-Hitler and pro-Irish Republican Army (IRA) nonsense didn't seem particularly off-key. He was keen to explain he rejected the modern IRA's Marxism and the 'reddening' of the Republican cause, and even lied how he'd engaged with republicans still involved with the armed struggle. As a group, NA didn't particularly take to him, but Christopher Lythgoe, now the regional organiser for the North West of England, was intrigued.

Lythgoe had studied books on the IRA and the avowedly Marxist Irish National Liberation Army (INLA) as well as a host of other Marxist terror groups. Lythgoe insisted Helm would be "fine" as a member, particularly when Helm bragged he could bring the sort of "expertise" Lythgoe so admired to the group.

But Helm was nothing if not an enigma. As well as the Irish Republican armed struggle, he was obsessed with the occult and supernatural. He referred to himself online as 'The Noble Wolf' and used a Twitter account 'Aethelwulf', which translated from Old English as 'Noble Wolf'. Ashley Bell, whom Helm had followed into National Action, was happy to hand him over to Lythgoe.

Helm would soon be the group's first martyr. Even before meeting with National Action at Lime Street in Liverpool, he'd thrown himself headfirst and full throttle into online organisation and agitation. He began contributing to stories about NA, posting on forums and Facebook, enthralling others with his and the group's revolutionary potential.

Helm also became enamoured to the point of obsession with a female National Action sympathiser from Wales, someone the leader, Alex Davies had earmarked for himself. The young woman had been actively encouraged by her mother to make friends and join the group, travelling to London earlier in the year for a protest against the treatment of white farmers in South Africa. She soon became Helm's and Davies's mutual obsession, writing a blog with provocative pictures of herself along with extreme anti-Jewish graphics and childish anti-Semitism. The young woman would eventually break from the group after opening her front door to discover a NA member on her doorstep with beer and pornography, demanding they "fuck really fucking hard" on a live feed for others in the group to see.

Helm had bragged just how revolutionary he was by running a Twitter campaign of hate directed at high profile members of the Jewish community. In October 2014 he was sentenced to four weeks in prison for tweeting a 'grossly offensive' anti-Semitic tweet to one of Liverpool's Jewish Labour MPs, Luciana Berger. The tweet showed a Holocaust-era yellow star superimposed on the MP's forehead using the hashtag #HitlerWasRight. When police searched Helm's home they found Nazi memorabilia, including a flag bearing the SS symbol and material from National Action and the Satanic Order of Nine Angles.

The young neo-Nazi didn't fit the image of university-educated revolutionaries NA was trying to convince the world it was. Despite overwhelming joy they had their first martyr, there was anger in the group that Helm not only pleaded guilty to the crime but that he also agreed to apologise to Berger and pay her £80 as a victim surcharge. In court, Helm was described as a jobless loner who trawled the internet for hours in search of friends and enemies. He'd convinced himself and tried to convince others that his tweeting and racial hatred was somehow protected by the USA's first amendment.

Helm's case piqued newspapers' interest in National Action and they reported how his mother had a nervous breakdown and how he'd been expelled from college, where he was regarded as a disturbed and disruptive loner desperate to stand out. While in prison for just two weeks, Helm wrote long and flowery poetry to his National Action love interest.

The mother of the young woman at the centre of the dual obsession was becoming more and more concerned about the general nature of the group and its fixation with her daughter. Far from being disciplined and decent young men, there seemed to be a culture developing around hardcore pornography and snuff movies that National Action members shared with each other. A culture developed, as often it does with excitable and lonely young men thrust together, of an 'anything goes' attitude with regard to sexual attitudes and also a climate of competitive jealousy when a young woman entered their orbit.

With his anti-Semitic trolling Helm was propelled to the sort of infamy he dreamed of. Even Larry Nunn of the London Forum, whose every word the National Action leadership held in high esteem, took to his *Western Spring* website in sympathy with Helm, saying he'd been the foolish victim of some organised Jewish plot, and his imprisonment was a "martyrdom". But it was in the United States where Helm's and NA's stock rose dramatically.

The American Nazi website *The Daily Stormer* had long admired and promoted National Action's brash, unhinged anti-Semitism – all the more, given Britain's strict laws on hate speech. A report from HOPE not hate later claimed as many as ten thousand UK users visited the website each day. It was a horrendous website, childish, hateful and crude, full of Nazi insignia. Latching onto the publicity surrounding Helm's imprisonment, the website unleashed a troll campaign the likes of which Twitter and other social media outlets had never previously seen. The size, ferocity and vulgarity of the campaign shocked MPs in the House of Commons – so much so, that the matter was raised on the floor of the House, further encouraging more trolls, more publicity, more hatred and even more childish vulgarity. *Daily Stormer* boss Andrew Anglin declared his troll war against Berger, saying:

> *"Following the Jewess Berger's successful lobbying of the British government to have the valiant hero Garron Helm locked in a cage for having identified her as a subversive alien parasite on Twitter."*

In order to press the point, Anglin suggested the use of rude terminology, while explicitly condemning any threats or allusions to violence of any kind. The brave soldiers of *The Daily Stormer* heeded the call and assaulted the "Jewess" on Twitter in the name of freedom. National Action's comment on the matter of the harassment of Luciana Berger was simple: "We hope the cunt gets PTSD".

CHAPTER 5: THE MOULDING OF A FOOL

The Crown Prosecution Service said the men, who "shared right-wing views", aimed to disrupt an antifascist benefit gig in Bold Street on 6 July. Ahead of the concert, the men targeted a group of people walking along the road to the event, police said. The men all pleaded guilty to violent disorder at an earlier hearing at Liverpool Crown Court.

**BBC: Men jailed for attack on antifascist group in Liverpool.
26 September, 2013**

National Action leader Raymond revelled in his group's new visibility. The drama of the NA's "bravery" and an increasing interest in the group both online and off, was being driven by stunts and Raymond's mastery of the art of dramatic license. By the end of 2014 he was waxing lyrical:

"What we are building is a network of cadres who are genuine believers, comrades who know what they fight for. With such people we can elevate this movement to a higher level – in this country we could build a war machine that can tear through the tired institutions and rip them into bloody shreds."

Money flowed into the group's PayPal account from abroad, as the ever-present overseas interest in the British far right peaked. The young journalist Colin Cortbus had even obliged with an article splashed across the *Daily Star* about the group's training camps, as part of the Sigurd network, supposedly named in honour of Norwegian mass murderer Anders Breivik and showing masked men with rifles at the prehistoric site of Silbury Hill in Wiltshire.

In one internet post, a 21-year-old rebel called 'Wolf' wrote: "Sigurd separates the men from the boys." His Twitter account revealed a string of rants and posts about Hitler with the caption: "Hitler was right." Garron Helm was most likely 'Wolf'. The response from the US was overwhelming. Not only was the internet flooded with hateful and threatening memes about

Jewish Labour MP Luciana Berger, National Action was at the centre of the storm. Regional email addresses were set up to allow local members to carry out local recruitment and to also alleviate the stress on the main account and Raymond's time. By mid- 2014 one former NA insider claimed the NA main email account was getting more than 1,000 requests for information, news and interviews per week.

National Action was also lauded on the popular image forum, 4Chan, a natural home for right-wing trolls, some of whose members later went on to manipulate images around Muslim terror attacks in order to sow further hatred. To keep up with the demand, the group mass-produced stickers, designed over the internet, to push its message of hate and division further to casual supporters who requested them.

But there'd been noticeable frustrations for the leadership too. Although they had members and masses of publicity, actual membership was surprisingly low and activists not always easy to direct and control. The British National Party (BNP) hadn't entirely forbidden dual membership of the group and Raymond, Alex Davies and Paul Hickman were becoming desperate the BNP should proscribe them, forcing the hand of their young members. Instead, BNP leader Nick Griffin decided to counter National Action by, as promised in Brussels, sending the Young BNP into battle in the almost entirely pointless campaign to save his seat in the European Parliament. His seat representing North West England was, as everyone knew, as good as gone anyway, and he thought he could prolong his position as leader by endorsing and promoting prospective NA personnel to key positions within his party.

In May 2014, the BNP released a video showing their radical young members bemoaning Britain falling into the hands of Zionism, Islam and "militant homosexuals". It was Griffin's first salvo of his new radical campaign. Kevin Layzell, Person B and Jack Renshaw all took lead roles in the ludicrously comic and wooden production, which caused hysterics when it aired. While Griffin thought the video projected the party as young, upbeat and radical, it was viewed exactly as what it was by the rest of the BNP's leadership: another horrific embarrassment. The party's ruling body would hasten plans already afoot to remove and dispense with Griffin as party leader.

There was also was very little National Action recruitment going on in university campuses. Even though this alleged campaign was the source of much publicity and confrontation, few students bothered giving Raymond's confused literary ramblings much more than a mocking acknowledgement. NA's proposed new, modern and disciplined man was also not always quite as disciplined as Raymond hoped. Members of the group may have willingly taken part in physical training camps, but they'd also taken to heavy drinking and drug-taking when socialising with other, more worldly far-right groups. Raymond himself hardly lived up to his supposed Aryan ideals either, with what appeared to be in our opinion, a developing fetishisation and fantasies about raping, defecating and urinating on political opponents.

In September, National Action activists went to a demonstration in Rotherham where both the National Front and the English Defence League (EDL) faced off with one another. NA turned up, armed with its growing reputation around training camps, and allegedly running around with guns hoping to recruit people from either group that was bored of the same old NF or EDL routines of getting drunk in pubs and then being shoved in car parks for their ever-diminishing protests. However, the young NA activists were battered into retreat by the EDL, along with the NF members, for being "Nazis". It was a humiliation. Despite the drugs and the drinking, a coalition of the NF and North West Infidels (NWI) could at least hold their own in a punch-up and did so in front of bemused antifascists after coming to NA's rescue. So much for National Action and its desire to be the new neo-Nazi vanguard.

Davies was increasingly antagonised by Garron Helm's stardom. As the group's founder and leader, Davies saw himself as the most dynamic individual in National Action. Not only that, but Helm had let the group down by apologising to Luciana Berger. Helm had little idea, interest in or sympathy for what Davies was going through, trying as he had been, to survive at university while building a revolution. Not only had Helm's stardom impacted on the prospects of a personal relationship Davies was trying to ignite, but it had overshadowed his own great achievement in being thrown out of university earlier in the year. In fact, by mid-2014 the University of Warwick had taken out a court order out against NA. In comparison to Helm's 'martyrdom', Davies' genteel poverty and well-deserved exclusion from university looked like very middle-class problems.

Helm's two weeks in prison hardly made him Rudolf Hess, but it was a period of incredible and intense scrutiny for National Action. Their sense of paranoia and their ability to hide themselves and their identities on- and offline served them well. NA was an almost impossible nut to crack, with nothing leaked and few mistakes made. There were no ex-members, no schisms or public fallouts. The media could only report what NA wanted them to report and they obliged by helping on one or two of the more notorious 'undercover' exclusives or special investigations about themselves. Nobody knew anything about them or just how serious or dangerous they were going to be.

Raymond and Davies, in particular, were relative unknowns and it was impossible for the media to understand how big National Action was, how clinically professional it was or how it was ticking over. What NA didn't want to be known, wasn't known, giving it the ability to boast and exaggerate, offering journalists a host of wild and provocative headlines and scandals to feed their lust for stories.

National Action was becoming a media sensation, and Raymond, who dealt with the group's publicity, had an eye for the drama, shock and choreography of running a constant attention-grabbing publicity stunt. He was always demanding photographs and reports for the NA website and his monthly activist report.

On the day of Helm's release from prison in early November 2014, a dozen National Action members led by Ashley Bell arranged to march to Luciana Berger's constituency office in Liverpool to greet their freed colleague, hoping to generate more publicity for the American market. Davies didn't show up and neither did NA's local leader Christopher Lythgoe. Before the group could meet up with Helm, Merseyside police swooped, arresting eight people. It was the first real dedicated police action against NA. The arrestees were held facedown in the street, searched and humiliated. Their homes were raided later in the day by armed officers. Those held by the counter terror police had their phones and computers taken for examination. The arrests, close to Berger's Parliamentary office in the city, were the beginning of an extreme antagonism between NA and the city of Liverpool that was to continue until the group's demise.

There was an air of excitement and outrage about the arrests but also the early beginnings of mistrust opening within the group. News of the arrests took a while to filter out to the wider movement, given so few of those arrested were actually plugged in to it. It wasn't until the next day that news slowly filtered through and came to Davies' attention.

Lythgoe, as leader of the group in the North West, was expected to be among those being held, but – ever paranoid about security – he reported he hadn't attended the demonstration because the whole thing had been organised on open text messages. Not heeding the good sense behind Lythgoe's paranoia, Davies made an appeal on Facebook for anybody arrested the previous day to get in touch. He even included his own phone number. Questions were asked as to why Davies hadn't led the demonstration, but he could hardly answer that he was having a jealous hissy fit about Helm over a woman who liked neither of them.

Helm claimed he'd seen the police swoop on the group and ran away to avoid detention. That in itself raised eyebrows. Surely Helm would now be a heavily-monitored individual and perhaps in the course of his climb-down and apology to the MP, he could have co-operated with the authorities in some way? Perhaps he'd even told the police about the planned demonstration? It would later transpire that Helm had also been under the government's 'Prevent' programme, desperately pleading them to help him to leave the far right.

Police raids and continuing national headlines made National Action more attractive to those in the movement tired of constant electoral defeats and disorganisation. But we're still talking about very small numbers. One of those who responded to Davies' appeal for news on the whereabouts of his arrested activists was Liam Pinkham, an already notorious Nazi from Birkenhead, near Liverpool.

The 25-year-old was well-known in Nazi and antifascist circles. He began his political life, in his late teens, living in a series of Nazi squats around Widnes, not far from Liverpool. The Widnes Front and Widnes White Boys had a loose connection to the Blood & Honour music network, an ageing and often volatile neo-Nazi skinhead movement promoting neo-Nazi music.

Pinkham's gangs spent their recreational time drinking cheap lager and cider, listening to punk and looking for fights with other gangs.

Despite their racist views, the Widnes squatters had rejected the politics of the BNP and the National Front. But Pinkham was attracted to the formality of the proper fascist movement and began dating the daughter of a well-known member of Blood & Honour. This came about only after Pinkham was criticised because a previous girlfriend was underage. With his new girlfriend he would later have a child, permanently cementing him as an upstanding member of the movement.

By his mid-twenties Pinkham had developed a reputation for violence and obedience. He was active in just about every far-right group going – even, on the odd occasion, with the English Defence League. After an earlier prison sentence, he was welcomed home to a newly-acquired housing association flat in Stockport with freshly painted swastikas on every wall.

In June 2012 Pinkham and up to nine other NWI members carried out a violent assault in Liverpool city centre on a father and his two sons who'd been to an anti-racist benefit concert in the city.

The assault, carried out in broad daylight, was captured on CCTV and footage of the attack was shared on social media by hundreds of British neo-Nazis in a macabre celebration of the strength and audacity of the gang. Not only was the gang 'fearless', it was an open secret it dealt Class A drugs in towns around the north west area, from Blackburn to Blackpool. That members of the gang were prepared to carry out violent and 'daring' assaults on antifascists gave them a notoriety not seen in the British far right since the days of another gang of violent neo-Nazi drug couriers, Combat 18. It was the daring and violent pranks that had also attracted the BNP's leader, Nick Griffin to the group – that and its joint hatred of the EDL and their leader.

Pinkham and five gang members were sentenced for the attack at Liverpool Crown Court in September 2013. Already on the fringes of National Action by this time, Pinkham was jailed for 17 months. Sentenced alongside him were Shane Calvert from Blackburn, who'd founded the gang – he got 14 months – and Michael 'Mayo' Kearns, the son of a Labour councillor, who also received a 14-month sentence. Police congratulated themselves that not only had they dealt a blow to a group capable of significant public order concerns, but also to a significant distributor of class A drugs.

Upon his release in 2014, Pinkham was keen to cement a relationship with the dynamic-seeming National Action. During the period of the NWI's imprisonment, NA had a free rein recruiting across the region. Pinkham was markedly different to the others in the NWI, most of whom were older and never worked, preferring instead to live off the proceeds of crime. Unlike himself, they were hardly ideological adherents to fascism. The strict rules about family and morality Pinkham so wanted to adhere to were not present among the self-proclaimed 'Infidels'. Its leader, Shane Calvert, seemed to have children abandoned with single mothers all over the place. He was also not keen on the NWI's industrial scale drug dealing. Calvert, a scrawny, unclean-looking and physically underdeveloped thug, had fathered eight children. He even had a conviction for criminal damage at the home of a woman who was pregnant with his unborn child.

Prison was an unpleasant experience for Pinkham. He'd let down his partner and disrupted their plans to have Aryan children brought up the right way. In prison the NWI gang had no problem making friends with a black gang on the wing at HMP Liverpool, sharing drugs and mobile phones with them. Pinkham had planned to keep fit and come out of prison wiser, fitter and smarter than he went in. The others took to it like a holiday camp on drugs. They spent their time smoking weed and a new drug, spice, that was later to fund most of NWI's activities.

Ideological and increasingly violent, Pinkham's experience convinced him the next time he went to prison it would be for something with people slightly more dynamic than the drug dealers and low-lifes of the NWI. He wanted more Hitler and less hedonism. The National Action leadership was just as keen as Pinkham on having a tie-in between the two groups; money and violence were no obstacle. NWI members were certainly able to handle themselves and they had no fears about going to prison for their criminal and political activities. It opened up a whole network of violent reprobates that would bring NA closer to the National Front and begin a connection into the dark and murky world of potential drug funding. The revolution NA had been planning was starting to take a very different course.

(Three years after Pinkham's jail spell, the NWI's Michael Kearns was sent back to prison for his part in a drug racket that ferried £5m worth of cocaine around the M6 motorway. At the time of his conviction he was a National Front organiser, an NWI enforcer and a financial contributor to National Action.)

Joining National Action, Pinkham offered his thoughts on what had happened in Liverpool and to those who went to meet Helm. The police's heavy-handed action had been to "protect there [sic] token Jew", he wrote to Davies. Approval and commiserations from the likes of Pinkham were exactly what NA's leaders wanted, never mind their idea about wiping away and destroying the rest of the British far right.

Although there was growing acceptance National Action was now part of the movement, it came with predictable criticisms. The attention-seeking behaviour that so titillated tabloid journalists bored older hands in the far right. And it wasn't just antifascists who thought little of Raymond's internet ramblings; even in the London Forum some questioned the sense in some of NA's musings and the sudden descent into vulgarity. NA had promised it would be a cutting-edge and cultural youth movement, but aside from the facemasks and persistent Nazi salutes, there was little to tell them apart from the moronic EDL.

Raymond was by this point hinting he had Asperger's Syndrome, a mark he considered of some untapped genius. It also appeared he wasn't overly concerned by some inside National Action in the North West of England dealing drugs. He'd been working on a theory that the group would eventually have to 'self-mutilate' anyway.

Young journalist Colin Cortbus was part credited with inventing the term 'White Jihad'. Raymond liked the idea and theory behind such a term. White Jihad, to him, meant total and utter devotion to the cause, achieving the final aims by any means necessary ... as long as he and Davies were the leaders. Raymond was having the most fun he had ever had in his previously sad, ignored life. So too was Helm.

In an interview with Hickman's *Renegade Radio* at the end of 2014, Helm talked about himself and National Action being on a "war footing". He also casually mentioned that he'd been visited by special branch officers earlier in the year when he was, at most, an incredibly peripheral figure in the far right who'd been only to a few events with the National Front and an NWI demonstration. Maybe he was bragging, maybe this is when he first began working with the government's Prevent programme. In a paranoid world, especially one where increasing fame and infamy could (hopefully) get you access to ever-elusive money and/or women (or simply sent to prison), such an admission – however inflated – did little to endear Helm to others. Helm bragged further that he was known online previously as "The Jew Hunter" and, one presumes, the Jewish MP Berger had been his prey.

The broadcast was revealing. Helm isn't gifted with the greatest intellect. Two Americans rang in to chat to him and his host, former BNP organiser Hickman. Hickman told one caller they were jealous of Americans who had the right to bear arms. The American grunted in appreciation and then it was Helm's turn to talk:

"In reference to the guns... a lot of us lads here are sitting here and waiting for you guys to rise up and start it all because you have the manpower and you do have the weaponry to get shit done.... We're waiting for you guys to step up to the plate.

"What the left don't understand is that NA and National Socialism is a brotherhood. And that's why they'll never win us... one would lay down his life for the next man next to him, I'll take that to my grave."

Of Luciana Berger, the Jewish MP he'd actually apologised to:

"She's a dog, she's a piece of shit. The only way they'll stop me is if they choose to put a bullet in me."

CHAPTER 6: **WHITE JIHAD**

"It isn't illegal to be part of our organisation, however if you do decide to become an activist you will need to become anonymous. You will receive further instruction on how to do this."

National Action website, advice on how to join.

Garron Helm's apparent desperation to be a martyr, to die by bullet for the cause if necessary, had struck a chord with Christopher Lythgoe, his sponsor inside the group and National Action's North West organiser. But if Lythgoe had been excited by Helm's earlier commitment, he'd been bitterly disappointed Helm had apologised to Jewish MP Luciana Berger after sending her an anti-Semitic tweet.

Lythgoe was a secretive individual. His semi-detached home on Greymist Avenue in Warrington was co-inhabited by his parents and a sister, but when people visited there was never any other sign of life. Lythgoe made visitors wait on the doorstep. If it was raining and they asked politely enough, they could stand just inside the front door.

You couldn't help but notice how dark and cold it was in the house; there were no furnishings to make it feel homely. The only noise was a clock that ticked somewhere in the darkness. The front garden was unkempt, with a tree and bushes shielding the living room windows. Despite being in his late twenties, Lythgoe's hair was beginning to recede. He favoured caps and hats and dressing down in tracksuit pants, old jumpers and thin jackets. He was a scruff.

National Action members were encouraged not to ask such questions of each other. Lythgoe never spoke about what he did for a living or where he got his money from. Even when later arrested, unlike others in NA, nobody came forward to say they knew him. Not even the people at the Warrington Warjukwai judo club where he trained. He just liked books – and onions.

But Lythgoe believed he was born to lead National Action. Though he got on well with co-founders Raymond and Alex – even liked them! – he didn't respect them. They were careless. Lythgoe saw NA as being able to take the next step of going to war with the state.

Although others had little time for it, Lythgoe liked Raymond's writing: it had a revolutionary air similar to some of the obscurities he liked to read on the internet or in books he had under his bed and on a small desk he used. There was a vulgar, revolutionary quality to some of Raymond's confused and contradictory nonsense. Despite this, Lythgoe was the first to doubt whether Raymond, who acted more and more like a spoilt rich kid, was actually committed to the next step.

Lythgoe thought he was invaluable to the group and it helped that, unlike Raymond, he could spell properly. He began communicating directly with Raymond over the spelling and grammar errors he made on the group's website and blogs. Whether or when he actually began contributing directly isn't entirely clear, given how protective Raymond was of the site, but it wasn't long until Lythgoe was editing and overseeing all Raymond's written work.

The phrase 'white jihad' also pleased Lythgoe. It evoked an image of selfless determination and sacrifice. At a training camp in Wales the previous year, attendees had adopted it as their mantra after watching Islamic State (ISIS) propaganda videos. There was no reason National Action could not be a similar outlet for angry white youths, he thought. Some members, like Lythgoe, even grew little beards. Nazism, National Socialism, was all about killing people after all. Lythgoe had long ago developed nihilistic, far-ranging interests.

Like ISIS, Lythgoe demanded National Action moved strictly to using encrypted-only messages when communicating. The messages would expire after sending and become irretrievable. In the evenings, Lythgoe took his dark desires and evil thoughts to the pub with him and sat alone downing pint after pint in silence. Most mornings he rose early to run off the excesses of the night before.

Helm may have had a careless, big mouth, but what was to say he'd be around forever anyway?

Health: We cannot accept persons with serious mental issues into the group for reasons of liability; Schizophrenia, Autism, and Homosexuality may result in discontinued involvement in the group.

***

2014 had been a good year. Recruitment had been slower than they'd wished or anticipated but that wasn't a terrible thing. In terms of image, reputation and appeal, National Action had arrived on the scene and looked very much like the sort of choreographed nasties Raymond and Davies had wished for. The BNP's decision to expel Nick Griffin from the party would, they felt, hasten both the BNP and Griffin's demise and send dozens of young BNP activists into NA.

To the growing numbers of YBNP members facing expulsion or being driven out of the party, National Action looked dangerous and interesting. NA hoped YBNP members would look to them as the next logical step in their journey. The party had failed; the political process and electioneering had proved pointless. Whether they thought it or knew it, terrorism was the natural progression for them.

Every fascist group had, at sometime, crossed the line from racism and vulgarity into terrorism. The National Front, the BNP and even Britain First and the EDL, relative newcomers, had members who wanted to kill and maim others. It came with the rage, the angst and vindictiveness that defined them. Few of the hatched plots made by British fascists ever came to fruition through a combination of cowardice or a simple inability to cross over the line from wannabe to actual terrorist.

What defined this impotence was the sight of the National Front and the BNP in the 1980s and 1990s, and how many of their members found their ways into little fan clubs of Northern Irish terrorists or strutted around wearing and displaying the tat of terror gangs like the Ulster Defence Association (UDA) and Ulster Volunteer Force (UVF). By the mid 1990s the terror group Combat 18 graduated to carrying and collecting guns and drugs for the UDA, even going as far as to pose with guns destined for terrorism, but they never actually went and actually carried out a (successful) terrorist attack, even though they had a murderous internal feud some time later.

The jihadis had their virgins waiting for them and National Action was developing a system of similar beliefs around death and sacrifice. Unlike Combat 18, NA were hardly gregarious types. They were lonely, sad, little boys in the main with nothing else but dreams of murder and genocide. Helm, with his tweets to the MP Luciana Berger, had been the first to exhibit a burning desire to be martyred, or at least noticed. The publicity and infamy he gained had titillated the others. Who would be the next to go further?

On January 14 2015, a 26-year-old called Zack Davies, from Mold in north Wales, walked into his local Tesco supermarket and attacked a Sikh man with a 30cm machete and a claw hammer.

Dr Sarandev Bhambra had been walking down the aisle of the store when he felt a "huge blow" to the back of his head. The 25-year-old dentist from Leeds was later left with two deep cuts to his scalp and another to his back. Caught completely by surprise, he turned to face his white attacker, who was swinging again, trying to behead him – just like ISIS did with its victims.

A fellow shopper Leanne Jones said she heard the words "white power!", recalling Davies was acting "like a lunatic" as he hacked away at Dr Bhambra with his machete. Another witness heard Davies say: "Come here, this is for Lee Rigby."

As shoppers fled and Davies continued with his sickening assault, one man stepped forward to protect Dr Bhambra. Former soldier Peter Fuller had been making his way along the homeware aisle when he heard shouting. He later recalled the words: "Remember Lee Rigby!", the name of the off-duty soldier murdered by two Islamist fanatics in 2013, and "white power!" Initially he thought the noise came from children messing around, but what Fuller saw was two men, one white with a large knife and a hammer, and one Asian, flinching in terror with his arm raised to protect his head. He walked forward a few paces to investigate further. The Asian male was now on his knees and the white male was standing over him swinging a machete towards his head. He saw one blow land with full force, hitting Dr Bhambra in the back and shoulder area. The former soldier described it as being the most evil thing he had ever seen.

Fuller then saw Dr Bhambra get to his feet and run away towards the bakery section of the supermarket, with Davies in pursuit with both weapons raised. Bhambra and Davies did a small circuit in their chase before Bhambra ran past Fuller, Davies behind him, still with both weapons in hand. As Bhambra passed, Fuller deliberately stepped into Davies' path. He said he was an ex-soldier and told him to "calm down" and that what he was doing was madness. As suddenly as he'd started, Davies stopped.

While Fuller waited with Davies for the ten minutes it took the police to arrive, Davies confessed he'd actually intended to go to the local post office to find a victim, but saw Dr Bhambra heading to Tesco's and decided to attack him instead.

"I've lost it, we're under attack mate," Davies told the former soldier. "You've stopped me."

***

It turned out that Zack Davies was known to the police. According to Robbie Mullen, National Action themselves were amazed Davies still had a machete: he'd bragged to them that police had visited him only the week before and found it in his possession. His bedroom was a Nazi and ISIS shrine. He even had flags and stickers from Combat 18. Among the books found in Davies' possession were many neo-Nazi tracts, including *The Turner Diaries*. There were also publications from the Creativity Movement, a pseudo-religion based in the US that held your race was your faith and which published books such as *On the Brink of a Bloody Racial War* and the *White Man's Bible*. Its leader, Matt Hale from Illinois, was already serving a 33-year prison sentence for trying to arrange a hit on a US federal judge. A 'reverend' of this 'religion', James Mac, was already embedded with NA.

Zack Davies hadn't mistaken Dr Bhambra, a Sikh, for a Muslim. The only thing that mattered was he wasn't white. The "Lee Rigby" shouts had only come to him while he was carrying out the attack.

"It was irrelevant what religion he was. It was his appearance, just the way he looked. It did not matter to me what religion he was, it was his racial appearance." – Excerpt from Zack Davies's police interview

If he thought calling out during the attack would get shoppers onside, he'd made a big mistake. His cries had the opposite effect, attracting former soldier and hero, Peter Fuller, to the scene. Davies told the police he was a member of National Action and an admirer of Islamic State's resident executioner, Jihadi John. He'd posted an image of himself in a balaclava with a large knife and the National Action flag on Facebook only hours before the attack. In keeping with standard and confusing White Jihad protocol, he'd also posted texts from the Qu'ran on his Facebook page which was wide open for everyone to see.

Posing with his National Action flag, Davies wrote:

"...the wrath of Allah is about to come down on the kaffir. I will have my revenge."

Everyone swallowed the bait. This would be no ordinary attempt at a racist murder. Davies came from a family with deep emotional issues. There'd been murders and murderers in the family before, according to journalists who worked on the case. It was hard for them to fathom which was more exciting: a neo-Nazi on a rampage, or an apparent Islamic convert in a little old Welsh town.

Police raided the homes of National Action activists in Wales. Very, very quickly, Raymond moved to disassociate the group (and himself in particular) from Zack Davies. This wasn't an entirely popular decision with some of the members, but in the immortal words of Lythgoe, it was a "fuck-up" after all. Activists carrying out Jihad were supposed to get away with it or die doing it.

Although Zack Davies had been active in National Action for at least a year, a public campaign began very quickly to ridicule him. He was described as "autistic", a "mentalist" and an internet troll. Raymond, NA's public face and somewhat of a coward, didn't disclose that he and Davies had been very close after meeting online. Davies had swallowed hook, line and sinker the murderous admiration of ISIS and Jihadi John. Even though the two had fallen out (like so many British Nazis) over the civil war in Ukraine, in his own words they were "still friends" and Raymond had even warned him on Facebook that people were trying to cause disharmony between them.

From as far away as America, people wrote in to say the Mold attacker – now known on line as 'Zack Ali' – was a Muslim convert. Five days after the attack, Nick Griffin was pushing the same message:

"The serious assault in Mold was rightly given wide media coverage. Much attention was paid to the fact that, according to witnesses, Davies was shouting 'white power'.

"But what the Lying MSM [mainstream media] have totally failed to report is that it has emerged that Zack Davies is a Muslim convert who now calls himself "Zack Ali"...

"It is of course no coincidence that a radicalised Muslim convert would attack a Sikh. Sikhism has its origin in the struggle to defend the Unbelievers of India against wave after wave of Islamist atrocities."

Two months later still, a tiny far-right party called Liberty GB, which had links to both the EDL and UKIP and a large following in the 'counter jihad' (anti-Muslim) movement in the United States, was still pushing the lie:

"British newspapers initially portrayed the attack as a "racially-motivated attempt" by a right-wing extremist promoting "white power." It later emerged that Zack Davies is actually a Muslim convert who goes by the name Zack Ali."

So, if Zack Davies was a Muslim convert and had attempted to murder a Sikh, it would be more than brilliantly helpful for everyone. American neo-Nazis, linked to the group Atomwaffen Division, which mirrored and mimicked much of what National Action did, was also toying with encouraging its members to convert to Islam in the warped belief that such a conversion would remove the fear of death.

Davies had got his jihad wrong. There was now real pressure on British fascists not just to deflect what had happened but to also find the conspiracy behind it. The Sikh community, through no fault of its own, had become the far right's favourite ethnic group, bizarrely allowing the far right to deny anti-Muslim hatred was racial hatred and that fascists were racists. In addition, a Sikh had become the first non-white member of the BNP, and the EDL formed a 'Sikh Division'. Nick Griffin saw a Jewish conspiracy afoot and the EDL and its offshoots saw an Islamic conspiracy in the media's attempts at portraying Zack Davies as a neo-Nazi.

Griffin did acknowledge the role of National Action in the case, but satisfied himself and convinced others this had been another Muslim attack. The police, charged with understanding and countering the far right, appeared non-plussed. They were apparently unaware of this supposedly-monitored group's six-month love-in with Jihadi John and ISIS. They certainly did little to help diffuse the situation.

After Zack Davies' conviction for attempted murder in June 2015, HOPE not hate published private messages between National Action members, revealing they were confident that they'd caused enough confusion to muddy the waters and avoid a deeper focus on their embryonic activities. Writing to friends using the name 'Charlie Guile', Raymond concluded he'd put out so much disinformation about the Zack Davies case that "the Sikh community or whatever will give up trying to generate a buzz. I think we can be pretty chill about the issue from now. RIP Zak."

Like a Jihadi should be, as far as National Action was concerned, Zak Davies was now dead and only much later, would he be properly martyred.

It was as simple as that. NA was off the hook. Nobody called for its banning and the same noises were still made about monitoring far-right extremists who posed an enormous threat online. Davies was just some mad kid, an internet troll with issues, a mad kid who liked both Hitler and ISIS. That's not an ideology, is it?

People had all kinds of ideas about how to tackle extremists like this. Take them to a mosque, feed them foreign food, make them feel guilty about being white, expose them further to cultures they didn't like, show them films about the Holocaust. National Action member Jack Renshaw would one day post a picture of himself on Facebook declaring he was a White Jihadist going about his terrorist business. It's pointless doing anything to tackle an ideology by telling people it's nasty if you don't tackle *the actual ideology* itself and the reasons people choose to follow it.

Members of National Action were now shedding their online identities as they went along, catching up with each other again somewhere down the line under new names. So clever were their communiqués to each other they didn't even need to know each other's real names or phone numbers. Rarely did they communicate in full view or, under Lythgoe's insistence, show their faces without cover.

"Also of concern is NA's use of skull imagery to hide the faces of its activists. The subconscious message sent out by this – to its followers and the public alike – is blatantly negative and unhealthy. If you focus people's attention on death and in such a way, whatever you say about keeping the white race alive, etc, it's pretty much inevitable that impressionable youngsters will become fixated on death." – Nick Griffin, January 2015

***

As things were accelerating with National Action in 2015, the rest of the British far right wasn't standing idly by. There were signs, if not of growth, then certainly of a resurgence; old networks of racist thugs and recreational fascists were becoming more active again. Small numbers of former EDL and BNP members were moving into Nazi street gangs drawn to confrontation with the left. When Nick Griffin was expelled from the BNP in late 2014 after a humiliating and debilitating battle, small numbers of hardline neo-Nazis spilled from the BNP into a host of other groups such as the National Front and North West Infidels. The NWI dominated much of the NF's apparatus in the north of England, keeping the party afloat with drug funds donated under the table and by providing small numbers of violent muscle on its growing list of desperate activities.

Jack Renshaw, the brash and upfront young man with startling self-belief, had led a spirited defence of Griffin, gatecrashing an anti-Griffin meeting held in Manchester with 20 others prepared to confront the BNP's new leadership. Many of the BNP's internal problems spilled out in the city and its surrounding towns. Although many had little time for Griffin, the NF and NWI were more than happy to help attack his former party. The youthful Renshaw was central to all of this, having longed to be next leader of the BNP. With Griffin gone, his opportunity had evaporated.

Renshaw had become something of a media celebrity. Hot on the heels of his plastic performance on the viral YBNP video, he made national news when he lamented (hilariously) on social media that his beloved dog, Derek, was challenging his principles by licking the genitals of other male dogs when they were out for a walk. Some people now stopped to shake his hand in the street; others stopped to spit at him.

Renshaw had also taken to blogging, which had come to the attention of his university. His blogs were a vicious party piece in the BNP's internal problems, and included deeply offensive and illegal anti-Semitic content. In London, an Anglo-Turkish pornographer, Steve Squire, had helped hasten Griffin's departure after the BNP leader was the centre of a minor sex scandal in the car park of an Indian restaurant with Squire's erstwhile former lover. Squire was determined, along with the party's new leaders now based in Cumbria, to eradicate the party's youth wing along with Griffin. In the course of his blogging, Renshaw had attacked Squire for allegedly selling date-rape drugs in the sex shop he ran in London's Soho. Renshaw pointed out that Squire, who ran a sort of "save the white family" campaign for the BNP, marketed DVDs featuring black men with large appendages "drilling" Aryan women.

The puritanical rants by those within the BNP, now linked to National Action, ensured Squire went about his work with gusto. As a pornographer he knew only too well how big a lust there was for porn inside this new group of upstarts, much of it way beyond what a Soho porn baron was into. Squire pinpointed two individuals he wanted out of the party. In response to Renshaw, Squire verbally attacked the young man in a radio interview, calling him a "faggot." He claimed that at the party's 2014 conference in Blackpool a number of people had told him Renshaw was acting openly gay. Despite Soho pornographers supposedly having fearsome underworld reputations, Squire had to weigh up his joy at eliminating the youth members with the worry about being targeted by them. Years before, during the 1990s, those charged with expelling or ridding Combat 18 members and supporters from the party had found themselves attacked on their doorsteps, even beaten unconscious. In one case, a senior BNP member lost an eye after an attack. The threat posed by NA wasn't a particularly physical one, more of a cyber one. NA members, if they put their minds to it, could cause the BNP all kinds of humiliation and difficulties.

Squire found himself confronted by a far more nuanced insolence when it came to expelling National Action members. Person B, became his immediate nemesis. After being confronted by Person B at a BNP meeting in October 2014, instead of raising the alarm that the young man had undergone a transition from an ordinary, plain-looking schoolboy into something dark and more radical, Squire rather took issue with Person B's dietary intake. In a bizarre text message sent to already stressed BNP organisers, Squire took it upon himself to expel Person B from the BNP in October 2014, writing:

"Dear Officers,
Former member Person B is no longer to be invited/welcomed at BNP meetings. His general attitude towards the [sic] us isn't in the party's interest, his appearance is desending [sic] into Nazi ss style black clothes, boots & razor haircuts. Yesterday at a meeting in East London he ponced tap water of [sic] the venue bar staff whilst bringing his own (sainsburys [sic] branded) salted peanuts."

It was comical. Squire was stranded in London by the party leadership, the party was in chaotic uproar over Griffin's expulsion and Person B, a growing menace with dark thoughts about violence, could only be expelled on the basis of not buying a pint at a branch meeting. And of course, eating home brand peanuts.

Person B had actually intimidated Squire with the threat of violence. He may have been just a gangly teenager, but he'd been attending the training courses run by National Action and the Sigurd and 'Legion' networks it worked with. He was also beginning to fill out, thanks to his use of weights. At a meeting where Squire took a pre-destined offence to him, Person B refused to leave, instead offering to sort it out with Squire outside. There was a similar picture unfolding across the country. In Manchester and Salford, NF and NWI thugs took great pleasure in disrupting BNP meetings to such a point they refused to meet any more.

Things were falling into place very nicely for National Action. Recruits were coming in, the website was getting plenty of hits, Zack Davies had carried out NA's first real "hit" and invitations were now flowing in from overseas to visit likeminded groups. National Action was now in fashion.

CHAPTER 7: ROBBIE MULLEN

"There really wasn't anything else. I was one of those abandoned white working class blokes, or kids, really. There wasn't anything and no-one to guide me through those later teenage years and by the time National Action was on the radar, it was hard to resist the temptation to make myself heard."

Robbie Mullen, speaking to the author March 2019

In 2015, the man who was later to blow the lid on National Action and its murderous intent, Robbie Mullen, began taking an interest in far-right politics.

Born in Widnes, not far from Liverpool, in 1993, he'd lived with his mother, his father – a former horse trainer who'd worked in Canada until forced by injury to retire – his brother and sister until he was 16. It was an unspectacular childhood, punctuated by some financial shortfalls caused by his father's illness. Despite his father's disability – he was kicked by a horse – the family got by.

School appears to have been a minor inconvenience and irritant to Mullen. He was regularly excluded: not for being particularly nasty, just for being a bit of a waster who liked fooling around. When he still could, his father took him to see Manchester United at Old Trafford and so, as a young boy, his weekends were taken up with football and rugby league (he could have been a pro, he thought).

At 13, Mullen's parents decided to turn to homeschooling. He'd been bunking off school and they were facing prosecution. Although he loved them, he had no idea of the stresses and strains he placed on his family. From then on, he stayed up all night and slept in late in the day like an immovable object.

At 16, he agreed to go to college and study for GCSE exams. He'd grown tired of being naughty and staying up late. His parents had grown tired of him, too. He had to get an education or never get a job. Roaming around the streets with other kids was boring. It was either college or, most likely, a term in prison.

In fact, in Mullen's mind there was an almost casual assumption that at some stage in his life he probably was going to prison. It seemed an inevitability, a rite of passage. Aside from his father, just about every male he knew had been to prison. How bad could it be? But he gave college a go. Worse than prison would be to go through life being 'thick'. More importantly, as tempting and easy as a life of crime appeared, his parents didn't share such a lax attitude.

In September 2009 he enrolled in college. It wasn't all that bad. At 16 he was suddenly treated as an adult. And then, just as he thought he could really give it a go and one day get out of Widnes, came bad news.

His father, whose health was deteriorating with sharp pains, was diagnosed with cancer. Mullen carried him to a taxi, bound for Royal Liverpool Hospital, but the vehicle got stuck in the snow and the driver gave up after two hours. He waited with his dad for two hours for an ambulance to pick them up.

Mullen senior lay in a hospital bed next to a dead body for a day before deciding he wanted to die at home. He lived for another month with his family by his side. Minutes before his death he asked for a Kentucky Fried Chicken meal. Robbie and his brother drove to get it, but they hadn't even made it to the takeaway before they were called back home, witnessing the absolute injustice of death.

In 2017, in another dark hour and with his own mortality in jeopardy, I spoke to Mullen's mother on the phone. I'd travelled to Runcorn under the cover of darkness and whisked him out of his house where he lived alone. He'd been unable to tell her about the awful mess he was now involved in, a mess she'd warned him about so many times. She had known so little about the dramatic turns of his life in recent years. During our brief, traumatic conversation, Mullen's mother said he'd never recovered from his father's death: the popular, naughty, but not unkind, boy had vanished that awful day in January 2010 to be replaced by the quiet, methodical loner he'd become.

***

"We are not a social club – as much as we would like to just be your friend we cannot afford to extend the enormous trust that comes with being part of the group if you won't return it. You will eventually be expected to participate in activities. You will need to be able to provide for yourself to at least reach the next town over twice a month if required. If you lose interest in us we will lose interest in you." – National Action Website advice about becoming a member

After his father's funeral Mullen threw himself into looking for work. He took anything that put food on the table and kept him occupied. The family home felt empty. Mullen separated from friends, who soon stopped calling, and worked every available hour. He juggled three jobs, working cash on the market during the weekends and stacking shelves during the week. In the evenings he sat in front of the television, surfing the internet or playing on his Playstation. He became a recluse. Eventually the family went their own ways and moved away from Widnes. Mullen opted to move in with his sister for a while, helping with her kids, before finding a small cramped place of his own. He found himself in and out of work due to a crippling and debilitating stomach pain linked to stress. The early symptoms of depression were probably upon him.

He moved to working night shifts – the pay was better – and it allowed him to sleep through the days, which seemed painful and empty. He found himself leading the shift team, a few more pence in the pocket for a laborious job. He was the only worker on his shift who spoke English as a first language. Moving from shift to shift made him feel even more isolated.

It wasn't until 2015 and after a long period of not working that Mullen applied for a 'proper' job in a business just outside Runcorn. He amazed himself when he got it. He had no qualifications, but he did know about stock control. He moved to new digs to be closer to his new adventure, to start anew another period in his life. By this point he had already discovered National Action on Facebook. He'd been browsing far right and far left politics on the web for a few years. Although he was attracted to the group, he wasn't sure he'd ever get involved. NA said they wanted new recruits, but would they want someone shy, someone quiet, like him? If the website had said they particularly favoured disengaged loners, he may have got involved a little sooner.

But National Action looked perfect: it demanded you shed your old skin and adopt only fellow activists for friends. Life as he had known it in Widnes would be well and truly left in the past. His mum had met someone else by now too; he didn't begrudge her that. Her life had been miserable. He never doubted she had always and would always love his dad, but her life had to move on too.

It was a big company where he now worked and he threw himself into the new job, provided people didn't keep stopping him to chat. Mullen wasn't a 'people person'. They'd just come into the warehouse, hands in their pockets, and chat fucking nonsense to him. The weather, the football, television, what they were having for dinner and where they were going on holiday. It was endless nonsense, but he had to put up with it because he liked the job and the money. With a little bit of overtime he could clear £300 a week into his pocket. The lives of his co-workers were so boring, but unlike them, he'd never even been on a plane or anywhere more exciting than McDonalds for his tea.

During the night Mullen trawled the internet, reading updates from far-right groups about their latest over-inflated adventures: stories about Islamist outrages, endless immigration, child-grooming gangs, the British National Party (BNP), the English Defence League (EDL), the National Front, HOPE not hate, groups like Antifa and more. This life, on the fringe of society and surrounded by notoriety and secrecy, looked exciting, like a fantastic bubble where nothing mundane ever happened. These groups shocked and upset people. One day he hoped someone would walk into the warehouse and say: "Them Pakis have been grooming kids down our street and I'm gonna cause a fucking riot." But they never did. He took himself off to the gym and began to train. He was tall and plump. Soon, if he hit you, you'd feel it.

Once he thought he saw National Action members at the train station in nearby Warrington, dressed in black and standing in silence. They were an eerie bunch. The train arrived and five of them got on in silence and continued to sit in silence until they got off at Liverpool. He didn't approach them. Mullen had seen NA stickers, bemoaning 'White Genocide' and some graffiti on the wall at the ASDA supermarket carpark. The things he saw on the internet were coming to life.

***

As Robbie Mullen slowly slid towards National Action, in February 2015 the group held one of its outdoor training camps. It was led by Jimmy Hey, a mixed martial arts (MMA) instructor with gyms in Blackburn and Heywood in Lancashire. How Hey became involved with NA isn't clear. He was both a serious and sanguine character, a businessman with an interest in the cause of the far-right Ukrainian paramilitary group Azov Battalion. A favourite of worldwide neo-Nazis, the Azov was fighting against Russian separatists in the east of their country.

Despite his views, Hey's gyms trained people from all backgrounds, including blacks, Asians and National Action members. He schooled NA's youthful recruits in the art of MMA, discipline and fitness. That day in February 2015, he marched some 40 young men and women up to the top of series of hills and then let them loose on one another.

National Action was particularly embedded in the North West. Copying the example of autonomous German neo-Nazis, who had no identifiable hierarchy, NA members followed instructions from founder and publicist Ben Raymond to send exciting, arty photographs to the group's website. They were particularly drawn to a disused power station in Huncoat, near Accrington, where they could wear black masks and take shots of themselves looking menacing. The group even had a graffiti artist, Ivan "the Lithuanian Lion", who would claim in an interview published by the group (not long before disappearing with some of its money) that he was fascinated with pederasty (homosexual relations between men and boys).

As already noted, there was an emerging fascination with sex and violence inside National Action. Few seemed overly concerned by just how far their fantasies went.

Ben Raymond may have gone out of his way to distance National Action from Zack Davies' attack on the Sikh dentist in north Wales, but everybody inside NA was seemingly convinced not only was a race war coming, but there were actual real people on their side willing to fight and take action for it.

No longer their primary or even favourite martyr, Garron Helm – who had harassed MP Luciana Berger with vile anti-Semitic messages – felt shunned, however. His online relationship had failed to materialise into anything sexual, adding to his frustrations. People were beginning to complain about his weird and attention-seeking behaviour. After all he had done for them – so he believed – NA had very quickly turned into a bunch of ungrateful bastards.

Following his release from prison, a sympathetic law firm in Liverpool had taken on Helm and given him some work. Nothing serious, just a bit of pocket money, but it was work all the same. Others in National Action were convinced he was talking to the police and he didn't help those suspicions when he told them he'd been offered a leg-up the housing ladder by Special Branch.

Despite these new opportunities, Helm entertained some extreme beliefs. For example, he believed Nazism was compatible with Satanism. This wasn't so much about devil worshipping as the spiritual ability to summon dark forces. It seemed like a natural progression from all the old world English mythology he'd gotten into before.

Helm began taking himself off camping in Lancashire, encouraging others in the group to join him for "contemplation". He believed he could harness an energy to summon wolves to help in National Action's bitter struggle. The rest laughed at him when he turned up to activities with new ideas about spells and sacrifice. Their ignorance frustrated him and drove him into further isolation.

In February 2015, Helm considered sacrificing himself for the greater good and the love and respect of his comrades. Writing as Bruce Wilhelm on Facebook, he stated:

"I'm not a lunatic for embracing martyrdom, I've just accepted that I could be more use in death than life. People need a reason to fight."

Nobody tried to talk him out of anything he was planning, not even the young woman who was the target of his affections. They all just clicked 'like'.

There was too much serious business going on elsewhere to worry about Helm doing something stupid. Raymond, who until now had controlled all of National Action's publicity and administration, was pleasantly horrified by how much support the group was picking up. Despite the denials that Zack Davies had been a member of the group, NA rode a massive wave of recruitment after the Welsh supermarket attack.

***

The Zack Davies attack should have heralded a warning. A new era for National Action was fast approaching. Despite all his confrontational bluster and outrageous blogging, for Raymond the group was a radical, Nazi, 'street art' project he hoped would mimic anarchist situationists – avant-garde artists, intellectuals and political theorists – active in Europe from the late 1950s to the early 1970s. Yet it was clear his pet project had been taking on a life of its own. Doubts had begun to surface about how much control he could exert on the group, even how much it needed him. Having embraced the 'brute' inside NA, Raymond was becoming bitterly disappointed that, in return, the group hadn't embraced or even paid attention to the intellectual challenge, endeavours and pursuits he felt Nazism offered. Raymond opted out as much as possible, preferring not to attend demonstrations.

By now the muscle that National Action needed to bulk up its activities was being funded and powered by drugs sold and used by the North West Infidels. To organise the sort of confrontational activities they desired, they had to collaborate with the equally unappealing National Front. Ben Raymond conceded that his members had to associate with, even at times look inseparable from, the "scum" or "*Der Untermensch*" that had been such a destructive, lumpen obstacle to the advancement of British fascism.

The majority of National Action members were still unknown at this stage; many only appearing in masks during public demonstrations. Exceptions such as the heavily-scarred thug Wayne Bell (aka Wayne Jarvie) from Castleford, who used social media to dish out threats, were rare. When NA activists met they began adhering to the new secrecy codes devised by Christopher Lythgoe, the secretive North West organiser. While Raymond studied texts from his favourite historical and political extremist figures, Lythgoe was studying similar books about the secrecy and planning of revolutionary armies and terror groups. He'd assumed right from the start of his involvement in NA that it would be subject to scrutiny from the state and possibly infiltration – or, more than likely, somebody would turn 'grass' and become an informer. It happened in every revolutionary context: from the serious revolutionary groups on the continent, to the Ku Klux Klan in the United States, to the IRA in Ireland, even small and insignificant Trotskyist groups, animal liberationists, and (bizarrely) health and safety campaigners.

For Raymond, more naive than Lythgoe, the attention of the state was an exciting prospect. It added extra spice to everything he wrote and did, knowing he was a centre of attention and possibly even considered seditious by the government. He tested his notoriety by taking flights to visit his family in Spain or other far-right groups on the continent, wearing baseball caps and dark sunglasses at the airport. Every innocent question at passport control, every hold-up and bag-check at the airport gave him a sense of supreme importance.

However, Raymond's behaviour was beginning to disquiet Lythgoe. In his January 2015 New Year address to members, Raymond had written excitedly about National Action being featured in an academic article. It seemed to please him immensely. Having amassed a large personal collection of academic books on terrorist and revolutionary organisations, Raymond felt the group deserved better coverage than the humiliating and disruptive mentions it got in blogs written by HOPE not hate and others.

Until now, the group had been lumped in with all the other horrendous little neo-Nazi gangs operating in the UK. Becoming the focus of academia meant, in Raymond's bizarre worldview, that he too, as the group's ideologue and spokesperson, somehow inherited a sort of academic mantle.

Whilst Raymond marvelled at what he thought was his own intellectual brilliance, in February 2015 the group suffered a jolt when its Welsh members were raided by counter-terrorist police investigating the Tesco attacker, Zack Davies, for a second time. Although the attention excited Raymond, for others the attention was becoming a growing worry.

Co-leader Alex Davies was by this time living with his grandmother. He slept all day when he wasn't scraping a living at a variety of low-paid, casual jobs and then was up and out all night doing God knows what – and it worried her. Her grandson had become dark, moody and secretive since being thrown out of university. With his boyish acne and squeaky voice, he'd always been loveable but troublesome, up to some kind of antics even as a young boy. Joining the BNP as a teenager had only made him more argumentative and from there it had been progressively downhill. He'd wasted his opportunity to get a real or good job and had frittered away thousands of pounds chasing disinterested girls and political dreams.

Half a dozen mobile phones scattered around Davies's home rang constantly, all hours of the day. He'd taken to answering the phones outside the house in hushed whispers; he was becoming obsessed with the group's security. Raymond, his partner-in-crime living by the seaside in Sussex, seemed to revel in the sort of difficulties and obstructions driving the group further towards a hardening of its views.

Soon, in response to the "constant police harrassement", Davies stepped down as leader. All the time, it was alleged, he was still on the government's Prevent programme.

Davies' decision to resign caused no end of turmoil for Raymond. It was the first real indication to him that if anything, he was being tolerated by some of the members. The decision on who should lead the group he'd founded was taken without him. There was no public announcement and the leadership secretly passed to Ashley Bell (aka Tommy Johnson), the straight edge Leeds Nazi who'd been illegally importing the group's flares and pyrotechnics.

***

"The threat from NA is less political than physical. The organisation appears hell-bent on continuing its provocative actions and the individuals within it are becoming increasingly erratic, unpredictable and potentially violent."
– 'Young, Nazi & Proud', HOPE not hate, March 2015.

Davies's resignation also placed an unwelcome stress on Ashley Bell. Although the title 'leader' was in some ways symbolic – what with Raymond orchestrating the website and the group's choreography – Bell's very apparent disdain for humans shone through. Lythgoe manoeuvred himself into a position to lead the group should Bell tire of the responsibility, appointing himself National Action's internal security adviser. At this stage, nobody outside the very inner core of the gang knew Lythgoe existed.

Raymond, Davies, Lythgoe, Ashley Bell and Person B sat on every messenger group National Action was now using to communicate. Or at least they thought they did. Messages between members were set to vanish within half an hour. Lythgoe had chosen Russian and German messaging apps because those countries' governments, he thought, were less likely to hand over information to the British security services. The messages went on throughout the day and night, with members' phones pinging with constant communications. The messages could be banal, childish, threatening or sickening. In one message to one group they even discussed raping my mother.

There was never any danger of individuals breaking away or forming factions, even if it did increasingly cross Raymond's mind. National Action was a gift for everybody that could run with it. Once accepted into NA, as long as they were loyal to the group, members could do whatever they wanted. There were no limits to how vulgar or offensive they could be.

As the group's self-declared choreographer and intellectual, Raymond thought he was being helpful and instructive, but in many cases his frequent longwinded interjections when serious discussions were being had were off-putting and divisive. Away from the leadership group however, angry young men (and women) wanted to do the very things Raymond's writings hinted at, even if he himself seemed to believe they were only words.

Despite his transparency and encouragement, some members – particularly Lythgoe – were growing tired of Raymond's comments. Lythgoe viewed many of the recruits as already wildly hardened and disaffected. They wanted adventure and they came to National Action to find it. Training camps were now frequently taking place and a little fight club had opened up in East London, where members trained in kickboxing and MMA with Polish neo-Nazis. For Lythgoe, there was a growing and pleasing obsession with death, terror and destruction running through the group.

Lythgoe wanted National Action's recruits to remain aloof in the company of other fascists (though by necessity the gang would have to deal with them). Not only were the majority of other gangs heavily dependent on drugs and alcohol, but there was little doubt they'd also be compromised by police informers, perhaps manipulated by the state on account of their addictions and stupidity. NA had to be something different, he believed: it had to be an 'elite' like the early and almost forgotten demands of NA dictate.

The dour leader-in-waiting went about his business quietly and methodically. Despite the countless frustrations he generated, Raymond's self-obsessions about his image and intellect were a good camouflage for Lythgoe. Lythgoe even suggested that wherever Raymond went he should have a bodyguard with him, as he was the group's 'public face'. This pomp and importance appealed to Raymond though he still had little interest on doing more than the bare minimum public activity. He also suspected Lythgoe was setting him up as a patsy. If anybody was going to be a risk to the security of the group, they'd go for the likeable and confused buffoon that was Ben Raymond.

Raymond's international travels were now adding to the group's growing international visibility. He hoped by cultivating links with fascist groups overseas he could impress others with his 'cutting-edge' intellectual project. It didn't seem to hurt if he was photographed holding the occasional firearm along the way. He travelled to Finland in January 2015 to meet up with members of Suomen Vastarintaliike, the Finnish arm of the Nordic Resistance movement that operated across much of Scandinavia and was obsessed with primality and Nazi activity. In the report of his trip, published two months later, Raymond wrote: "I would actually meet a lot more women during my time in Finland, so people preoccupied with this issue should take note" – quite possibly a reference to the excessive sexualisation of National Action, and the whispers, rumour and general assumption that he was gay.

More interestingly, perhaps, was Raymond's admission that he, like the Finnish neo-Nazi leader Kai Murros, was a fan of the Khmer Rouge, the murderous Maoist group that took control of Cambodia in the mid-1970s and ushered in a genocidal reign of terror. Maybe Raymond had, at least, an understanding of Freud:

> "We agreed on a Cambodian solution to the problems afflicting our nations. I would meet Kai again in Helsinki where he would elaborate on this theme 'It was my anti-communism that led me to support the Khemer [sic] Rouge' – as this was a movement for the destruction of intellectual life."

***

There were now nearly 100 members of National Action meeting regularly around the country. Many carried out autonomous actions, often low-level graffitiing and postering, but there was also violence. Universities remained a favourite hunting ground for the youthful extremists. These seats of learning were ripe for confrontation. Of course, both Alex Davies and Jack Renshaw had been removed from their studies because of their far-right activities, making them increasingly targets for retribution. University was now an enemy hunting ground, not the place of intellectual challenges and equals Raymond and Alex Davies once dreamed it would be.

With almost £10,000 in the group's PayPal account, National Action could now afford to pay for materials and travel expenses. Raymond and Alex Davies took the step in early 2015 of giving half a dozen of their most trusted organisers the log-in details to pay for what needed doing in the name and cause of white jihad. This helped ease some of the financial stress on Davies, but also helped pay for more than 20,000 NA stickers that soon arrived from Poland.

In Borehamwood north of London, a campaign of intimidation against the area's Jewish community was up and running. National Action stickers and posters were plastered across the area, with gangs of hooded men intimidating anyone who came across them as they did so. Although these actions were the work of NA activists, the main muscle was provided by Polish neo-Nazis from the National Rebirth of Poland (NOP), a skinhead gang made up of Poles living in the UK. The Poles were members of a tiny organisation in Poland that masqueraded as a political party. Even in Poland, which had a large number of competing far-right groups, the NOP was considered an unpleasant aberration. Although anti-Semitism is common among such Polish groups, the adoption of German Nazi imagery isn't always as welcome: after all, as well as enslaving their nation, the Nazis had regarded the Poles as an inferior race.

Mainly centred in London, Manchester and the south east and west of England, this relatively small group of Polish extremists had been operating under the radar of their host country's fascist and Nazi groups since 2010. It was active in trying to recruit Poles living and working in some of Britain's poorest neighbourhoods, often where Polish migrants lived cheek-by-jowl with other immigrants. Formed in 1981 as an underground movement under Communist rule, NOP was the longest surviving post-war Polish Nazi group. Originally a youth movement, it registered itself as a political party in 1992, in its own words for "legal convenience". Since 2001, the party has taken part in the electoral process in Poland, but polled miserably. Its website – which had an English section for its UK-based members and supporters – called for the death of the "Enemies of the Polish Fatherland."

The BNP had been the first to embrace the influx of Polish EU migrants into the UK back in 2009, when it cynically used imagery of Polish World War Two fighter pilots and Spitfire planes from the Battle of Britain in its election materials. It certainly unsettled some of the BNP's more blue-collar members, who found themselves in competition for jobs in the building trade with desperate Poles they felt were undercutting their salaries. The Poles, though, were lauded by the BNP for being hardworking, Christian, white and prepared to have white children.

In Manchester and Norwich the NOP held leafletting sessions at the cities' train stations, handing out leaflets in English and Polish demanding the release of Janusz Waluś in South Africa. Waluś is currently serving a life sentence for in 1993 assassinating the African National Congress's general secretary Chris Hani. It was an obscure demand to make of a wholly disinterested England.

As well as attending National Front Remembrance Day marches, the NOP began ingratiating themselves by attending London demonstrations in support of Greek neo-Nazi party Golden Dawn, as well demonstrations in support of Ukrainian neo-Nazis and the paramilitary Azov Battalion. In the absence of any particularly intimidating British muscle, they also guarded the meetings and protests organised by the highbrow London Forum.

The NOP cared little for British laws, sensing a freedom here its followers weren't necessarily allowed in Poland, where even other neo-Nazis wanted to attack them. Like National Action, they viewed the British far right as physical and intellectual weaklings: it wasn't long before the two sets of extremists, NA and the NOP, had fallen into bed with one another.

In Manchester the NOP had a link man in British-born hotel worker Radoslaw Rekke. Based in Wythenshawe, Rekke had a habit of posing on Facebook with a collection of large hunting knives and (supposedly deactivated) firearms he collected. He'd long been an admirer of Polish neo-Nazis. Once Polish migrant workers began arriving in the UK, he began to look for like-minded Poles. Still a teenager who'd hooked up with plenty of Polish fascists and neo-Nazis on trips to Poland, he was conscious he spoke Polish with a noticeable Mancunian accent. Like many who found their way to National Action, he was something of an outsider.

Feeling ostracised from society, Rekke threw himself completely into the National Action / National Rebirth of Poland tie-in. On training camps, they talked at great length about what weapons they could carry legally in public. Small penknives on key rings were the most favoured. Through it all, Rekke was making a name for himself by walking through Manchester city centre with Nazi badges sewn on his jacket, carrying a knuckle-duster and a knife concealed in his pocket.

He soon joined up with National Action activists, including a Latvian man and a teenager from Stockport, to plaster mosques and Jewish schools in the North West with both NA and NOP stickers. Like everything else NA did, it was carried out in a methodical frenzy. In Prestwich, in the north of Manchester, the group was busy with desecrating Jewish buildings and property. Renshaw, by now heavily embedded in NA, had even gone on social media to broadcast himself putting up "Stop anti-White Genocide" stickers on the office of the local MP. There was a growing sense of invincibility.

CHAPTER 8: A WAR IS BREWING

"A war is brewing it is inevitable. We will be the ones fighting it… we must be ruthless and if innocent people are cut down in the process then so be it….Blood must be shed, the blood of traitors and our enemies."

– Matthew Hankinson, speech to National Action's 'White Man March', Newcastle, March 2015.

The north east of England has a long association with the extreme right and also a proud tradition of trade unionism and organised anti-fascism. It could often be a bit of a battle ground. In its early days, the English Defence League (EDL) could call on hundreds of supporters across both Newcastle and Sunderland. Before that, the British National Party (BNP) had stood a full slate of candidates across the region at local elections.

After both the BNP and EDL went into decline, EDL splinter group, the North East Infidels (NEI) led by convicted drug dealer Warren Faulkner became the pre-eminent far-right group in the region. It stayed mainly in Sunderland to avoid conflict with what remained of the EDL in Newcastle. Another gang, the Sunderland Defence League, operated in both Sunderland and Newcastle, as did the National Front and another neo-Nazi outfit, the Northern Patriotic Front. It wasn't uncommon to find the rival groups brawling with each other after heavy bouts of drinking on a Saturday afternoon.

Despite being linked to another EDL splinter (the North West Infidels), the NEI wanted nothing to do with the Nazis of National Action. This didn't really matter to NA's scarred thug Wayne Bell, who was entrusted with organising the group's first public demonstration. The White Man March would take place in Newcastle in late March 2015. There were plenty of other big-hitting local Nazis to provide security for the small number of marchers. They'd meet at a rally point on the Blacksmith's Needle monument at Newcastle's Quayside, where Bell would lead masked and black-garbed NA members down to greet them. The Quayside was once the industrial hub of Newcastle's docks and after years of decay had undergone gentrification. Small bars and cafes now lined the area, overlooked by new apartments: it was becoming the hip place to be away from the hustle and bustle of Newcastle's busy city centre.

With an openly neo-Nazi group coming to town, nobody was entirely sure what to expect. Rallies and marches by the EDL had attracted hundreds, even thousands, in the not-too-distant past. The previous month, 400 people had attended a Newcastle rally by the anti-Muslim group PEGIDA UK – an attempt to mimic the German anti-Muslim street movement from Dresden. The leader of PEGIDA UK would be, for a short while, Stephen Lennon who had formed, led and then abandoned the EDL.

Newcastle was grey and overcast as a crowd of around 100 far-right activists gathered in the spitting rain. Thirty National Action members stood on the Blacksmith's Needle monument dressed in black, their faces covered, giving Nazi salutes. Garron Helm, hair slicked back and looking everything like a young Nazi should, removed his mask on a number of occasions so he could be photographed and immortalised. Christopher Lythgoe mingled in the crowd listening to speeches with his head and face covered.

Robbie Mullen had left home in Runcorn early in the morning to be there on time. He was excited by the prospect of finally seeing the mighty National Action in action. Maybe there would be a riot, maybe he would be jumped by antifascists who had vowed to "smash" the march. Other than finally meeting NA members in the flesh, he had no other real expectations. Like the others, he wore all black. He grabbed himself a pasty at Liverpool Lime Street station and prepared for the journey to Newcastle, constantly checking his phone for updates. He hadn't been this excited about going anywhere since he was a child and his father had taken him to Old Trafford to see their beloved Manchester United.

Mullen was settled now, both in work and at home, but he was lonely. When he closed his front door at night the silence surrounded him. He kept in touch with his mother and his siblings, of course. His sister always had a plate ready should he pop around, and he loved spending time with his nieces and nephews, but they weren't friends. A young man needs friends, needs to get out of the house and meet people. His mum and his sister told him as much. But at least he wasn't in trouble (they thought), at least he was working and looking after himself: maybe the rest would come? Perhaps there'd be a nice girl at work. He'd even been for the odd pint with a work colleague, but everything was still bland and unexciting compared to the great bubble of fascism he saw on the internet.

He didn't tell his mother or sister about National Action. He wasn't a member or anything like that, they just "interested" him. There was this whole other world that he looked in at night: a world of revolutionaries, Nazis and anarchists. That's where he actually wanted to be.

Where he'd settled was quite rural compared to where he'd grown up. He'd taken to cycling everywhere. After walking the dog he'd get back on his bike and cycle down the narrow lanes and over bridges and along empty paths in the quiet darkness. Occasionally he'd imagine he was in France or somewhere else exotic: the Manchester Shipping Canal was beautiful and it was peaceful, but it was hardly exotic.

When we first met, we discussed his cycling trips, rides that often went on for hours. I asked him what he listened to while riding. He shrugged his shoulders, confused. "Music?" I asked. But he cycled without such noises in his ears. He said he didn't like (or didn't know) music. "Just the thoughts in my head," he answered. I didn't push him further. Even at my own most lonely and distraught at least I'd had music.

As the train to Newcastle pulled out of Lime Street someone crashed into the seat opposite him, dressed head-to-toe in Adidas gear. The figure was restless, constantly shifting in his seat and fidgeting with his hands. Mullen kept looking at his phone, trying not to make eye contact, but the young man seemed desperate to make conversation, talking in a thick, drawling Scouse accent. Never a great conversationalist, Mullen tried to ignore him, nodding and taking quick sideways looks. The other man was unshaven but had paid great attention to his hair, manicured to look unkempt but actually held firmly in place and brushed to look blonder on top than it really was. Maybe it was dyed? His kit was flash and expensive, even if it was just a tracksuit. He made and took a series of calls on separate mobile phones, sometimes loud, other times hushed. Try as hard as he could to ignore him, Mullen had met Andrew Clarke from Kirkby.

As they got off the train at Newcastle, Clarke tried one more time to engage Mullen in conversation. Mullen was having none of it. Clarke gave a shrug, pulled on a National Action t-shirt and walked off. Mullen felt a little deflated. He could have spent a good couple of hours at least talking with Clarke about NA, but he hadn't believed someone like Clarke, 30 years old and so confident and flashy, would have been a member of a group like NA. He seemed so criminally... mainstream?

Clarke was in fact a central player inside National Action. The grandson of one of Liverpool's much loved and admired former councillors, he used the name 'Longshanks' when online, in honour of Edward Longshanks, England's king during the 13th Century. Clarke was a massive exponent of the 'beat the bailiff' movement and 'barrack-room' legal endeavours by small groups of people on the left and right in and around working class movements in Liverpool. He could quote any number of obscure laws that were still not entirely wiped from the statute books. Rent was theft, credit cards were to remain unpaid, you don't have to pay your TV licence fee, and to Clarke, Jews were settled in this country illegally. According to Clarke's mantra, you didn't need to be a lawyer to practice law, you just needed enough gob to tie people up knots. And threats of violence.

Clarke was also a small-time supplier and user of Class A drugs. It's what made him fidgety and contributed to a temper and uncontrollable urge to offend. Despite his hectic lifestyle, he managed to find work on a number of high-paying construction jobs and in architecture. As soon as he found a job, however, it wouldn't be long before he'd walk out after an argument. He had a reputation for leaving jobs in style, causing scenes and storming out of offices and buildings, or screaming and shouting on building sites. He wasn't allowed to see his own child, but would later gain infamy when he posted a picture of himself and his very young nephew giving Nazi salutes. To give Clarke an even more authoritative air, he was the nephew of notorious Liverpool gangsters Peter and Stephen Clarke who in 2013 were sentenced to 10 and 15 years, respectively, for drug dealing, illegal money lending and amassing an arsenal of weapons. With a combination of drugs and bravado, Andy Clarke feared nothing and no-one.

The Newcastle White Man March was to be the first time the public could get a proper look at the darlings of the Sunday press. Choreography would be the key. The stewards wore yellow vests and small numbers from tiny, almost mythical neo-Nazi groups such as the British Movement and Combat 18 mingled with people from the London Forum, which acted as a sort of 'nexus' or meeting point for many far-right figures both UK and international, joined by others as well from the National Front.

Everything about the day had an air of expectation about it. Could National Action really pull this off? They'd done well by avoiding up-close public scrutiny and it wasn't lost on them, the vanguard of neo-Nazi aggression, that it wasn't just bloody anarchists and violent antifascists who wanted them to fail. Nor was it lost on them that the security for the rally was provided by other gangs of fascists and neo-Nazis that NA felt were physically and intellectually inferior.

Interested neo-Nazis and fascists formed a small crowd at the monument waiting for the National Action circus to begin. Among the crowd was a recruiter from Ukrainian Nazi paramilitary group, the Azov Battalion. Puffing hard on cigarettes as well as vaping from an electronic substitute, Francesco Saverio Fontana had travelled from Italy to meet British supporters of Azov and cast his eye over the infamous NA.

A well-known member of the Italian far-right scene, Fontana had seen military action in the Ukraine against the Russian-backed separatist movement in the east of the country, until a mixture of age and indiscipline saw him moved to the Misanthropic Division (MD), the international front group used to recruit supporters and soldiers to Azov. MD had members as far afield as Australia, Japan and Brazil, with supporters prepared to travel to the Ukraine and fight.

A small group of MD supporters in the UK had encouraged Fontana to come over to see National Action first hand. In fact, two of MD's most senior members in Britain were NA's martial arts instructor Jimmy Hey, based in the north west of England, and former Combat 18 and Ulster Defence Association (UDA) man, Rob "The Postie" Gray, in London.

The choreography was, as expected, quite spectacular. Wayne Bell led masked and uniformed National Action members and their closest supporters down some steps to the monument where their flag waving and assault on common decency could begin. Soon Jeremy "Jez" Turner from the London

Forum was speaking, followed by an incoherent and blind drunk Billy Charlton from the Sunderland Defence League. Matthew Hankinson, the "posh lad" from Newton-le-Willows, spoke for NA, shouting loudly about the coming race war. He issued a threat, a warning, that there'd be murders, that blood would be spilt and that they were preparing for this eventuality. He was surrounded by young men with cigarettes hanging from their mouths, carrying a banner proclaiming "only bullets will stop us".

"We must be ruthless. If we don't fight and we don't cut out the cancer... Britain will die."
"We are racial national socialists, our nation is our blood," he continued, as rainbow flags were burned in the crowd. "We need the strongest of our race, we need ordinary people who in time will become extraordinary."

Hankinson told the crowd they should "get our hands dirty" amid shouts of "traitors" and "fuck the system". "Blood must be shed, the blood of traitors, the blood of our enemies!" he cried out.

Echoing an infamous white supremacist saying from the USA, the 14 words, Hankinson ended by shouting: "Stand up white men and set our people free, we must secure a future for our people and a future for white children."

The leader of the National Rebirth of Poland (NOP) then gave a speech about solidarity between white peoples. Mullen walked around the crowd taking in the atmosphere, nodding at people and saying hello. Wayne Bell, with his intimidating scarred face, was ironically the most friendly one there. Mullen both liked and feared him. Known mainly at the time as Wayne Jarvie, Bell had developed a reputation for an unhinged hatred of the left and Jews, often calling publicly for both to be murdered. A welder by trade, Bell's commitment to violence and Nazism had earlier convinced National Action founder Raymond that the group should adopt "the brute" over the intellectual. Bell convinced and recruited Mullen on the spot.

Mullen recognised Lythgoe, despite his face being covered and even spoke with the infamous Helm who was recognisable because he kept telling everyone who he was. Mullen walked along the Quay to where antifascist activists were standing and shouting abuse at the Sieg Heiling Nazis. Here he was, Robbie Mullen from Widnes, so long alone in the world and with his thoughts, now thick in the middle of the bubble he'd watched from afar for so long. It was like his very own Freshers' Week at university, and National Action seemed without a doubt the most dangerous, different and exciting thing he had ever witnessed.

Fontana the Italian saw the same as Mullen and was impressed by the choreographed display of Nazism and the angry, violent words pouring out. Fontana would hang around in Britain for several months, embedding himself with groups such as the London Forum, where he could get a fuller picture of the movement in Britain.

The day ended with a series of arrests: Andy Clarke, the man from the train, was thrown in the back of a police van after burning the Israeli flag. As they shoved him in the back he told the police his rights, then told everyone else their rights, and spat venomous anti-Jewish tirades to anyone that would listen. Others followed, nine in all, for a range of stupid acts. National Action's new front man, Ashley Bell, was also thrown into police custody along with some Poles and, of course, Helm, who as good as demanded the police arrest him too.

After the rally there was a serious brawl involving locals, the National Front and the Polish neo-Nazis. No amount of white brotherhood could stop a growing resentment about the Poles organising in Britain better than the British.

But Mullen travelled back to Runcorn in an excited mood. Like National Action, he was feeling bullish. Ben Raymond, who stayed at home to edit any video footage that came down the line, was already taunting antifascists in an open statement:

"We have just held the first advertised National Socialist rally in decades. You did not turn up because we have built a new terrifying force in this country that would have torn any opposition limb from limb should they have been attacked. The human material you turned out for this event was pathetic, your ranks were filled with the elderly and the disabled...

"The system and its leftist tools will regret the day they were unable to smash the nucleus of our young movement, we are now unstoppable and will continue to grow from strength to strength – as promised, mailed, signed, and delivered. Hail Victory." – National Action report on Newcastle

CHAPTER 9: WE ARE SUPERMEN

"Whether we, the dedicated few from the march, are to survive the revolution, let it be known that all of our enemies will receive their reward from us. Retribution. There are no excuses for betraying or defiling the race."

National Action report

A week after the Newcastle demonstration, the National Front, one of the world's longest surviving neo-Nazi groups held its own White Pride World Wide demonstration in Manchester. There was a growing resentment in the NF's leadership about just how far National Action had come, and just how much of a distraction it had become for their own dwindling numbers. The relative success of NA's Newcastle rally, followed by NF members brawling with Polish Nazis in a pub afterwards was driving a deep resentment in the leadership. Despite an influx of a few dozen former British National Party (BNP) types, the NF was more than a little lumbered with EDL types who found a home in the NF to carry on their hectic schedule of drug dealing, drug use and alcohol abuse. The North West Infidel (NWI) drug gang, who had poured so much of their drug money into the party also appeared more enamoured with NA than they did with the NF's activities. NA enjoyed watching the NF squirm and now, led by former NF member Ashley Bell, NA wanted the NF finished completely.

More than 100 neo-Nazis and white supremacists from across the UK made their way to the centre of Manchester to drape white power flags and make Nazi salutes for the NF's White Pride demonstration. Robbie Mullen, now a member for exactly a week, sat on the train with other NA members making their way to the demonstration; for the first time he felt part of something. He was now inside the gang. In just a week he'd been completely accepted into the secretive bubble that had titillated him on the internet. NA was in many ways disappointingly unspectacular but in other ways, driven by a disturbing drive and dedication by its members, it was everything it promised. From the moment Mullen met with them they assumed him as one of their own; his relative silence, his grunting answers, his age and what the *Daily Mirror* would later pinpoint as a "dark aura of angst and sadness around him" made him a perfect fit. Their conversations in person were stilted and often trailed off in unfinished, but online, on the series of apps and hidden email accounts they used, they communicated with each other much more comfortably. He'd been for a drink with Christopher Lythgoe who'd struck him as monotone but with a penchant for terrorism and an almost chilling bloodlust. Dour and methodical in conversation, it was often over the apps where Lythgoe would really spring to life as a fearsome, secretive intellectual and revolutionary who barked orders, instructions and encouragement. From those early moments Mullen could tell Lythgoe was the leader in waiting.

To join, Mullen surrendered to National Action everything they needed to know about him. They bragged someone in Homeland Security (!) could run a check on him. They scrutinised him on- and offline, advising him to change a number of details about himself and how he, particularly, could hide "from the Jews at HOPE not hate" and immerse himself wholly and fully in the revolution. In that brief week, he felt an almost complete change in himself. Maybe he walked differently now, but he couldn't quite put his finger on it. Maybe he spoke differently, he actually felt different and felt it was noticeable. He felt others at work might have known his dirty secret. He was a Nazi now.

Early in the day in Manchester, Polish neo-Nazis clashed with local antifascists. There was fighting in the city's two main train stations, before the Nazis made a rearguard action that saw dozens exchanging blows in and around Moseley Street, just off Piccadilly Gardens in the city centre.

In Piccadilly Gardens drunken Polish boneheads ran a gauntlet of kicks before running into the police, who threw them to the ground after drawing their batons. Later in the afternoon on the backstreets of the city the two groups clashed again. Liam Pinkham, not long out of prison and by now a part of National Action, was chased down and beaten by antifascists who took one of his shoes as a trophy.

The whole day had been terribly disorganised and nothing like the event National Action had organised the week before. There'd been no choreography, no great arrival. Instead, drunken bores and boneheads had gathered in pubs and shuffled to the rendezvous point risking a beating from antifascists. The NA members present were less than impressed. For many, seeing the National Front up close and personal was a bitter disappointment and proof that they, NA, were superior in every way.

Despite asking, National Action wasn't given the chance to address the rally by the surly National Front leadership. This affront didn't entirely matter because, with its youthful militancy, NA reminded others in Britain's far-right movement of the dark past, when Combat 18 had terrorised not just "reds" but innocent people who found their way onto horrendous and scruffy hit lists the gang had put together. With NA's arrival on the scene, militancy had returned once again to the decimated and fractured British far right. C18 flags were flown at the Manchester rally by some old hands and NA saw this as an almost homage to themselves.

But National Action was a different animal to C18. It attracted violent loners and sociopaths who mimicked much of what they liked in other political movements. And thanks to Ben Raymond's antics, it had a dramatic, almost 'arty' feel to it. C18 (the 1 and the 8 representing the numerical place in the alphabet of Adolf Hitler's initials) had been the original "brutes", bullies and psychopaths who'd expressed a violent Nazism fuelled by drugs, terrorising fellow far-right travellers in the BNP and National Front.

Now in their late 40s and early 50s, these homicidal and pot-bellied men of yesteryear had witnessed the very real 1980s and 90s street violence that National Action dreamed of. Like many in NA, C18 had been a part of the BNP and, like NA, had rejected the electoral path. Had C18 been good to their word or their potential, Britain would have been a very different place for the young NA members.

Raymond had tentative discussions with some former C18 men curious about his group. Despite their age, what was left of C18 cast a heavy shadow over what National Action wanted to do. The newcomers knew only too well that C18 members had been involved in bomb plots and even a murder twenty years before; David Copeland, the murderous London nail bomber who had terrorised London for three weeks in 1999 had also been linked to C18. Now a small and fractured shadow of its former self, C18 laughed at Raymond's apparent madness when he presented himself to them. To Raymond, C18 came across as vulgar, ageing yobs, with little or no understanding of what Raymond and Davies were trying to build with NA. Had C18 stayed off the drugs and out of the pubs, in a period with little CCTV and no internet or surveillance, who knows, the race war may already have been won.

***

There were further stunts and demonstrations that day across the country. A Jewish monument in Birmingham was vandalised by National Action members. Another EDL splinter group, the South East Alliance (SEA), which had gone full-blown Nazi very quickly, also held a demonstration in Rotherham. Jack Renshaw, who'd now moved firmly into the NA camp, even gave a speech calling for paedophiles to be hanged – words that would come back to haunt him.

Other National Action members, led by Raymond, made trips to Lithuania and Latvia, where they met with militia gangs in support of Ukrainian neo-Nazis. Raymond seemed far more at ease travelling to foreign countries meeting foreign neo-Nazis than he did talking to their British counterparts.

Lythgoe simply believed that Raymond was a coward. Having sured up National Action's internal security, there should be no reason for Raymond not to turn up to demonstrations and events. Mullen was quickly aware that Raymond, assumed by those outside of NA to be leader, actually enjoyed very little real power or support inside the group. As the militant with obsessions about physical training and terrorism, Lythgoe had demanded and received respect from the moment he joined. His dry-humoured intellect and aloofness impressed the others, and he drove a constant narrative that Raymond was to be respected, but ignored.

Raymond's co-founder, the failed philosophy student Alex Davies, was supposedly taking a back seat in National Action. It may have been simply a ruse to get Raymond to stop the constant clinging phonecalls and emails, because to Lythgoe's chagrin, Davies still commanded the absolute respect of the members. Even when Leeds-based Ashley Bell was supposed to be the leader, he and everyone else still deferred to Davies who was now working in a call centre. Davies, the angst ridden revolutionary, loved the choreography that Raymond demanded but was also drawn to the secrecy and dark arts that consumed Lythgoe. What also made Lythgoe attractive to Davies was that Lythgoe had access to small amounts of money, enough to keep him off the dole and out of work and so presumably off the state's radar. The money was provided by a monthly payment being made to the North West National Action by a Liverpudlian businessman based in Spain who ran a series of hothouse call centres. The same businessman was also prepared to pay for travel expenses and mobile phones for the North West contingent.

While being deferred to, Davies began, in turn, to defer to Lythgoe. This pleased and placated Lythgoe who had picked up on the animosity between Raymond and former BNP organiser Paul Hickman. Lythgoe established a second power base through Hickman in the Midlands but was mindful that although he was certain he would lead the group nationally eventually, he shouldn't cause a split. Raymond's absences and childish behaviour may have been a hindrance but they were also in Lythgoe's favour. So were Raymond's constant panicked pontifications, which massively irritated other members of the leadership group. They soon began to realise he wasn't the intelligent being he pretended to be; he was an irritant.

By mid-2015 Raymond was churning out even longer essays on the National Action website, such as the July 2015 work *Seeking synthesis between ideology and action in new generation nationalism*. Even by Raymond's already high standard for nonsense, this one was an absolute masterpiece. In his own words, he was now a "political soldier". His essay misquoted right-wing philosophers and corrupted history in flowery tones, but conveyed little else beyond his travels and sense of self-importance. It must have taken him long and painstaking hours to concoct. He followed up again later that month, this time tackling Lythgoe's assertion that 'white jihad' literally meant blowing up and killing people. Despite the numerous calls for death and destruction on the website under Raymond's own pen, it appeared that in reality he didn't want the natural consequences of his writings, framing instead, jihad in terms of a "culture war" and humour:

"The role of the White Jihad is twofold. On one level it is satire, it is so ridiculous that it mocks comparison – humour is the most fantastic weapon because with it we can make ourselves understood while alienating those who are driving the narrative, using their own cheap lies against them, and inciting them further down a path of their own making...

"Our struggle is a culture war where we fight and win every day just by being who we are. We don't have to blow ourselves up or cut people's heads off in order to get noticed, we have already been condemned...

"Everything we need to become the rebellion of the age is in place; the fear, the glamour, the terror, the presence, it is all there for the taking, all that is left for us is to embrace it. We don't have a choice in this matter."

Raymond could hardly claim innocence from National Action's glorification of hedonistic violence, though, as much of the more outrageous encouragement of thuggery was in the group's internal messaging. Many of the group also used these channels to share sick fantasies about rape and bestiality.

For Mullen, as well as the excitement about his new venture, there was also a tinge of disappointment with how small the far right actually was. Although he knew National Action's size was relative to the nature and goals of the group, behind all the huff, headlines and bravado, and the media screaming and wailing about the rise of the neo-Nazis and fascists, there were actually very few people not just sitting behind a computer tweeting racist abuse at MPs and celebrities. Groups such as the EDL had boiled down to an incestuous orgy of drink- and drug-related thuggery. By contrast, NA had to be small and perfectly-formed to remain ideologically pure and avoid the sort of messy joke the EDL became.

Raymond and his website were the public face of National Action, making many people assume his ramblings were the sum total of thinking in the group. But Lythgoe, although he now edited and often approved of the nonsense Raymond was writing, saw himself as the succinct ideologue of NA. The North West was by far the biggest NA unit and by far the most active. From Stockport, Liverpool, Manchester and surrounds people came to listen to Lythgoe hold court two nights a week at the Friar Penketh pub in Warrington. It was upstairs at this Wetherspoons hostelry, a large two-floored circular brick building on a roundabout in the centre of town, that Lythgoe built his gang, or unit. Members of the drug gang NWI would occasionally drop in from Blackburn or Blackpool to provide class As and listen to Lythgoe's plans, but most of the group that met upstairs at the pub were becoming the core of what Lythgoe saw as his court as he expanded on a "truly dystopian vision."

Lythgoe kept a notepad at home where he envisaged himself as a medieval king and those around him as crusaders. Having taken his A-levels late and then an Open University course in engineering, he'd become obsessed with graphs and charts where he could plot and explain his theories. Lythgoe was a violent, psychopathic dullard, but to those around him, initially at least, he had formulated the race war: how it would happen, how it would and should be fought and why it should be fought. All the choreographed photo opportunities Raymond requested for the website were promptly delivered as Lythgoe knew, in the age of the internet and with the easy manipulation of the media, it would continue to deliver crusaders to the cause. Despite the heavy drinking, the creeping emergence of class As and the occasional interaction with undesirable types from groups such as the NWI or worse still, National Front, Lythgoe was closer to building the perfect Aryan fighting force than silly Ben Raymond, cowered behind a computer and a packet of cigarettes in Bognor Regis, ever was.

There were similar meetings ongoing around the country in Yorkshire, Birmingham, Newport, Cardiff, Swindon, Bristol, Cambridge, Edinburgh and London. Alex Davies, supposedly on leave, made it his mission to visit each one, but it was in Warrington he saw the greatest advancement of ideals. When he visited Warrington and he needed somewhere to sleep, Mullen had a couch for him.

Davies particularly liked one Lythgoe synopsis; National Action was to lead a revolution, not be its mass body. They'd be like the Bolsheviks in Russia at the turn of the twentieth century; the smallest but most cutthroat part of the revolution who would rise above all others to lead a country dripping in the blood of Jews, blacks and Asians.

And the analogies didn't stop there. The Provisional IRA lived in small cells, often not knowing if their neighbour was a member. They only ever appeared in public with their faces covered and when they struck, nobody (supposedly) knew who they were. The same with the Red Army Faction (Baader-Meinhof gang) in Germany during the 1960s and 70s. Lythgoe could reel off any number of masked terror gangs – most of them leftist – who could strike from the shadows and spread terror anonymously.

"Let the walls be covered in our symbols and our names, but those who write it don't have to know us."

Mullen learned very quickly National Action wasn't about blacks, "Pakis", immigrants and gays, as everyone who viewed the group from outside assumed. That kind of low-grade EDL/BNP vulgarity was almost passé to NA. It turned away prospective members who simply mouthed off vulgarities about non-whites.

Two examples of these low-grade low-lifes were Garron Helm and Zack Davies, the north Wales supermarket attacker. They were both stupid enough to get caught.

***

"Imagine you are on a march right now and the camera zooms in on you, are you consistant [sic] with the image put out by the group? If not that is OK, but we expect to see an improvement, if after two months nothing has changed then we will be obliged to discontinue your involvement. Presentation also includes sticking to the dress-code on demonstrations and looking good in general." – National Action website, advice on becoming a member

In July 2015, nearly 100 British neo-Nazis headed to the Brecon Beacons in Wales for further martial arts and ideological training, engaging in semi-naked fisticuffs before marching up and down hills. People attended from as far afield as remote Scottish Islands and the Republic of Ireland.

As had become the norm on these camps (a mixture of physical fighting and ideology), ISIS propaganda and ideals were distributed and discussed. Watching propaganda videos of people being ceremoniously murdered excited the attendees; ISIS made brutal murder look so easy, and it took an adherence to ideology that was apparently admirable. Not fearing death, not being afraid of martyrdom was another ball in the ISIS court. While most other British fascists and neo-Nazis shared the world's terrified abhorrence of ISIS – a stance that had helped recruit many a footsoldier to the NA cause – could any of these bedroom-dwelling wannabe Nazi terrorists match ISIS for dedication?

Instead of fearing them and hating the Islamic Jihadi, what could they actually learn from them? People had already drawn wildly excessive, wildly stupid parallels between ISIS and groups such as the EDL.

ISIS had their own state (a caliphate), an army engaged in military struggle and adherents across the world prepared to strike with murderous terrorist acts. The EDL were drunkards engaged in racist stupidity and alcoholism while standing in car parks singing football songs. Sure, ISIS was a great recruiter of beer-swilling blokes who hated Muslims and wanted to fight ISIS from the comfort of pubs, but NA wasn't like the EDL, the failed BNP or the completely useless NF.

To mark them apart, to make National Action really cutting edge, they had to embrace new ideologies that tested their faith, their commitment and not just shock Mum and Dad at home and the readers of the *Daily Mail*. Those ginger-haired kids converting to Jihad should be converting to *white* Jihad. There were kids from the same towns and cities as them in Britain heading off to Syria and Iraq prepared to commit to and embrace barbarism and genocide in the name of Islam. Despite their own vulgarities and childish behaviour, this is one of the reasons NA quickly developed the idea of eschewing those who used racist language. It's also why, although they hated the left, they didn't so much hate leftism, implanted as it was in the arts and culture. So much of what the NF, EDL and BNP believed in was flawed. Quietly admiring Hitler like the NF and BNP had done for fifty years was pathetic. Similarly, the EDL's drunken Nazi tactics were an embarrassment. Waving Israeli flags because they knew it upset Muslims? How pathetic was that?

It bore a striking similarity to Nick Griffin's former Political Soldiers who for a brief time inside the NF during the 1980s embraced the idea of dying ('Long live death' was one of their slogans) and also the alignment with Islam against Judaism. Hitler, simply put, wasn't enough. They had to be nuanced, had to make people sit up and properly take notice. They discussed another similar obsession they shared with ISIS; as well as genocidal fantasies, they shared ISIS's well-documented obsessions with hardcore pornography, rape and sexually humiliating opponents. Young men who spent most of their lives in their bedrooms surfing for porn and genocide were very open about their penchant for raping those they hated. A whole host of names were thrown into a mix for gang rape and humiliation. In the main they were female MPs, left wing and antifascist activists. It then broadened to celebrities, black footballers and historical figures.

The training camp had been a success. Even if not everybody present had necessarily embraced National Action's not-so sudden slide into nihilism, they'd embraced the idea of broader idealism and sacrifice. The only problem was, as Mullen understood it, nobody had actually stood up and said they were prepared to unleash it.

"Zack Davies, the failure from Mold, became the benchmark for not just failure but also success," said Mullen. Sending tweets to MPs and then apologising like Helm wasn't really a martyrdom anymore. Lythgoe bragged he'd been to visit Davies and met with him prior to the attack in Tesco's. Although they'd deny it now, Raymond and Davies would also claim to Mullen they had met him.

"The feeling was Zack had been too premature. He hadn't planned what he was going to do properly, he had fucked it up and just gone for some random bloke he saw walking into Tesco's. He mimicked a jihadi but he had not died like a jihadi. I guess that was the difference between White jihad and Islamic jihad; we knew there would be no virgins waiting for us in heaven. We'd be dead. Like Hitler." – Robbie Mullen, March 2019

The camp came on the eve for what was National Action's most audacious plan yet: They were going to hold a White Man March in Liverpool that August. The drive for the march however didn't come from the North West's organiser. The last thing Lythgoe wanted was a riot on his doorstep while he was building a terrorist cell in and around the city. Adding to his angst was that the organiser was the dubious idiot, Garron Helm. He'd gone straight to Raymond, leader Ashley Bell and co-founder Alex Davies with the idea of marching in the city. By way of probably reining Lythgoe's ambitions they had readily agreed.

A resentment about the march had quietly simmered inside Lythgoe for weeks. His attitude towards Helm had changed dramatically once the North

West unit was up and running properly. Helm had a habit of waltzing in and out of National Action meetings with horrific stories he'd conjure up about his activities with the IRA or hunting down and strangling foxes. To upset Helm, Lythgoe had one evening brazenly appointed the newcomer Mullen as his deputy. The affront was taken as it should be by Helm – very badly. During a subsequent police statement during operation Harplike, Helm made much of the fact he hadn't been given the job or at least appointed as the organiser for the city of Liverpool. The truth was in fact, he had been. Lythgoe just chose to ignore it.

As the date drew closer it became very apparent that every walking, talking leftie in Britain would be making their way to Liverpool to counter the march. Lythgoe became nervously apoplectic. He was refusing to attend. He told his group in the Friar Penketh pub that were there to be trouble, the police would raid all of their homes, and reasoned Lythgoe, aside from people like Pinkham, this small group was unknown to the police. The "backwards celebrity" that was Helm would probably be enjoying meeting with the police and "ratting like a shit-cunt all our names to them."

But after the relative success of Newcastle, it appeared many within National Action wanted to continue its antagonism not just of "reds" but also the entire city of Liverpool, which with its Jewish MPs and lofty, leftie traditions, antagonised NA just by existing.

Although still a small group in terms of numbers, National Action had proved it could create and generate headlines. Lythgoe showed a general disinterest in the march on the group's internal messages, but even he was surprised by how much publicity (negative or otherwise) it generated. The rest knew their mettle would to be severely tested – more so than at Newcastle or Manchester – but they felt they had trained for this. To them, the left was nothing but unkempt, middle-class, flag-waving students who'd face the highly trained and committed NA activists – and be crushed.

Co-founder Alex Davies, usurping both Lythgoe and nominal leader Ashley Bell, issued instructions to the members wishing to attend. They were to be "Black bloc from head to toe" with a face covering, sunglasses and a hefty belt buckle.

"The quality of what you're wearing is important," he instructed. "No tracksuit bottoms, jogging bottoms or generally scruffy clothing."

It appeared he was having a sly dig at Lythgoe's attire. Two months previously Lythgoe had been upset by the demand that everyone should wear expensive trainers. Raymond and Davies also insisted Raymond would be the only National Action speaker at the Liverpool march, which seemed to please most of the group. Another Lythgoe irritant, Alex Deakin from Birmingham, who was a firm fan of Raymond and Davies, was in charge of getting the West Midlands members to the march. Lythgoe could feel he was being reminded of his place as a mere regional organiser.

On the eve of the march there was panic and outrage when Liverpool's Mayor Joe Anderson revealed he'd received a threatening letter from National Action that promised a race riot if the march was banned. Anderson had been the focus of much abuse from NA over his outspoken opposition to the group. Members genuinely believed they hadn't sent Anderson the letter. The story made national news and helped raise the temperature further around the city. Raymond and Davies were furious. The letter hadn't been sent by Raymond. They thought it had been sent either by "reds", or by someone close to Lythgoe. (Mullen has since said he believes the letter was written by one of Lythgoe's people, a taxi driver from Huyton, who had taken to ferrying Lythgoe around.)

HOPE not hate was no different to anybody else in the run-up to the Liverpool march. Sure, National Action had gotten away with it in Newcastle, but Liverpool? The city was, after all, the self-declared People's Republic. If NA got away with this, there'd be real trouble. Maintaining a mantra of antagonising and upsetting the neo-Nazi group, we wrote about the threatening letter to Liverpool's Mayor:

"And so, with this letter not having been approved by the kid who failed philosophy and the double glazing salesman who is sickly and bed-bound whilst searching the internet for skin flicks, there was angry rage. White rage, too."

We then quoted Raymond's response to the letter itself:

"At no point have we been contacted by this piece of shit journalist or asked to comment on the authenticity of this letter. We demand all news outlets redact or put reasonable uncertainty on the assertion that this message came from our group, please have some ethics."

Raymond was infuriated by our reporting. He put on a brave face to prove he wasn't 'bed-bound' and even accepted an invitation to crash on the couch at Helm's place before the march (he would later tell Mullen he had to wipe his feet before leaving).

There were stories and rumours that neo-Nazis would be attending the proposed march from as far away as Sweden and Poland. The rumour mill even said antifascists would be heading over from Germany. Coachloads of antifascists were booked to attend from London and Kent, with Unite Against Fascism saying it would march with the mayor on the day, away from where the fascists were organising. The lead-up to the march began to take on some kind of historical importance to both the left and the far right. There was panic in the latter about a potential humiliation. For the left and antifascists, it was a simple case that if NA could march in Liverpool, then the idea that certain communities and cities could hold firm against Nazis would be forever lost.

Worse still, people might even accept that the likes of NA had some kind of right to protest.

Genuinely large-scale street victories against the far right were few and far between. There'd been an almost methodical, militaristic approach to ridding communities of fascists. In the 1990s, the BNP had been driven from its favoured stomping ground of Brick Lane in east London after a series of (almost weekly) clashes. The smart people knew the defeat and humiliation of fascists had to be as political as it was physical and it had to be final. The crushing defeat of the BNP at the ballot box had to be done on doorsteps and had to be carried out simultaneously and nationally where they were both sitting and standing.

In 2012 hundreds of EDL marchers were forced to flee during a confrontation on the streets in Walthamstow, east London, and its leadership was forced into a humiliating retreat in the back of a getaway car.

Now in August 2015, our intelligence relayed a very real sense of nervousness leading up to the White Man March in Liverpool. Both the fascists and antifascists were hoping for some kind of miracle intervention by the people of Liverpool. Until the very morning of August 15 neither really had any idea how it would turn out. The night before the march, Helm accompanied the police for a walk along the planned route and realised he hadn't actually told the rest of the group where they were supposed to meet before the demonstration.

For Raymond the impending event held great personal and political importance. If he could assert his leadership and his vision over the group, then marching dressed in black and delivering a vulgar, hate-filled speech would be all it would take to deliver a victory. Again, as in Alex Davies's instructions to members and supporters, there would be the choreography and the drama Raymond so wanted: they'd march in threes, women in the middle, larger men on the outside. Absolutely nobody was to talk to the media except for Raymond. He seemed quite prepared for a confrontation with Lythgoe if necessary. Before bed the night before, Jack Renshaw, another problematic abhorration for Raymond, fired off some tweets in the direction of antifascists:

"Antifacists who use the Spanish phrase "No Pasaran" [sic] forget that the Spanish fascists did pass! Just like we will pass today!

"In years to come, your grandchildren will speak [sic] this day and how NA made history. Prepare yourselves."

Renshaw had made a name for himself by being confrontational. Despite being kicked out of university and occasionally attacked by antifascists, he showed little sign of curtailing his confrontational approach. Whereas Helm adored Raymond because Raymond could be warm and welcoming and accepting of Helm's weirdness, Renshaw was another, like Lythgoe, who saw Raymond as a barrack room coward.

Few National Action members slept the night before Liverpool, their messaging systems pinging and buzzing with every outrageous idea and thought they could muster about the next day. They'd been promised at least 300-500 people would join their march.

"This isn't the time to be despondent – we dared to dream. When the WMM organisers said we would march on Liverpool, the most militant left wing city in Britain, we said we would march. We had never been stopped before – 150 brave souls said 'yes' and walked into the lion's den just to see what would happen." – NA report on Liverpool

By 11am on August 15 there were hundreds of antifascists and curious locals outside Liverpool Lime Street station. Everyone was tense. Antifascists had already occupied every pub that had opened for business. Just before midday a train pulled into the station and Jack Renshaw emerged, looking like a confident, naughty boy holding a shopping bag. Our photographer greeted him there, reporting back his surprise just how small, almost frail, Renshaw looked. Renshaw was all on his own, his cheekiness evaporating momentarily as he scoured the concourse for any sign of others. The only Black bloc he saw was Antifa.

"You're just Jews, doing the work of the Jews," he began, but he was quickly drowned by an angry counter-narrative and found himself shoved and hidden behind protective police lines. It was clear very early on, that National Action would have a fight on its hands.

Helm had reported during the night that the police expected a couple of hundred counter-protestors marching in the opposite direction for a rally about "smashing fascists." The police felt the National Action march would go ahead without too much trouble at all. But the station was filling up quickly – and noisily – with an ever-greater number of antifascists. There were reports of some trouble on a train from London, when a group of fascists had been forced to disembark when an antifascist "patrol" found them sitting meekly in their carriage.

The train into Liverpool Lime Street from Warrington had a noticeable omission: wannabe leader Christopher Lythgoe. He said he'd developed an upset stomach overnight and wouldn't be coming. Helm had dictated National Action meet outside the lost luggage office on the station concourse, which is where they found the police helpfully already standing there waiting to protect them.

Small groups of Nazis sauntered into the station trying discreetly to make their way to the rally point, their faces covered. All of them were confronted at some stage by antifascists. There were clashes outside the station and the Nazis took cover inside, trying to make their way to the lost luggage area. They were soon surrounded by a massive black block of antifascists who converged on the same point and demanded it be closed.

Garron Helm leads NA into Newcastle, March 2015. © HOPE not hate

Early joint NA protest outside American Embassy, London, May 2015. © HOPE not hate

Alex Deakin, Swansea 'White Pride' demonstration, 2015. © HOPE not hate

Larry Nunn. The Nazi boss NA so wanted to impress. © HOPE not hate

The Polish neo-Nazi group NOP. Provided muscle to NA when they needed it.
Newcastle, March 2015. (c) HOPE not hate

White Jihad, Newcastle, 2015. © HOPE not hate

Jack Coulson relaxing at home (Instagram)

NA cartoons had a
penchant for sex and
violence (Facebook)

Shane Calvert, criminal and leader of the North West Infidels. © HOPE not hate

Adam Thomas and Darren Fletcher, imprisoned in 2018, on an EDL march in 2012.
© HOPE not hate

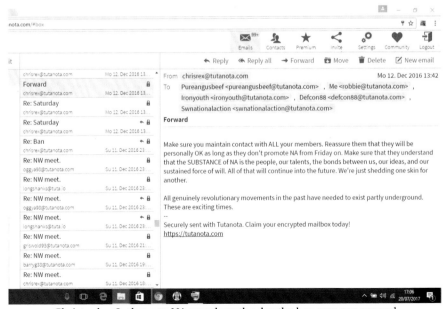

Christopher Lythgoe to NA members the day the ban was announced

Robbie Mullen, Liverpool,
February 2016.
© HOPE not hate

Andrew Clarke St Helens Dec 2016

 National Action NE @NANorthEast_ · 1h
#VoteLeave, don't let this man's sacrifice go in vain.
#JoCox would have filled Yorkshire with more subhumans!

  2 4 ● ● ●

The horrendous tweet
in the aftermath of the
Jo Cox murder that led
to the banning of NA

Italian mercenary Francesco Fontana (right) in Newcastle 2015. © HOPE not hate

Robbie Mullen meeting with NA members Dan Cotterill, Matthew Hankinson and
Radoslaw Rekke despite the ban, July 2017. © HOPE not hate

Ben Raymond and Ashley Bell. © HOPE not hate

Wayne Bell, Liverpool, February 2016. © HOPE not hate

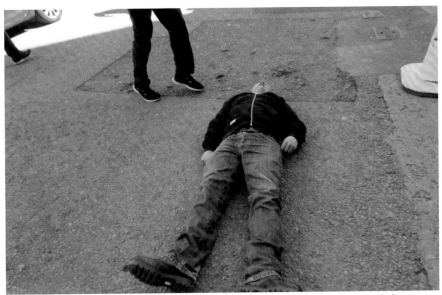

Liverpool, August 2015. Antifascists responded to NA's antagonism with fury.
© HOPE not hate

Alex Deakin gives Nazi salute with Raymond (glasses) and Renshaw (front right).
Liverpool, February 2016. © HOPE not hate

Polish hooligans arrive at
St Georges Hall Liverpool,
February 2016. It was the
signal for rioting.
© HOPE not hate

August 2015. Hankinson and Bell confronted outside Lime Street station, Liverpool.
© HOPE not hate

Kevin Layzell. National Front member that straddled the NF, National Action
and Polish Nazis. © HOPE not hate

Lythgoe never wanted public centre stage. Newcastle, 2015. © HOPE not hate

Matthew Hankinson (left)
and Wayne Bell, Liverpool,
August 2015. © HOPE not hate

Nazi, paedophile and Satanist Ryan Fleming (Facebook)

Alex Davies, Swansea 2015. © HOPE not hate

The iconic picture of NA
hiding in the left luggage at
Liverpool Lime Street station.
August 2015. © HOPE not hate

Alex Davies pleads with the police to let NA out of Lime Street station, August 2015.
© HOPE not hate

Wayne Bell, National Action's angry scar-faced action man, tried to assault as many of them as he could, coming out of a pub with a pint glass and demanding to fight one-on-one, in single combat.

Alex Davies and a few others took their chances by trying to find a way in to the station, mingling with the similarly attired antifascists. The size and scale of the counter protest was already a thing of legend: you could barely squeeze into the station by one o'clock. It seemed as if hundreds of people were arriving at every moment.

Outside, Wayne Bell and Matthew Hankinson put on an impressive display of their fighting skills as they tried to make their way in. The two of them had met up with members of the NWI but found themselves fighting for their lives with some locals who had casually asked if they were Nazis. Bell saw no reason to deny the charge, but when he and Hankinson were set upon, the NWI leaders, usually masters of bullying and violence, simply stood on the sidelines, watching. The NWI leader, the criminally vulgar Shane Calvert, demanded a police escort into the station to join the rest of the (now-beleaguered) National Action group outside lost luggage.

Inside the station, National Action members pleaded with police to be allowed their march. According to Mullen, the police officer in charge simply raised his eyebrows.

"Alex Davies," says Mullen, "took to whining like a little boy. His voice sounded cracked and upset, like a little kid before he has a tantrum."

Meanwhile Raymond acted, according to Mullen, "like an excitable little kid who never gets taken out much. He was making daft noises and walking up to people to introduce himself."

"He introduced himself to me; he was weird but nice. He spoke with a sort of nervousness, like he was self-conscious about the way he sounded. Then fruit, eggs and other objects began flying into us, hitting people in the face and head and he seemed oblivious to it. He seemed oblivious to everything that was going on around him."

Eventually the fascists were forced into the lost luggage office by the police, for their own protection. After weeks of antagonism, the sick images of genocide, the goading and stupidity of some National Action members online, antifascists were driven by an almost historical hatred. Mullen, himself forced into the lost luggage that day, said it felt like the antifascists' Cable Street.

As eggs and a whole array of fruits and vegetables (most notably bananas) rained down on the 60-70 gathered there, the police pulled down the office shutter. A deafening roar of approval went up inside the station, which caused pushing, shoving and celebration outside as everyone wanted to see the moment for themselves. Hundreds of smart phones captured the moment of supreme humiliation, broadcasting the images and video straight to Twitter. Tens of thousands of people retweeted the images. There'd be no White Man March: it was a moment of horror and humiliation for the neo-Nazis.

"You could hear objects hitting the shutters and there was a lot of really angry people locked inside," said Mullen. "To a man, we all wanted to march still, we still believed we could march. But, as gradually the fuller picture emerged of thousands upon thousands of people trying to get in and kill us, our thoughts turned to how the fuck we would get out of there alive."

Inside the office people looked to Raymond and Davies to find a solution. Helm, who'd been the nominated organiser for the day, sat quietly in the corner. Raymond tried to cheer up two visitors from the Antipodean Resistance who had travelled from Australia to be there, sharing handy hints on travelling to Europe on the cheap. They stared at him aghast, bewildered that he seemed to have absolutely no care for what was happening outside and the absolute humiliation his supposedly 'cutting-edge' gang was suffering. Renshaw, who'd committed so much of his energy to winding the day up to be a confrontation he could never win, sat in the corner sobbing.

Jeremy Bedford Turner, the main speaker at the far-right London Forum, decided it was best to go straight back to London no sooner had he arrived at the station. Turning to leave, he was confronted in the ticket office by antifascists, making him run away, leaving his glasses and diary behind. Phone calls to and from the lost luggage were both heated and depressing. Where was the cavalry? A small team of neo-Nazis holed up in a pub about a mile from the city centre attempted a kamikaze mission to fight their way into the station. Led by Liam Pinkham, his partner and her father, they made it within sight of the station before they had to be rescued by the police under a shower of boots and fists.

The humiliation was horrendous. A minibus of Polish thugs, led by National Front official and former YBNP member Kevin Layzell, was arrested in Wigan from where they'd wanted to catch a train into Liverpool. It was nearly five o'clock in the afternoon and they had still hadn't made it to the city.

Back in Liverpool itself, down by the docks, hundreds of antifascists held an impromptu party, letting off flares and smoke bombs. National Action's combative Twitter accounts were deluged with pictures and messages about their humiliation. NA had manage to attract perhaps 100 people from across the world to marvel at what they thought would be a significant victory and a turning point. Swedish supporters sat bloodied and tearful in pubs out of town while others, from places such as Scotland and Ireland who couldn't even get as far as a pub, were turned away like the Poles at Wigan railway station. Why people were even traveling to Wigan, part of a daft masterplan, remains a mystery.

Possibly only Christopher Lythgoe, at home in Warrington and watching the whole thing unfold on social media, was happy.

CHAPTER 10: "A RIDICULE UNPARALLELED IN NATIONALIST HISTORY..."

National Action put a brave face on its humiliation, but Liverpool was a massive wake-up call. The group had made its mark by bullying small groups of leftists and students, convincing itself it was bigger and stronger than any organised or militant opposition. The group's inner core had believed their own publicity, that they were 'dangerous' and 'well trained', and more than enough to cope with the antifascist movement which they'd assumed wanted to hide behind police cordons.

The earlier Manchester White Pride demonstration had shown them and reminded others there were still militant and organised antifascists around, but such was National Action's strong self-belief they thought they'd simply sweep away any opposition after beating up some students on campuses. Ben Raymond, rarely brave enough to face opposition himself, had spent many enjoyable hours dedicating column inches on the group's website to denigrating antifascists and claiming antifascism was dead. He wrote in one post in April 2015, titled *"NA commandos humiliate communists by going to their rally and stealing their stupid flags"*, that:

> *"The deciding factor was that antifa are hobbyists who do not possess the camaraderie or organisation of a tight knit group like NA, absolutely none of them seemed to know each other, pretty much anyone can go there and do whatever."*

Locals in Liverpool had responded with a militancy to National Action's presence that shocked the group to its core. They had believed the public's opposition to racism and Nazism was waning; that immigration had finally become the tipping point; that ordinary people would sit back and allow them a free run of the city.

With their humiliation sealed across social media, next came the condemnations that would set back for many months their relationship with the rest of the British far right. Their sheer juvenile ignorance had particularly upset Joe Owens, a notorious Liverpool criminal and far-right figure who had once been bodyguard to British National Party leader Nick

Griffin. Owens went public with his condemnation, calling Liverpool and its fall-out "a ridicule unparalleled in Nationalist history."

Garron Helm responded to the criticism by publishing Owens' address on the internet. Christopher Lythgoe watched the debacle unfold from his home in Warrington, commenting only to his closest members. Despite the bravado from behind the closed shutters of the lost luggage office on Liverpool Lime Street station, the internal communiqués were horrific. The anger, the fear, the terror of the day was expressed over a period of three to four hours. Even getting home had been a nerve-wracking event. The police, the 'reds', the antifascists and the whole of Liverpool had made National Action look small and silly. From as far away as Sweden and Australia people had come to see this new, lean and mean fighting machine and they'd left deeply unimpressed.

Wayne Bell assumed responsibility for the failure. Writing on VK, Russia's version of Facebook, he heralded the beginning of the group's dark age:

> "For those there yesterday were the bravest we have, those not there showed us exactly why we're doomed, say what you want, if you weren't there then you can't say fuck all but you will. We don't play things safe like others do, no city in Britain is off limits to us.
>
> "On a brighter note we had a meeting in Manchester and now have full backing from our friends from Poland. This was a defeat but we showed that we won't be intimidated by the rent a mob. It was a set up from the start.
>
> "Revenge will come!
>
> "We will take the fight to them. From now on we won't be doing many demonstrations in the future. An elite unit will now be drilled. We got the strongest fittest fighters in British nationalism.
>
> "The best have been identified and will be taking a different route than the rest. Demos serve a certain purpose but there are too many groups. We should have had hundreds out yesterday so the only positive was we know the bottlers from the brave."

Robbie Mullen didn't share any of the shame. He was exhilarated – what a day! He'd been there on the front line, like a fully paid-up member of the gang. He'd stood with them all and cemented his standing in the group: Alex Davies, Ben Raymond, Andy Clarke, Matthew Hankinson, Garron Helm, Jack Renshaw, Radoslaw Rekke, Wayne Bell. They were the frightening National Action and they were all friends for life. No-one else would ever matter again.

***

It was after Liverpool that HOPE not hate believed a split had occurred within National Action. Wayne Bell's assertion it would no longer be doing demonstrations and would become an elite group was potentially the first evidence NA was moving (or some within it wanted to move) closer to a terrorist outcome. Of course, we had no actual idea at the time that anyone other than Ben Raymond or Alex Davies was leading the group – or was even capable of leading it. It was clear from rumours and little bits of gossip we picked up that Raymond was the only one of any real independent means. It was also clear that when HOPE not hate wrote about either himself or National Action, he became agitated. Our style, or perhaps just mine, was brash and dismissive, designed to antagonise him because we'd always seen him as the weak link in the group. I thought he was a charlatan from the off. But never in a million years did I believe he could build an organisation of dark, homicidal maniacs.

Raymond liked to pretend he was the orphan of Catalan parents, living off a bequest. But by this point media organisation VICE was forensically investigating his background and came to us for a chat. Like us, though, they were unable to find anything of substance about him. They'd turned up a number of potential parents living and dead both here and abroad. How could it be so difficult to track down his background? Raymond was keen to spread the idea that he had money saved up in Ibiza or that he held property there. VICE turned up a gay cabaret singer in Sitges, near Barcelona, who had sung fascist ballads in drag as the most likely paternal suspect. And when I occasionally alluded to it in my blogs, Raymond had by all accounts exploded with hurt rage.

According to Mullen, who was now part of the North West England cell led by Lythgoe, HOPE not hate was either incredibly perceptive or, in Raymond's eyes, stirring trouble for the group by asserting there was a split. They were simply not in the habit of going to war with each other or airing dirty linen in public. Yet.

For all intents and purpose, Raymond was still the public face of National Action, blissfully ignorant and overly-concerned with his writing, international travel and self-image. The leader and direction had changed, or at least shifted, but it wasn't a schism. Raymond would occasionally become panicked or distressed when he missed out on making a decision. But these were lonely boys, all of them in some way damaged, socially awkward. If Raymond still led them in any way, it was because they saw a more driven and unfortunate version of themselves.

Meanwhile, Lythgoe and those he gathered around him had realised the true nature of National Action. The group had been a way of boosting popularity and airing their desires and darkest sentiments with likeminded people ... and it had been Raymond's writings that had driven the group darker and deeper into something more sinister. There was never any way those embedded in the group would throw it all away over some silly mistakes. Excuses were made for Raymond because, after all, he had created the group along with Alex Davies.

The other upshot of the Liverpool debacle was recruitment. Laugh at them the world may have been doing, but three days after the event, thousands of emails were flooding in demanding more information about the group. Raymond, Davies and Lythgoe were taking turns in clearing the backlog, making sure every membership enquiry was answered and dealt with. It wasn't just lonely young men writing in: young women were also interested. On the internal message groups there was much excitement every time another young woman applied for information about joining. Members went off to check their Facebook profiles and then come back with a picture they could all comment about. "Looks like she's a slut" or "this one wants raping" were not uncommon responses, but still they came in and still they were recruited. The only real problem was, what to do with the female members?

In the group's early days, the very few women involved had been harassed, almost tortured by requests for gangbangs and group sex. Numerical and availability issues aside, why did so many young men want to have sex together at the same time with the same person? The young woman who had met with us very early on in National Action's history said she suffered never-ending series of requests to join the rest of the gang for bukkake parties and gangbangs.

Out of a humiliating disaster, there was still something to salvage. Perhaps it was Raymond, perhaps it was Lythgoe, but someone in their number was abreast of the Leninist concept of revolutionary defeatism at least. The sheer weight of the Liverpool humiliation had played into Lythgoe's hands and the huge interest in membership was now almost debilitating. Mullen got something of a shock when during one of the weekly ideological browbeatings Lythgoe held for the group in the Warrington Wetherspoons, he replaced Matt Hankinson with Mullen as the North West regional organiser.

Mullen may have been surprised – delighted – with his sudden elevation but there was method in Lythgoe's decision. Hankinson was tall, handsome, university-educated and in National Action circles at least, on the cusp of normality. And Mullen... well, he wasn't. The lonely kid from Widnes had almost nothing else in his life outside of NA, which is what Lythgoe wanted.

Ironically, it would be Hankinson that Mullen remained closest to during his time in National Action. The former's strong sense of independence and confidence was a greater pull than Lythgoe's dark and sour ramblings. Mullen even went to watch Hankinson fight in a charity boxing event where, by all accounts, Hankinson dealt his opponent a ferocious beating. What stuck in Mullen's mind wasn't the bout, however, but Hankinson's pre-occupation with preventing his name getting out to any wider circles, and ensuring his face wasn't photographed. Someone told Mullen the Hankinson family owned some stables somewhere. Mullen's father had been a horse trainer when he lived in Canada, so there was already some kind of connection or assumed bond in Mullen's mind between the two already.

***

For the rest of 2015, National Action was almost paralysed by the need to regroup and retrain. Its zealots travelled to various gyms and venues around the north west of England, taking instruction from Jimmy Hey, the mixed martial arts specialist. It wasn't just the North West where the group trained either. There was a shift happening across the country, as those no longer willing to simply be part of Raymond's avant-garde Nazi boy scouts travelled to the North West to be tutored by Hey.

Hey was held in high esteem by National Action. Although the MMA fighter liked them in return (enough to have joined them on the fateful outing to Liverpool, with two of his fighters in tow), his interests lay further east – in the Ukraine and the Azov Battalion's front group, the Misanthropic Division (MD). Wayne Bell and Lythgoe were similar adherents. While there was little more public activity for the rest of 2015, NA was more than just licking its wounds. It began laying plans. Saturdays were earmarked as training days, where the group could meet, train, then engage in heavy drinking sessions. Plans were made to follow the lead of other fascists in simply abandoning London: it wasn't a place where NA could comfortably organise and it was overrun with non-whites, Jews and 'reds'. Yes, the Polish neo-Nazis from National Rebirth of Poland (NOP) were there, but Lythgoe reasoned that NOP – "wogs" themselves – could operate within the capital as foreigners anyway.

Plans were floated to move the group to West Yorkshire. A White Homeland project was mooted and a website set up to raise funds for it – something that had echoes of plans by 1990s neo-Nazi organisation Combat 18. Raymond became one of its cheerleaders. Davies was sent to investigate the possibility of buying an old farmhouse, somewhere close to or on the outskirts of a rural village. The two looked at Haworth, a village in the area, but it was too expensive and too middle class. Lythgoe suggested members without jobs should be sent to live in West Yorkshire and encouraged to live in cheap accommodation; they could continue to train and agitate in the local area, then wait for the rest of the group to move there when the time was right.

Some mused you could fire rockets from above the hills of Bradford and hit the city's mosques. One young member from Bradford, Jack Coulson, began building what he thought was a rocket launcher. Such was the kind of mindset now developing.

There was a genuine belief, at least among some in National Action, that West Yorkshire would be the birthplace of the race war. One more Muslim riot in Bradford – or in Leeds even – and NA would be prepared to lead the fightback. Demonstrations as grandly advertised as Liverpool were now off the agenda. Everything would be done on a need-to-know basis from now on.

It wouldn't matter where members were based; war would come to them.

It wasn't a new idea. British Nazis and fascists had for almost a century dreamed of taking control of small parts of the country. In the United States, Nazis quite often lived in compounds dominated by guns and incest.

In the UK, Combat 18 had once had a similar idea: its Aryan Homeland would involve moving en-masse to Essex and taking over a local area. The group's ideological guru, former monk and Satanist Priest David Myatt, had wanted some sort of back-to-the-land compound out in the Essex countryside, a cult-like setting to raise race warriors. For some of the others, the dream was about taking over the local council and pub in a small village (and most likely getting drunk) while waiting for the race war. C18's erstwhile leader during the period, Charlie Sargent, had claimed they wanted to control council estates in Essex much like paramilitaries in Northern Ireland. Some, like Sargent, had already taken that dream as far as it could go, ending up in mobile homes on the outskirts of Essex towns. But the dream would collapse under C18's inherent contradictions and the murder that Sargent would help initiate as the group collapsed in bitter recriminations and civil war as factions struggled to control its direction and control of a lucrative music business.

Other fascists had had similar ideas. In the 1980s Nick Griffin had run off to live in a rural fascist commune in France and then, after the BNP collapsed, had tried moving himself and his supporters to Hungary. These ideas would always seem to involve fascists moving away from civil society and retreating into the darkness of their fetishes.

But National Action was different. Its followers had few of the distractions plaguing groups such as Combat 18: there were no girlfriends, friends, wives or even public profiles to really worry about. The move to a West Yorkshire village might have been a real possibility, but like with most fascist plans, underlying it always appears to be a subplot to either enslave one another or simply vanish from the modern world entirely.

National Action's core believed it could fund this project with its own modern skills, such as building commercial websites and video editing. Raymond and Person B, the troublesome teen from east London, were commercially good enough to sell their wares. Person B had a real flair for art and design, and was already busy selling website shells to the hotel sector. Alex Davies, the principle character in self-promotion and bullshit, insisted he could front a company offering all of these things. Davies had moved into the sales game, going door-to-door to generate enough money for his ever-increasing international travels on NA business.

The idea of this had been put into plan by Lythgoe before the Liverpool debacle, but it was only after that failure the plans had really swung into action. Things were escalating. For Mullen there were no more lonely nights pounding the cycle paths beside the Manchester canal or sitting at his PlayStation eating cold pizza. He was getting fit, putting his weight behind punches in training and using the martial art kali sticks imported from Asia that looked nice enough, but could break bones very easily.

When they weren't training, the group was meeting potential recruits. Sent to quiet train stations at inconvenient hours, the recruit would be studied at a distance before being approached. Normally National Action would send "Rad" the Pole from Manchester to retrieve the individual from where they'd be delivered to a nearby pub for scrutiny. If they looked "weird" or "queer" they'd be left at the train station to rot, and the group would get drunk before going home.

They were prepared to travel to recruit. Chris McCartney, Lythgoe's driver and an imposing figure who was a cab driver and small-time drug dealer by day, had taken to driving the group to recruitment meetings. He was well over six feet in height and weighed close to twenty stone. He was an absolute beast of a human being. With his imposing and heavily tattooed frame, he added a menacing air to proceedings. If the recruit was "mad" and spent the whole time speaking about how he wanted to kill all blacks, Jews or Muslims, the group would dump him in the pub and walk off. Taking that into consideration, Mullen often wondered why McCartney himself hadn't been put through the same process:

"Some [recruits] would turn up to these meetings and look kind of normal. We'd all get a drink and then sit down to chat. Very few made it through the interview process because quite often they'd open up with 'I'm prepared to kill as many people as you tell me.' Lythgoe didn't want people who were prepared to kill randomly: we'd had that with Zack Davies. Lythgoe wanted people who understood there would be a process to this stuff. Random killings were pointless and cruel and the person doing them a danger to the rest of the group. I mean, who goes to a pub and just starts talking like that?"

I asked Mullen if he believed Lythgoe, that there had to be murders. "Yes and no," he replied. "Does that make sense?" I told him I wasn't sure. "Well, I guess looking at it now it was inevitable. But as he was turning people away who were prepared to do it, I sort of thought…. it's years away like a pipe dream, a bit of a fantasy?"

Were any of those in your group capable of committing murder? I then asked.

"I think that was the process. We would be ready when we were ready, not when some nutter decided to go to the supermarket and do some random Asian bloke in."

So was National Action against racist attacks? "Yes and no. Does that make sense?"

Yes and no.

***

In September 2015, Raymond appeared on the BBC's daily current affairs programme, the *Victoria Derbyshire Show*, on a slot exploring radicals.

For many in National Action it was the first time they got a good look at Raymond and how he spoke – which was softly and with a slight drawl. He claimed to the interviewer that his parents were dead. It wasn't his worst performance in front of the camera and the show went soft on him, presumably assuming he would have enough rope to magically hang himself in the eyes of the public.

On the National Action internal messaging as the programme went out, and Raymond and the interviewer walked around Bognor Regis before settling for fish and chips on the beach, some mocked him.

"Ben looks like from Ernie from Bert and Ernie," wrote one. "Looks and sounds like a poof," wrote another. But overall they were happy with his performance. Within hours there were more people searching for the group online, discovering its website and even donating. Raymond again went online to entice the Americans to send money and watch the interview on YouTube.

In the North West, Lythgoe was able to withdraw some more money for expenses, stickers, train fares and beer. Raymond also confirmed in his BBC interview that the idea of removing non-whites from the country ("repatriation") was a fantasy, something not even National Action believed possible. He also reaffirmed NA believed it was superior to other groups on the British far right. The National Front, to which it was close, didn't take the interview well. Publicly the NF was still the only far-right party that believed it possible and necessary – and called for – the removal of all non-whites from these shores, even those born in Britain.

Raymond also told the BBC that he didn't rule out the possibility that National Action could one day become a political party. Sure, he was part-showman, but he had avoided the temptation to be the lunatic he was behind his computer screen. More than anything, although he'd been racist enough to either settle or unsettle who watches the BBC current affairs programmes that early in the day, he was making clear that he'd still decide the future direction of the group. His self belief in his monstrously over-exaggerated political acumen played out again. Lythgoe was unimpressed.

In the same month, Jack Renshaw (now firmly ensconced as the gang's spokesperson/motormouth in the North West), took to Twitter with a series of horrendous tweets about Jews that would continue for at least another year. His personal Blog, *Renshaw's Corner*, was even worse for its extremism.

In October 2015, I was sent a picture of the North West Battalion of the Misanthropic Division, the Ukrainian Azov Battalion's front group in the UK. It was grainy and not of much use, but Lythgoe was visible front and centre with his face covered. Sometime around then, Lythgoe had snatched control of National Action. Ashley Bell from Leeds had tired of being a dummy who nobody knew was leader and while the group's founders, Raymond and Davies, prevaricated, the title fell to Lythgoe. Now, NA would have a proper new leader. Raymond, for the first time in the group he formed, knew he would become subordinate. Except nobody was to know Lythgoe was the leader. Like everybody else, we'd never heard of him.

The photo was interesting, but of no use to us at the time. With Lythgoe would come Renshaw, the troublesome oik whose intellect and popularity troubled Raymond.

Lythgoe sent National Action back to Liverpool in November 2015, with Renshaw on a megaphone. NA's website claimed 30 of its number, masked and menacing, including Mullen, "smashed the red terror" that was the city of the Liverpool:

> *"At the initiative of our Liverpool group we started [an] online campaign immediately after [the] White Man March where we would announce our return. Sometimes with only a day's notice, coachloads of activists (assumedly paid for by somebody) would turn up to counter non-existent demonstrations (after the first time these only got larger). Sometimes in the confusion members of the Anti Fascist Network would attack their own in the belief that nazis were prowling the streets. This bait and ridicule also allowed us to test our security and patch up any leaks we had. The inadequate police at these demonstrations and their collusion with the opposition ruled out any planned demonstration as even if we were able to march it would put the health of police and civilians in danger. In the long run we must surmise that although Liverpool set us back 4 months, it was invaluable for saving us from future catastrophes and drilling into our supporters and allies, the need to adopt the new method."*

This time, no-one had even noticed they'd been there.

CHAPTER 11: THERE MORE YOU IGNORE IT, THE CLOSER IT GETS

"When using an anonymity service, it is important that all the traffic originating from your computer is routed through the anonymity network. If any traffic leaks outside the secure connection, anyone monitoring your traffic will be able to log your activity."

– Security and Anonymity in the Digital Age – A Nationalist Perspective.

A s 2015 drew to a close, the new direction inside National Action was in force. Nobody doubted that Christopher Lythgoe, who had what a judge would describe as a "dystopian vision for the future", had spent his time waiting, carefully planning to take over the group. A lot of things he may have been, but he was never idle.

Despite (or more likely because of) the visibility generated by the disaster at Liverpool Lime Street that summer, when the group was humiliated by much larger numbers of antifascists, the group had grown exponentially. It now had eight regions active around the UK, each led by a committed individual reporting privately to Alex Davies, Ben Raymond and, of course, Lythgoe.

Although it antagonised them both, Davies and Raymond went along with Lythgoe's demands for total oversight of the organisation. He wasn't going to lead National Action quietly: he wanted control but no scrutiny. No-one outside the north west area or the inner core knew he was the real leader. It suited him that way, but he was constantly antagonised by Raymond's dithering and Davies's prima donna outbursts.

Having given up the leadership after pressure from his grandmother, Davies had assumed it would find its way back to him. It hadn't; Lythgoe had snatched it and there was no sign he'd relinquish it. Lythgoe's control had been immediate and strict. For Davies, this kick in the teeth made him more keen than ever to make himself appear the leader, at least in the eyes of the membership. Each region and sub group had to meet during the week and do an activity at the weekend. Davies could be found at all or any groups during the week, sleeping on sofas and offering advice on how best individuals could protect their jobs and their identities; things he himself had supremely failed to do.

Davies now found himself caught between Raymond, his co-founder, and Lythgoe. Davies was loyal to Raymond, but getting bored of his tireless self-promotion and cowardice, particularly now the Lythgoe show was in full swing. Lythgoe continually highlighted Raymond's shortcomings: self-promotion, weirdness or cowardice. He was also able to pinpoint the things that agonised or antagonised Davies. He craved popularity and respect, but had no serious job and no money. Having lost the top job and having to take a backseat publicly, he still wanted a lead role in the organisation. When Ashley Bell had been puppet leader he'd readily acquiesced to the whims and demands of Davies and Raymond, even allowing them overall control of the purse strings though he had the opportunities like the others to help himself to funds as he went along. Lythgoe had demanded almost immediately he took over National Action that he would be the arbiter of who got what and when. Lythgoe also had to be wary because, despite Raymond's faults, it was Raymond's skills and self-promotion that kept the bank balance topped up.

Davies was surviving on a few pounds a week while the group footed his travel bills. Davies' travelling and pep-talks were another thing that kept the group going. He had kudos with the members and Lythgoe was canny enough to appreciate that no matter how infuriating it may be, compared to Davies and Raymond, he could hardly warm a room full of activists. No, Lythgoe's talent was in being a surly and softly-spoken unseen medieval king who could send his troops into battle. He jotted in his note book how he saw the organisation of troops and generals' falling-in behind and underneath him. He had a commitment too; a commitment to ensuring people would understand how final and important his work was. The work of moving National Action into a position where it could fight a race war.

To Davies, the uniforms, the secrecy, the flags and the physical training meant everything – it was the ultimate excitement – but he also longed to be taken seriously, as he thought had been the case during his days in the British National Party. When he made it to Warrington to sit with Lythgoe's group in the pub, Davies would do all the talking, squeaking excitedly about his plans for the White Homeland project and his travels to Germany to meet like-minded networks. He impressed upon them his importance on the international scene and that he had access to the group's administration, but he was also struck with excitement by the seriousness and solemnity of Lythgoe's new direction.

By the end of January 2016, National Action had 200 active members, training and keeping fit together on a weekly basis. Each member who could afford it paid £5 per week for this training, and for other materials. Lythgoe insisted everybody who wanted to be a member had to contribute to the group's upkeep.

Massive bundles of offensive stickers were now arriving in the post from Poland each week, the more offensive the better as far as all were concerned. And every now and then, the "brutes" could be let off the leash to practice the fine art of violence and intimidation.

In Nottingham, a former member of Antifa had joined National Action. While a militant antifascist, Person C had been a crossdressing teen known as 'Amelia'. When he joined NA he was plain old Connor again, but Davies and Raymond embraced him as proof that the media and antifascists could no longer pigeonhole NA. Connor offered up the details of his local Antifa members and his new-found NA friends obliged by organising a night out in Nottingham, mustering a 30-strong gang dressed in black to go on a drinking binge looking for a fight with Antifa members.

> *"Today we are exposing a fascist this is Person C you maybe confused to why Connor has a antifascist flag behind him. Well Connor was part of the antifascist movement in Nottinghamshire. Connor was known back then as "Amelia" as Connor was transgender girl.*
> *"Then Connor converted into Muslim (so he claims). Connor soon later joined National Action and was made to stop being transgender was made to become straight as Connor was homosexual. Connor on far right with a small group of fascists and he shouted out names and addresses of Notts Antifa."* – Person C Exposed, Redrev skulls. Believed to be Person C exposing himself in the only blog post on the wordpress site.

Everyone was playing cat and mouse with the police, a very real game where their local Special Branch [anti-terrorist] officers would desperately try and unmask individuals involved in the group, visiting them at home to look around their bedrooms. It was another reason for the Homeland project to get up and working – so that the 'revolutionaries' wouldnt upset their parents by having the police tearing bits of their homes apart.

Following his BBC interview on the Victoria Derbyshire show, Davies suggested Raymond leave Bognor Regis permanently and move to Swansea with him. At least the two together could try to keep Lythgoe under control without risking their communications being intercepted. It's not clear whether the two were objecting to Lythgoe's dark turn and determination that National Action should become an outright terrorist group, or his surliness in dealing with them. The move to Swansea made sense to Raymond and helped alleviate the growing pain of feeling ostracised by Lythgoe. According to Robbie Mullen, Raymond had already moved many of his personal possessions to Swansea anyway.

For Mullen, the days of loneliness were in the past. For all the time he was spending with the group, he said that (at that stage) he never picked up anything particularly 'political' about it. The group's racism was vociferous and its hatred for Jews was off the scale – almost inexplicable he felt – but he accepted it all as part and parcel of the bubble he was in. The group worked on an assumption, through the interviews it conducted when people joined, that everybody understood where it sat politically. Their world views were harsh and disturbing, but Mullen felt more self-confident in himself since meeting them. He wasn't a quiet, introverted boy anymore and in a world that had sent him more than the odd cruel blow, he could gradually feel himself hardening in the same way as the others. "Kick back," he thought. "Kick back at all and everything."

By embracing things such as White Jihad, National Action wanted its members to reject all of the emotional weaknesses that had made them who they were when they were lonely, bullied schoolboys, and instead embrace the absolute darkness of their most startling and deranged thoughts. Don't just dream of genocide, plan one.

Whenever the group met or communicated, the conversations were littered with hatred and vulgarity about society and the prominent individuals within it. A bond had developed between them all, a bond that made them feel invincible, like they could tackle anything or anyone. If you had troubles at work or at home with the neighbours, National Action would sort it by sending half a dozen masked individuals to your door. They included people like Andy Clarke, the vulgar barrack-room lawyer, who understood the power of intimidation and violence. Others appreciated it too, taking advantage to settle the scores and sores they had held dear for a long time. NA could be the disturbing and violent revenge of the nerds.

Wherever the group travelled, Mullen felt there was an aura surrounding them. Drinking in Manchester city centre, sometimes a dozen National Action members in total, they went hunting for trouble. Radoslaw Rekke ('Rad the Pole'), the British-born Pole from Manchester, would wear his Nazi t-shirt, deliberately seeking to cause offence, carrying a set of knuckle dusters in his pocket for when the trouble started. Everyone now carried a small knife. The group's confidence was infectious and it made them feel untouchable. They had an impenetrable bond they felt couldn't break. It was them against the world and as for the world, well, that wouldn't be around forever.

With Lythgoe's elevation to leader, former BNP youth leader Jack Renshaw firmly embedded within National Action, too. A likeable but dark joker, always seeking confrontations and arguments, Renshaw was clever. He believed he was cleverer than anybody else in the world, and certainly in NA. Having held a senior post in the BNP and having been of considerable importance at one time, he was a valued member of the wider movement. Lythgoe in particular preferred Renshaw's nonsense to the nonsense from the pen and mouth of Raymond. Renshaw's cunning wit and extravagant self-belief was certainly an arrow in Lythgoe's own often dour bow.

National Action were the darlings of the media, but few people writing about them knew the real truth. Having assumed (rightfully) there was an almost invisible schism inside NA, we had to keep up our written attacks, even if to only keep annoying Raymond (who passionately hated our work). He thought we were beneath him, but protested loudly that our attacks on his intellect were an attack on the whole group.

"In the case of National Action, they want people to believe that they believe they are the cutting edge of a movement that will one day grab power in this country and grab it violently. They used to portray themselves as the intellectual and youthful cutting-edge of the British far-right – not a particularly difficult task given the competition, but in reality it is only angry and childish words they spout with nothing like an ideology or a coherent sentence to format it. Even the rest of the far-right could see that. So now, they are "brutes", but not even very cutting edge ones at that." – National Action fill in their own school report once again. HOPE not hate, January 2016.

***

With promotions came demotions and Lythgoe, like everyone else in the North West, wanted Garron Helm to disappear. He had long since lost his pre-eminence as a pinup for National Action and had become something of a permanent irritant. He had been dating a young woman from the Polish neo-Nazi group NOP, upsetting Kevin Layzell from London who was the supposed link-man between the National Front, NOP and National Action. Layzell had also set his heart on a relationship with the same woman and began begging phonecalls to people in NA asking if Helm would desist with this relationship. Helm refused, and despite being perennially unemployed, even began traveling overseas with her.

Even before the disaster at Liverpool Lime Street station in August 2015, Helm had been shoved further and further to the margins. He took Mullen's elevation particularly poorly. Not permitted to have any role, he'd also taken umbrage over National Action's return to the city three months later. As time wore on, many of the group simply ignored Helm's calls or messages. Although he somehow managed to fly to Poland regularly, he was left out of trips that NA made there from around the UK. Even if he was in Poland at the same time as other NA members, they avoided and ignored him.

Speaking about him in February 2019, Robbie Mullen said:

"There was just something about him unlikeable, I dunno what it was exactly. Everyone had something against him. Apologising to [MP Luciana] Berger; his desperation and his lies. For some it was simply he was so poor and incapable. I think out of all of us he had more done for him by the wider movement who felt sorry for him. He had a habit of being a crushing disappointment and bore. He turned very weird very quickly."

Lythgoe even suggested Helm head to West Yorkshire as part of the Homeland project, but he refused. His involvement in the 'dark arts', making silly prayers to conjure spirits and often taking himself to Preston to camp alone, went from amusing to irritating very quickly. For a while, Rad the Pole had dated Helm's sister Ebony, and the three had gone camping together. Rad had tired of them both simultaneously and made disparaging remarks to the group about the Helm family that the group lapped up hysterically. In Helm, the once-lonely boys had found their victim. He made even the poorest, dullest and most unloved of them feel superior.

While on his magical mystery tour of witchcraft, Helm made friends with Ryan Fleming, an early fringe member of the group who had suddenly disappeared once before. Tall and slim, Fleming had a supreme, if not dark and mysterious, confidence about him. When Helm was spotted in Leeds, the group's erstwhile leader Ashley Bell met him at the city's train station and asked what he was doing. Helm said he was going to a friend's flat, someone who was "part of the movement". Very soon, this Ryan Fleming's flat became the centre of wild drinking parties. The group needed a place to call their own: despite hijacking the odd Wetherspoons for cut-price drinking, without their Homeland the group as yet had nowhere to meet in real privacy.

Fleming, who was a carer for a young woman and a part-time student, had smeared much of the walls of his flat with excrement and what he bragged was menstrual blood.

"There was shit everywhere," recalled Mullen.

Shit?

"Yeah, poo! Bloody tampons and all that stuff too. Also sheep's skulls on the floor that he and Garron [Helm] had collected on the moors to pray with. The living room was quite clean but I never went back, me and Matt [Hankinson] would go to the pub instead to wait for the others. Ryan [Fleming] was as sick as fuck, I can't put it into words," said Mullen, before doing so:

"Fleming went camping and training a few times and most of the group saw him and his sickness as some kind of revolutionary shit. I remember Wayne [Bell] who had kids and that, saying he would never let his kids near him. Ben [Raymond] went there for a party or something and seemed absolutely delighted with how weird it all was. He even tried to date the young woman Fleming was a carer for. He invited her down to Swansea to declare his love for her. He thought Fleming was a fucking artist or something."

Fleming, like Helm, was attracted to the writings of the infamous Satanist group, Order of Nine Angles. Fleming also had an obsession with "young meat", under-age girls and boys. He would share with National Action members what they thought was his fantasy about having violent sex with children or with the disabled. In NA, the more crude and more violent the conversations were, the better. Many assumed the Satanist stuff was just another part of White Jihad, that the summonsing of evil spirits would be their crutch, their Islam.

***

"I take huge inspiration from nature – wolf males don't act like female wolves and they do not fuck each other, wolves do not breed with sheep or monkeys, also they do not tolerate the weak – they hunt and slay the weak. Answer is – my beliefs are very normal, natural and healthy beliefs of a white young man." – Ivan, the "Lithuanian Lion" interviewed by National Action, April 2016. In an earlier version he claimed he was interested in pederasty, but the article was subsequently edited by NA to remove the offending references.

Although National Action had now established itself as a major player in the British and international far-right scene, it wasn't the only group experiencing a new-found confidence. Although the numbers involved were incredibly small, the National Front (NF) as well as the EDL splinter gangs, the North West Infidels (NWI), South East Alliance (SEA), there were a large number of people on the British far right prepared to travel for violence. So small but numerous were these groups that they were always on the cusp of a violent confrontation, mostly with one another. With its innate sense of supremacy, NA actively antagonised these groups. Castleford's Wayne Bell had even started issuing threats to other leaders.

Ryan Fleming, Garron Helm's new friend, was also about to cause all kinds of problems for National Action. On January 23 2016, NA was preparing a flash demonstration in Newcastle, where they'd turn up unannounced, hold a small demonstration and then vanish, leaving the world's media to report on their shocking bravado. A vicious rumour started to spread inside NA the day before. "Ryan's a paedo," was all it said. It was met with silence. A minute later the message appeared on another one of the group's internal messaging groups, moving from Signal to Telegram to Wire, where the group had something like a dozen different groups set up.

Robbie Mullen had been forced to silence the messaging apps on his phone because he was working. During his lunch break he excitedly logged on to see who was around for a chat. There were arguments breaking out on almost every group he visited. Because messages were set to expire after anything from 15 minutes to one hour, he was simply witnessing an argument that had begun hours ago and was repeating itself in different formats and forums. He had no idea what was going on. While he was reading there came a ruling from up top in the organisation: the arguments were to cease and the subject was to be dropped. Lunch was ruined.

Mullen knew not to ask what had happened. When something was to be dropped or stopped, it had to stop forever. This sort of discipline was what appealed to so many who'd joined.

After work Mullen went out for drinks with his work colleagues, a curious ritual he'd avoided until now. This time he went and even allowed himself a pint. The conversations bemused him. He sat through it all – polite chat about holidays, heavy boxes, big tits, small tits, new cars, mortgages etc – and found it all so *mundane* compared to his new life with National Action. He had to get himself the fuck out of there and back to his own bubble of sensible danger and hatred.

At 5am the next morning, the day of the demo, a car pulled up outside his cold little house. He'd already walked the dog twice since getting home the night before. She lay on the couch under a blanket, staring at him with one eye open. Did he never stop?

Lythgoe had made an edict that anyone getting a lift had to be collected directly from their homes and sighted actually leaving the house – there were to be no collections from the street, street corners or other locations. Thus at 5am Mullen had to open his door and go back inside his house before Lythgoe was satisfied. Matt Hankinson sat in the back of the car with a stupid grin. Beside him was Michal Trubini, a large Slovakian anti-communist who said very little but liked to fight. Lythgoe sat in silence next to a driver who said nothing the whole way to Newcastle. No-one in the car seemed to know exactly what the issue with Fleming had been about. Lythgoe had a face like thunder. Whatever had happened, Fleming had been promoted to North East organiser during the arguments, which Lythgoe had also known very little about. They agreed none of them liked him.

***

"A group of neo-Nazis carrying 'Hitler Was Right' banners and making Nazi salutes in central Newcastle this weekend have escaped punishment because they committed "no crime".

"Up to 20 National Socialists wearing masks and dressed in black met at The Monument and performed Nazi salutes in the centre of the north-eastern city before breaking off into smaller groups and making their way to the university." – Jewish News Online, 25 January 2016.

Our office phone had rung non-stop all weekend: "What are you going to do?"

What *could* we do? Police officers who approached National Action members in Newcastle were told they had been given legal advice that said their 'Hitler Was Right' was neither illegal nor offensive. The police accepted it. NA now even had a solicitor on tap in the city, it appeared.

A busker playing the saxophone had taken offence to the black-clad group standing on Grey's Monument in Newcastle city centre and made a valiant attempt to drown out their chants of "Sieg Heil". According to eyewitnesses who spoke to the *Daily Mirror*, some passers-by had even given Nazi salutes to the neo-Nazis. A small, part-bewildered, part-angry group surrounded them as they stood on the monument. Fleming, promoted to organiser for the day, told the crowd National Action would "fight for Hitler, fight for what is right. White is right." A video taken on the day also shows young girls seemingly quite taken with the black-clad men standing menacingly around. On the monument, the group felt in their element.

"Fucking look at us!" they whispered. "We're fucking untouchable." The saxophonist came closer, showing off now, drawing howls of approval from some of the hostiles in the crowd surrounding the National Action men. Lythgoe then gave the order – "fuck him up" – and Hankinson laid into him, breaking his instrument and punching him in the head.

The whole demonstration lasted no more than a quarter of an hour, but their point had been made. To avoid detection, Wayne Bell led one group off and Lythgoe led another: straight to Wetherspoons for a celebration.

"Lined in disciplined ranks, we announced ourselves and gave a fiery speech, denouncing the 1%, the refugee 'crisis' and the bankers and leaders who had orchestrated recent events and who continued to scam the British people. A few members of the public attempted a futile debate, but the group of young people at the front became very excited and were saluting us. a Crypto-Jewish busker began blaring on his saxophone in an attempt to drown out the truthful words being spoken. He was swiftly dealt with by a loyal operative, and began shouting and leering along with other Jewish elements, and they become more vitriolic and incoherent as our second speaker took the floor, but it didn't make much difference." – National Action report on the demonstration, 20 Feb 2016.

***

The outrage from their Newcastle activity was to generate news coverage for National Action around the world. Raymond would claim in internal messages that the attention netted another "couple of thousand shekels" within hours. But trouble was looming. An antifascist in Yorkshire had become obsessed with one of the National Action members in the photographs from Newcastle. He knew the face but couldn't put his finger on a name, nor work out how he knew them. It was Ryan Fleming: not had he only spoken at the rally, but he'd flirted outrageously with the young girls who stopped to look at the group.

On a following evening I took myself up to Yorkshire to meet the antifacist. He was like cat on a hot tin roof. He put an envelope on the table, beaming with pride. "You'll fucking love this," he bragged. I doubted it, but I opened it all the same. Inside was a newspaper cutting and an old photograph of Ryan Fleming. I bought the guy a curry and headed back down to London.

In honour or homage to Fleming, National Action later changed their report's subheading to "he who owns the youth gains the future", one of the sick social media posts we highlighted in our report into Fleming.

CHAPTER 12: IF YOU TOLERATE THIS, THEN YOUR CHILDREN WILL BE NEXT

"There has been much noise made about the violent children known as National Action making an appearance in Newcastle last weekend. The delinquent gang even assaulted a lone busker as part of their efforts to prove they are some kind of dangerous terror group.

"While that may be up for debate, what is clear is that they are not sort of people you would let near young children. One case in point is Ryan Fleming who made a short speech and carried a pink carrier bag on the day. A number of antifascists from different groups took an interest in Fleming and it seems we were right to.

"On one of his Facebook pages, he quotes Moors Murderer Ian Brady, the monster who tortured and murdered young children along with Myra Hindley.

"Fleming, originally from Horsforth, has a conviction for false imprisonment and sexual assault on a vulnerable teenager dating from 2011. For the imprisonment and sexual assault on the teenager he received 26 months in prison. He was also ordered to sign the Sex Offenders register for 10 years.

"The vulnerable young adult suffered a "degrading and humiliating" ordeal when he was tied up, attacked and sexually assaulted at a party by Fleming and his friend.

Fleming had told the teenager he had the option of eating Marmite or performing a sex act on him. He was made to eat the Marmite and then assaulted.

"Fleming uses various names like Alexander Morain when on social media. Like many in National Action, he hides behind various aliases for "security purposes" as they do not like- like Wayne Bell aka Jarvie standing next to him, to be uncovered. Often they close down one account as soon as they fear they are about to be exposed.

"Understandably, Fleming in particular, does not want people looking too hard into him, who he is and what he has done in his past- despite quoting Brady on his page. He also likes to quote extensively Adolf Hitler on "capturing youth" though we're not sure even Adolf Hitler had in mind

what Fleming has done. Fleming even brags that young people find him attractive.
"National Action do not seem to have a problem with him. They have even posted his speech from Newcastle on their YouTube page. We have also been told that the leadership of National Action are aware of Fleming's conviction and his adoration of the likes of Ian Brady and torturing young, vulnerable teenagers, but think it is a "hoot"."

– Meet the Nazi who abused and tortured a teenager, HOPE not hate, 29 January 2018.

"There is absolutely no question of caving into this ridiculous hysteria, what Ryan did was heroic and the morally correct thing to do – none of you have a clue.
"I am particularly disappointed (sic) that leading members of the National Front still continue to comment on here. I wasn't kidding earlier, I have very serious allegations about your party which unlike the marmite case are in no way defensible and will be very damaging. You are very lucky because I am currently thinking about Matthew Collins and the pain it is causing to deny him this information – dammit, more hard decisions. I don't really understand the NA/NF rift, please stop being dafties and engage with us in productive efforts for R&N. Inviting us to Dover was really nice, why don't we build on that instead of silliness?
"Considering that HNH have several paid employees running insider's blog which is created for the sole purposes of causing division and no other reason (not even the antifa read it) – I don't see why they didn't have guys to come here and go on the offensive in the hope that posters join them and rifts occur."

– Ben Raymond writing on Stormfront, 6 February 2018.

***

Ryan Fleming had taken a vulnerable young man out of a party, tied him up, held him captive, tortured him and made him suck Marmite off his penis. Within hours of our story appearing (which included a link to the original newspaper article about his conviction in 2011) National Action was in meltdown. Was the reality and seriousness of all their internal bragging about lust for violence and sex coming home to roost?

Not only had Fleming openly bragged about his Satanism and fetish for young women, he' d also praised and lavished admiration on Myra Hindley and Ian Brady, the notorious Moors Murderers who'd tortured and murdered Lancashire schoolchildren in the mid-1960s. No-one in National Action had batted an eyelid, even when he bragged he liked young girls and they, in turn, liked him. They had even accepted (except for Robbie Mullen and a few others) that smearing his home with excreta and menstrual blood was all part of his act. After all, Fleming was well-known in his village for riding a horse bareback to the pub. He was a "card" and a "real character".

Fleming had appeared a confident, committed good talker, an impressive individual. Mullen felt powerless to raise objections. Would his new-found friends sneer at him, make him an outcast? Was he just too working class to understand why so many National Action members liked lazing around in Fleming's disgusting "arthouse" flat surrounded by shit and piss? He needn't have worried, because there was anger, violent anger that would soil relations between many of the group until its very end. Ben Raymond was convinced Fleming was innocent of any crime, and worked hard to convince others. Even with the original news story linked to HOPE not hate's blog, and even with Fleming's own internal admission of guilt, people chose to ignore Fleming's sexual assault. The group could simply wait for the outrage to pass and move on. But Raymond was to be shocked with the response.

Wayne Bell, the scarred thug who we'd initially identified in our expose as Wayne Jarvie (his nom de plume), had once dazzled Raymond with his brutality. Now he would drive Raymond to distraction by stating Fleming should be killed. He even demanded permission to do it. Bell felt physically sick, knowing he'd stood there next to Fleming in Newcastle, the picture of them now there for all to see. Bell had known his instincts about Fleming – to not allow him near his children for a start – were right all along. Raymond found Bell's rage and fury an affront and would never forgive him for it. What really sickened Bell (and others) was they'd been duped into going along with Fleming's jokes and perversions without actually understanding, like with so many things that would unfold within National Action, this was a group that enjoyed acting out sickness. They'd all laughed about Fleming's open descriptions of his sick desires; others had even shared theirs. For many, the reality of sexually assaulting somebody was horrific. For others, not so much.

I asked Mullen about his recollection of these events. He admitted his confidence had been shaken to the very core. He'd met and even liked (to a degree) a sexual predator, and worse still, he became worried by not embracing the reality of others' fantasies becoming reality, he could be ostracised or seen as "uncool" by them:

"Wayne [Bell] wanted Fleming murdered and asked that he be given permission to do it."

What was the response to that?

"A silence of sorts. Everyone was getting their heads around it. Wayne felt that the only way the group could survive this, keep it pure, was to take out Fleming and murder him ourselves, show the movement that we really were a cut above the groups like NF and EDL who also had paedophile members."

Would he have done it?

"I dunno. Away from all his thuggery and violence he was a proper family man, you know. A proper dad with a proper home. He was one of the few that was very different to the rest of us who had no-one and nothing. I don't know why he put up with the group's constant obsessions with the idea that someone harmed kids made him, you know.....

"Ben [Raymond] said there would be an investigation carried out internally before a decision was made, but you could tell he wanted it ignored."

A decision about murdering Fleming?

"No, about whether we should expel him. Fleming has no idea how close he came to opening the door to Wayne [Bell] and a very large sword."

And how did you feel about the rather nonchalant way the group dealt with Fleming's sex crimes?

"I kind of gave way to the (prevailing) mood, I guess. But I did feel really uneasy with the way some of the group loved the idea of what Fleming had done proved us, as a group, to be something kind of like... different to the rest? I never doubted that there were loads of people on the far right who probably fancied kids. The EDL was full of them, you know, "nonces", but even when NA were all joking about raping kids and women, I just thought it was talk, because publicly we were all for killing nonces, and I meant it when I thought it or said it.

"Now (confronted) with having a nonce in our own ranks, all those jokes and fantasies seemed like the truth and our stuff about healthy life styles-already a massive lie given how much drugs and alcohol were being readily used, probably more bullshit too."

To others in National Action the initial horror and outrage gave way to a strange sense of bemusement. Fleming was claiming that he merely punished the (vulnerable) boy for ogling his girlfriend. All it had been was a sly blowjob, after all. Fleming's girlfriend had also been convicted, and so what if they also tortured the boy? Fleming told them, preying on their own insecurities and paranoia about the law, that he'd been forced to plead guilty, go to prison and be placed on the sex offenders' register.

What Fleming hadn't admitted was that this kind of behavior was very much linked to his apparent association with Satanic cult The Order of Nine Angles (ONA), which we revealed at the end of January 2016. For those who had listened to Fleming talk about ONA, their assumption had been it was a spiritual group that liked National Socialism.

The ONA was conceived and run by a former monk-turned-Satanist, David Myatt, who had been the chief ideologue to Combat 18 and later had morphed into a Jihadi-supporting Islamist militant.

As a war of angry words and threats raged in and around National Action, Fleming seemed delighted to have been exposed. He took to leaving messages about the story on the comment section of our website. But inside NA, there was a split finally occurring, mainly over Raymond's stout defence of the abuser. Over on the neo-Nazi forum Stormfront, NA found themselves humiliated. And it got worse the more Raymond tried to deflect Fleming's conviction and Satanist beliefs.

There were more than 30 pages of National Action humiliation on Stormfront. Many far-right extremists who had, until now, appreciated what the group had to offer to the otherwise-moribund movement, were incredulous that its mouthpiece, Raymond, could deny the facts as reported or laud a convicted sex offender with his claim that it was all a "Zionist stitch-up".

Some of the assertions National Action made publicly in Fleming's defence were horrendous and Raymond (writing as 'Goyles') and one or two others (one believed to be Alex Davies) kept digging themselves further into a paranoid hole. The damage was becoming almost irreparable, both internally and externally.

Of them all, it was Jack Renshaw who seemed most impressed by Fleming's conviction. "By the way, despite us ignoring your past, this will make brilliant banter," he wrote to Fleming, offering support. Renshaw also claimed that most users of Stormfront were "pretending child porn isn't open on their second tab."

Andy Clarke, National Action's barrack-room lawyer, was less than impressed with Fleming, telling him the group's condition was now "critical", saying: "I would never have allowed myself to be coerced into pleading guilty for such a thing. You may well have been coerced and you may well not have. This is bad for NA and is no laughing matter."

Clarke couldn't understand why Raymond was defending Fleming at all.

"We all wanted it and Fleming to just go away, but Raymond would not let it go," said Robbie Mullen, later. Mullen claims that Raymond started a rumour that National Front personnel had raped a fellow member at a gig, hoping it would deflect from NA's own problems:

> *"He just didn't want to give up on Ryan [Fleming] and at the same time he just seemed oblivious to our own.... angst over the issue. I wasn't the only one who felt the whole group was about to die. I read the thread on Stormfront and every time someone from NA made a comment about Fleming, all I could see was National Action ending prematurely."*

The Fleming affair further damaged Raymond's standing within the group. For so long he'd survived on a debt of gratitude from the gang for starting and promoting National Action. But the shyness, the little bouts of coy weirdness and pointless bravado had grated as well. He'd now pushed it too far, yet still seemed oblivious to the disgust some felt. "I guess there was a little split developing," recalled Mullen. "Those who wanted a race war and wanted to fight it, and those like Ben [Raymond], who sort of thought pedophilia was another string to our arthouse bow. We were meant to shock and offend, I got that, but not shock and offend ourselves."

Along with Garron Helm, Raymond continued to treat Fleming as a valued comrade. Helm would visit Fleming and the two would take long walks together to collect animal skulls for their morbid collections. Raymond kept pushing the line that National Action should be against the persecution of a white man by the Zionist state – but it washed very little.

HOPE not hate knew Fleming never stopped being a member of National Action, despite the ignorance of others inside the group. He kept leaving messages on our website, boasting about his superhuman powers and his ability to transform into a werewolf. The messages and threats kept coming for three months, telling us that he could transform into a bat (among other things) and fly into our office and bite us. It was most bizarre.

He also left what he presumably thought were tantalising clues about what was going on in National Action, even claiming that Raymond had dated his flatmate and taken her to a posh hotel in Swansea. This was later confirmed to us by former members of NA, including Mullen. When I showed Fleming's messages to colleagues in our office they were part-horrified, part-intrigued, but we never used the information Fleming left for us. Even an accurate weather report would be tainted by his disgusting behaviour.

Later that year, in April, we published a blog revealing Fleming had written a book on Satanism, the *Codex Aristarchus*, which apparently would allow "the reader themselves [to] step upon the black path of the Wamphyri – feeding upon the human herd." Written under the alias A. A. Morain, and published in the USA, he said the book derived from the blood-stained moors of West Yorkshire, England. If that doesn't give you an idea about what followed, the book was also a "genuinely amoral vampiric praxis melding the black arts of predatory astral vampirism."

In July 2017 Fleming was jailed for three years for having sex with a 14-year-old he'd groomed on the internet.

***

The Fleming affair had a debilitating effect both on the group's moral standing (such as it was) and also its relationship with the rest of the British far-right movement.

Some had been waiting for such a moment to put both National Action and Raymond firmly in their place. As Raymond had alluded to in his postings on Stormfront, the relationship between the National Front and NA had hit rock bottom. The NF would now refuse to take NA members to one of the biggest far-right riots in British history.

There'd already been a number of clashes between far-right groups and antifascists at the Port of Dover in Kent during 2015. Under the guise of showing support for British lorry drivers, the NF had been organising anti-immigration demonstrations in the town. Migrants living in camps in Calais in northern

France would attempt to stow away on lorries or trains heading to Britain. Dover was seen by the far right as the prime entry point for illegal immigrants to enter Britain.

The British far right was still very small, but the high profile of National Action invigorated them. A week after Fleming had been exposed, attentions had already turned towards an attempted unification of every far-right group in Britain for an almighty clash with antifascists in Dover. The far-right groups would be heading to the town on January 30 for a protest march. National Action hadn't been officially invited, but had assumed they'd form some kind of Black bloc on the protest. Instead, they were very sharply and publicly uninvited once Raymond and NA made clear it wouldn't be doing anything about Fleming.

Some in the NF had developed strong issues with National Action's innate sense of superiority, and of course, Raymond's longstanding attitude towards them. Within hours of our story breaking about Fleming, the NF held an emergency conference call and voted not to include NA in the Dover action.

As a compromise, some National Action members were privately told they could join the Misanthropic Division (MD) – the front organisation for the far-right Avoz Battalion in Ukraine – which was preparing to travel to Dover once more to cast its eye over an ageing and potbellied movement. For Mullen, there would be absolutely no stopping him from going to Dover. Some NA members still expected to be picked up in Middleton near Manchester, despite the ban on them attending. The NF minibus drove past them at the pick-up point, half empty, with the driver, a member of the NF's executive, giving them the finger.

The day that unfurled would reveal the far right's savagery and ferocity, as well as appearing to catch police unaware. The violence began early in the morning in Maidstone in Kent, when a minibus of Chelsea football hooligans attacked coaches from a London university at a service station. The violence would continue throughout the day.

In Dover, shortly after 1pm, anti-racist and antifascist protestors blocked the far right's route and sang the antifascist anthem '¡No pasarán!' ["they shall not pass"].

The far right responded with violence, attacking the police and trying to force their way through police lines to attack the antifascists. Within 15 minutes the police had lost control as hundreds of protestors traded blows. Antifascists forced the fascists to retreat. The police then used their vans to try forcing antifascists away from the march, but large groups broke away to continue confronting each other. Usually these clashes between fascists and antifascists are merely skirmishes, but in Dover, carrying lumps of rock and wood, hundreds from both sides ran amok for hours, at one stage forcing the police to flee and regroup. The violence engulfed the town. The police didn't seem prepared for the intensity of what happened, despite the far right going out of their way to promise and boast of their plans.

Both sides would later claim their victories and YouTube would very quickly fill up with trophy shots of gangs engaged in their warfare. The bruised and the battered were paraded for photographers and images of the anarchy were relayed across the world via live feeds. One clip showed antifascists smashing up the pavement, then launching pieces of paving into the assembled fascist lines. In other clips fascists were shown ambushing antifascists and trapping them against a fence, lining up to take turns launching kicks at their victims' heads. Everyone, even seasoned observers, were surprised by the ferocious violence of both sides. Certainly, antifascists hadn't been this bold since the days of Red Action in the 80s and 90s. On the ground, as Mullen was discovering, with the police having briefly withdrawn from the town, there was a belief on both sides that people were fighting for their lives. The blooded pictures and live footage being beamed all over social media gave the same impression.

More than 70 people were arrested and an investigation got underway to hunt down perpetrators from as far away as Scotland. More than 30 people were eventually imprisoned for Dover, almost all of them far-right extremists.

One of those also spotted at Dover was Wilf Browning, the infamous leader of Combat 18 (C18), who'd been living under the radar in the Netherlands for a number of years since taking control of the group. Browning had travelled to Dover to meet members of National Action, but was instead regaled with horror stories by National Front activists about the group's insolence and their hiding and protecting of sex offender Fleming. Browning was, according to one NF member, unmoved by their whinging and pleading. He was too long in the tooth now for the sort of squabbling and backstabbing that characterised the British far right.

***

Meanwhile, back inside National Action, Raymond was still fuming but deflated both with those inside and outside the group who'd taken umbrage with Fleming. His test, their test, to push the boundaries of decency and be as 'arthouse' as they were Nazi, had failed. The "brutes", the "retards" and the "autistics", as he called them, had missed a point. His fall from grace hurt him. NA would now take another step into the further darkness dictated by Lythgoe and those around him. Raymond, the bedsit revolutionary, was on the very cusp of being drummed out of the organisation.

"I think there's an inherent contradiction in fascism. On the one hand it's a very social movement, but on the other hand for the very same reason it attracts people who are also – for want of a better word- incredibly autistic." – Ben Raymond, interviewed by Counter Currents Radio, February 2016.

Lythgoe was infuriated Raymond had gone to such public lengths to protect Fleming. He'd humiliated himself and the group. Lythgoe settled into moody drinking sessions in the upstairs bar of the Wetherspoons pub in Warrington, the Friar Penketh, where he'd taken up an almost permanent presence. Surrounding him were his men and boys, as loyal as lapdogs could be. No-one was excused from joining him.

Lythgoe pulled the North West group ever closer as it expanded. Mullen was now attending the gym at 6am every day and cycling the seven miles to work after walking his dog. The early joy and excitement was draining out of the group and to everyone it was becoming clear Lythgoe wanted to go further than upsetting lefties and Jews with graffiti and low-level violence. He sent hundreds of messages to Raymond admonishing him, making clear he had to fall into line.

In February 2016, sitting upstairs in the Friar Penketh, Lythgoe outlined how he saw the future. Race war was inevitable. National Action was small, but it was ready to fight. There was a weight of expectation not just in the membership but of those around and those opposed to it, that something had to happen, a statement had to be made.

Helm was also under a further dark cloud for the Fleming affair, and Lythgoe was struggling with what to do with him. It was noticeable how Helm's appearance was also changing. Gone was the clean-cut image he'd worked on. Over a period of time his appearance would denigrate to such extent that he acknowledged he'd stopped washing entirely and, most nights, he was camped out in the woods, trying to conjure the inner werewolf.

Despite its inherent inconsistencies and the Fleming affair, under Lythgoe there was a growing level of security consciousness and obedience developing within National Action. When it worked, it was like nothing any far-right group in Britain had ever managed before. Throwaway phones were purchased and dumped regularly. Names and identities on social media were frequently created, changed or deleted, with members encouraged to completely dump their 'skins'. Few people ever had any real idea who they were talking to on the encrypted message groups that Lythgoe oversaw.

Yet Lythgoe was also turning a blind eye to the increasing low-level drug use, drug dealing and criminality within the group. He encouraged links with the North West Infidels and its criminality, occasionally inviting the group over to the Warrington pub for talks about strategies. Lythgoe saw the NWI as fodder, a drug-induced criminal militia, and although the NWI hardly saw themselves in such a degrading light or knew they were actually regarded as such, they were encouraged by the new NA leader's darkened depths.

After recovering from earlier police actions and several imprisonments, NWI quickly re-established itself in old haunts, peddling drugs and fake designer gear in the small towns in and around Blackburn in Lancashire. Unlike National Action, the NWI had no problems with the wider far right: it would work with anyone.

It's hard to put an exact figure on the number of people involved with the NWI, but it was probably no more than 50. Instead of the bolshy, youthful National Action, these were older and seedier men and women, some in their late 50s and early 60s, similar to NA in that they had a hierarchy but dissimilar in that there was also a matriarchy. Whenever the group seemed on the brink of collapse, after another drug arrest or conviction or a breach of a court order, a series of women from Blackburn to Wigan would take over the group's reins, maintaining its vicious social media channels, its funds and materials. On a number of occasions women within the group went as far as to smuggle phones and contraband into prison at great risk to themselves. The NWI leader Shane Calvert even relied on his mother to keep the group going in his long absences inside. It was a group that played together, lived together and in some cases, slept together.

One female NWI member was forced to flee a particular town after the death of a young girl who had taken a bad ecstasy tablet linked to the gang. She was in her late 50s and, at the drop of a hat, re-appeared in another town in the north west a week later, still part of the NWI. By using the NWI Lythgoe tried his hardest to signal to the NF there'd been a major shift of power within National Action. Like the NF and the NWI, the power of NA now sat firmly in the north west.

According to Mullen, Lythgoe advised members close to him to read the Qu'ran as a way of understanding the justifications of terror, a process he hoped would encourage their understanding of political over theological adherence. In his eyes, terror was as inevitable as it was necessary for National Action to survive.

Lythgoe had been a major believer in the White Jihad project the student journalist, Raymond and the American group Atomwaffen Division had initiated and ran with. Mullen, doubting his own revolutionary potential, simply ignored the advice to buy a Qu'ran and instead listened intently to the theological justifications for terrorism Lythgoe interpreted, like an Islamist, from the Muslim holy book.

***

A gang of Polish neo-nazis living in the United Kingdom has called for a demonstration in Manchester later this month by Polish football hooligans, in support of a "British white country."

The date set aside for the demonstration appears to have been borrowed from the nazi drug gang the 'North West Infidels' who had already planned their own demonstration in the city on the same day. The gang behind the planned demonstration have called their demonstration "Fuck Islam & Isis." This will be interesting. – Polish Neo-Nazis Plan Manchester Demonstration, HOPE not hate, 5 February 2016.

Wayne Bell, the Castleford neo-Nazi and the gang's original brute, had now moved firmly into the Lythgoe camp of thinking, though he was excused long-winded strategy sessions over in Warrington (and most certainly reading the Qu'ran). He was now the most infamous and seemingly fearless member of National Action. He and Raymond had been such good friends, but Bell had very gradually tired of Raymond's nonsense. Bell had first heralded a darker heart in the group after the disaster that was the NA's attempt to march in Liverpool in August 2015. A man with a ferocious temper and by far the oldest of all (male) NA members, it was Bell (who used the name Wayne Jarvie publicly) who announced the formation of a tougher unit of fighting men with the assistance of Polish gangs in the immediate aftermath of the humiliating disaster.

CHAPTER 13: RED TERROR, POLISH TERROR, ARE WE ALL IN THIS TOGETHER?

"In a show of defiance against red terror we will be participating in our first pre-advertised march since the White Man March in Liverpool. There will be so many of us that it will almost certainly go unopposed, especially after the communist tragedy in Dover, they'd be advised to keep well away. If you wish to join the NA bloc at the NWI demo war [sic] black be alert contact your local NA branch which can be found in the regions page to obtain the RV – this time we go in together, no individuals waltzing into Piccadilly station to be mobbed, you will be abandoned."

National Action's instructions to people attending Liverpool rally, Feb 2016

The pressure to keep marching, keep up confrontations with the left, was a movement-wide obsession. Few feared prison as much as they feared another long period of procrastination. As such, a far-right march led by Polish neo-Nazis was quickly announced after Dover, this time back in the north west, in Manchester.

It was to take place on February 27 2016. Except it was never going to Manchester at all. The true location was Liverpool. The more vociferously those on the far right claimed they were heading to Manchester, the more it dawned on us – and many others – that Liverpool was the true destination.

Having had a very enjoyable if not bruising afternoon of recreational rioting in Dover at the end of January, the hard men of British fascism (already depleted by arrests) had set their hearts on Liverpool in order to redress National Action's humiliation at Lime Street the year before. The plan was simple: wind up the left and antifascists, trick them into heading to Manchester for a riot, and then sneak into Liverpool and declare a victory.

A couple of minibuses were booked from the south to carry the National Front, British Movement and various members of English Defence League (EDL) splinter group the South East Alliance (SEA), to the fray. A mob of steroid-enhanced Polish far-right hooligans from London were mobilised by

North West Infidels (NWI) leader Shane Calvert and National Action's Wayne Bell (who had made the promise to 'mob up' with more Polish fascists after the previous debacle in Liverpool), along with Radoslaw Rekke, 'Rad the Pole', NA's Polish-speaking member from Wythenshawe in Manchester.

They promised the Polish gang unlimited rioting for an afternoon in Liverpool and, they hoped, a smaller number of disorientated and depleted antifascists to batter when they got there. Christopher Lythgoe and Robbie Mullen approached the National Front in an attempt to coerce them, either by drugs or cash, to send their members along too. It was time, according to the NWI, for the groups to bury the proverbial hatchet. The NF were told NA had undergone a change of leadership, and that NA was now serious about the race war. Such was the NF's hatred of Ben Raymond, they refused to budge. Infuriated, Lythgoe instructed Raymond to deliver the NA's speech on the day, to make up for the one he didn't get to make in Liverpool the first time.

People heading to Liverpool were to go in hard when they got there: the Poles would carry out all the violence, and then Raymond could deliver his speech. Not everyone inside National Action was happy with Raymond being offered the opportunity to speak, but a sense of duty within the group prevailed – many were unaware he was still friends with sex offender Ryan Fleming. By midweek, militant antifascists had made the decision to go to Liverpool come what may. Those less interested in violence were to go to Manchester. It was a risk, but one they thought they should take.

The rally (it was never going to be a march) began shortly after 1pm, when a small group from the NWI gathered in the Crown Hotel outside Liverpool's Lime Street station. Violence began early in the day, when a train arrived from Manchester carrying fascists and antifascists. The fascists had disembarked bruised and upset and found themselves stranded as their racist comrades had gone to the pub instead of greeting them. *The Liverpool Echo* reported although police tried to keep the two groups apart, they were heavily outnumbered and on at least two occasions a number of the NWI's Infidels group broke through police cordons and fought with antifascists. Liverpool would have the same ferocity and intensity as Dover.

The Poles then led a charge onto the steps of St George's Hall in the city centre, fighting their way through a police cordon as rocks rained down on everyone. Police officers fell down the steps of the hall, some were even attacked as they fell. Missiles, including bottles and cobblestones, were thrown at the neo-Nazis, who threw them back into the crowd. Innocent passers-by were struck by flying objects; a police officer suffered concussion when hit by a rock as he tried to clear a smoke bomb.

The previous August, when National Action had been driven from the city under a hail of fruit, there'd been an almost carnival atmosphere, but the 30-strong group of Polish neo-Nazis, in face masks and matching hooded jumpers emblazoned with 'Polish Hooligan', made for a more menacing environment.

On the steps of St George's Hall, as fascists were driven up the steps and towards safety in their own numbers, the thin police line held firm with batons drawn and riot shields deployed. The groups of fascists and antifascists continued to try and break through and attack the other. National Action made themselves busy by painting and daubing swastikas on the famous neoclassical St George's Hall opposite Liverpool Lime Street station, where they'd been so humiliated the year before. The Poles maintained a concerted attack on the police.

The minibus of fascists then arrived from the south. Foolishly those on board had been sending text messages asking for directions to those at St George's Hall. Plans for the violence that was breaking out were later recovered by police from those same phones. Among those who arrived from the south was Wilf Browning, the leader of veteran neo-Nazi gang Combat 18.

Browning held discussions on the steps both with Raymond and Alex Davies, and he too was surprised to hear neither was actually the leader of the group. Unimpressed with Raymond, who was according to Mullen "spitting and gurgling like a fool", Browning met with Lythgoe, but what they discussed is unknown to anyone.

Raymond read out his speech:

"We are the new generation, we are immune to intimidation, we are the faithful soldiers of the nationalist idea... we will continue to battle for the victory of our white race."

Among all the fighting and carry-on on the steps of St George's Hall, National Action looked like a queer bunch of little boys among the fighting men from Poland. Hiding behind a flag with a loudhailer, Raymond was joined by Jack Renshaw, who with Lythgoe's blessing, let rip an almost inaudible stream of a foul anti-Jewish tirade. Running around in a face-mask was Alex Deakin, the university student from the Midlands who had volunteered to be Raymond's confidant as he begged and pleaded to hold onto power within the group. Raymond and Davies had manoeuvred Deakin into position in the Midlands, replacing the other co-founder, former BNP organiser Paul Hickman who'd been another vicious critic of Raymond and the apparent source of much of the sporadic and anonymous information about him that was being sent to us to encourage HOPE not hate to humiliate and antagonise him.

Paul Prodromou, the leader of the SEA, was making himself busy shouting out orders to everyone to push against police lines. Prodromou had developed something of a reputation for instigating violence but always managing to avoid arrest. A foul-mouthed, almost comic-like character from Essex, Prodromou came to prominence during the rise of the EDL in 2010, where he was the regional organiser for Essex. In his mid-50s, he used 'Paul Pitt' as a more anglicised name, but his reputation had slowly denigrated over the years until he was viewed as a disastrous figure of ridicule and suspicion because of the way he spoke, his temper and antagonism.

Robbie Mullen recalled:

"We were all really excited to meet the Wilf Browning. He came along and spoke to all of us, offering us his hand. He was a serious individual but very friendly. Behind him, Prodromou was showing off, shouting abuse and swearing, 'cunt' this and 'cunt' that and we were all a bit embarrassed by him. I think Browning was regretting travelling in his minibus.

"Suddenly, an Antifa member was pulled into our crowd and everyone laid in with fists and kicks. You could hear the thud of the boots against his face. Suddenly, Paul Prodromou started shouting 'strip him naked, take his clothes off him. Get the cunt naked.' A couple of the lads started trying to get the Antifa bloke's clothes off. Prodromou was frothing at the mouth and kept demanding we get this bloke naked. "Thankfully, Wayne Bell stuck his arms in and pulled this lad out. It probably saved him a major hospitalisation. Wayne only did it because he thought the poor bloke could've been one of ours…"

***

£25,000 worth of damage was caused to St George's Hall, alongside a £60,000 police bill. National Action members were besides themselves with excitement. Thirty five people were arrested for violence on the day, mainly Poles, three of whom who were imprisoned almost immediately. More arrests were to follow once the police found messages on the phones of those who had organised the day's events. Just managing to stand on the steps of the hall was considered a major success by NA. Sure, they'd hidden behind the mass of Polish hooligans doing the fighting, but this was how NA and Raymond in particular, envisaged the race war. He'd taken up his position on the steps of the hall, hiding behind foreigners, as part of the officer class he believed the British far right was lacking.

"How did we do this? All the organisations worked and planned in secret using new/experimental methods that relied heavily on our opposition underestimating us. You will recall the planned demonstration in Manchester in our February review? This had been a ruse from the beginning and by cleverly rerouteing [sic] the counter-demonstration and announcing the venue at 24 hours notice it sowed chaos in the ranks of the antifa, soured their plans, and significantly delayed them. It also ensured that their forces would be split and those organising violence would have to improvise with materials on-hand (favourites of the antifascists are elaborate devices such as razor blades in potatoes – too impractical and risky to travel with). The formal/respectable face of the counter demo Hope

Not Hate was committed to keeping their part of the demonstration in Manchester, 100+ people who could otherwise have caused us problems – indeed it is their own claim that they are the ‹command centre› for antifascist violence and that their ‹intelligence operatives› are there on the ground to direct these assaults (why the CTU are not kicking in their front doors remains a mystery)." – The Battle of Liverpool. Review & Action Report, National Action Website, 19 March 2016

It had taken nearly a month for National Action's report on the Liverpool violence to appear. Lythgoe had refused to allow Raymond's earlier reports to be published because they were so childish and triumphant. He hammered emails and messages to Raymond until he got it right. The report made much of their new forms of communicating: encrypted messages set to vanish, for example. It's possible, indeed likely, this may have been written in order to humiliate the NWI and SEA members whose phones had been recovered by the police.

Problematically for National Action, although they encouraged it, the tone of their report made it clear they thought they had proven once again their superiority to the rest of the British far right. It infuriated those who'd actually engaged in the violence whilst Raymond and Renshaw shouted instructions from behind police lines. Better still, there'd been no arrests of NA members.

Back at the Friar Penketh pub in Warrington, Lythgoe gave a debrief of the event. It would be the first time he'd asserted his leadership over the whole group. Not only that but, in his opinion, the great Wilf Browning had come to see him, to admire his mighty National Action in action. He also felt Raymond now fully understood the force of his control and followed his instructions.

Away from Lythgoe and the debilitating sessions in the pub, Mullen had become close to "posh" Matt Hankinson, Radoslaw Rekke and Dan Cotterill, a Liverpudlian student who exhibited no real interest in the politics of the group.

Aside from Cotterill, they were obsessed with Nazism and keeping fit, taking long walks in Delamere Forest together or cycling. Hankinson was bright, he was educated and he was totally dedicated to Nazism. Mullen was more interested in conspiracies. Life had been so cruel to him, had taken so much away from him, that he wanted to believe that things didn't just happen by accident. Someone, somewhere, probably a Jew, had conspired to make his life go wrong. His father's cancer, he was told, could have been cured if the Jews were not withholding the secret cure. The most foul things in life – from the Holocaust to 9/11 – had been the work of the Jews.

The poverty Mullen had seen growing up as a child, kids who went without anything unless they were forced to steal, was also the work of the Jews. He felt the same way I had all those years ago when I'd been involved in similar groups, as a young member of the NF, BNP and C18, before I turned against them – that he'd been abandoned by the labour movement and the Labour Party. Mullen was quite capable of recognising poverty and injustice, he'd experienced it. There was a queue in life and he'd never had his chance to be at the front of it.

Yet class struggles seemed anathema to the gang: such an analysis seemed a distraction from the coming race war, from the unifying sense of fear, anger, panic and secret self-doubt that drove them all. It watered down the race struggle to have white people lining up with 'blacks and muds', talking about their troubles and never mentioning the Jewish angle.

As an organisation, National Action recognised the working class was rightfully embittered – *their* working class members were embittered – and Raymond, who slept most days to spend his nights trawling the internet, was most conscious of it. But like other fascists and neo-Nazis, NA had toyed with and failed to understand economics, having only ever conceived of an idealised future with factories full of obedient white serfs, or the green and pleasant lands of the killing fields of Cambodia. Those in NA who didn't work, or refused to work, could hardly be forced into working poverty. It's why both Raymond and Lythgoe allowed, even encouraged, minor criminality such as the selling of drugs, or accepted the occasional antisocial behaviour. It suited NA that so many of its crew didn't work or declared themselves as students. Those unemployed were meant to be preparing for life in West Yorkshire but, in the meantime, they ate into the group's finances for travel and treats. Raymond would also, when present, stand his round at the bar as would a few others, such as Andy Clarke, who would also have a small amount of Class A drugs to alleviate the stress and pressure the members genuinely felt they were under. Just thinking aloud about killing people (as they were increasingly prone to do on Facebook) had increased police interest, surveillance and harassment of members. Barrack-room gobshite Clarke seemed to spend all of his working day filling his social media accounts with pictures of the victims of the Holocaust. The most brutal, the most disgusting, the more graphic the better.

As a way of further penance, Raymond agreed to foot any legal bills or costs the group incurred. He'd also pay Davies's rent for the house they shared in Swansea, secretly hiding their politics and other persuasions from their other housemates. For Davies, Lythgoe and Raymond, no matter their differences over strategy, life in 2016 undertook all the breathless excitement of being full-time revolutionaries.

At night Davies would hear Raymond beavering away on his computer. Raymond would be waiting for Davies to get home from wherever he had been, like a jealous lover, and ask him lots of questions about who he'd seen and who he'd spoken to. Davies would go to bed and Raymond would begin work on his computer, sometimes knocking on Davies' door at two or three in the morning for advice or to show him something he'd done.

By living together, Raymond hoped they could take back National Action from Lythgoe, but Davies was tiring of him. He wanted to go out to nightclubs and pull women, but Raymond never wanted to join him.

"Raymond was always acting weird on the internet instead," said Mullen. "Alex [Davies] started coming over to the North West for nights out, joking he had 'left the wife indoors'."

There was an aura about the group, together, out drinking and socialising. They no longer felt like civilians; the group as a whole shared a revolutionary purpose. Their every available moment had to be spent together, drinking training or plotting. There was, as Mullen would recognise, a stifling inevitability the group would become terrorists. Everything was urgent and intense all of the time. Everything was secret, the countless new identities, the paranoia, the endless mobile phones purchased and dumped. The sickening, endless discussions about rape and murder, and the ultimate sense of belonging to a group where you could do or say anything, as long as you weren't caught doing it, like Fleming had been and would be again, abusing kids. Sometimes, it wasn't even about Nazism any more. It was for the sake of planning terrorism. This group would become, became, terrorists for the sake of terrorism.

***

The NF was never going to let National Action's insolence be forgiven. They persisted with antagonising NA with a series of posts about the Fleming story on its Facebook page. They also named and shamed a series of NA members who had shed their identities. The NF sent an ex-soldier armed with a baseball bat to visit a number of its own members, threatening to get them in line and not co-operate with NA. One of those visited, who was facing charges for the robbery and torture of a vulnerable female neighbour, would later kill himself. He'd been getting involved more and more with NA which is probably where the desire to torture a disabled woman came from.

The NWI and NA responded to the NF's threats with violence of their own. NA members were present during one attack on the home of an NF member in Salford when someone shat on the doorstep and sprayed "nonce" on the door while shouting threats through the letter box. The NF member cowered behind his couch in the living room.

National Action made it clear to the NF they'd "take out" every known NF member in the North West. The NF desperately emailed local members, claiming NA was "riddled" with sex offenders and perverts and they should be resisted. It was a pathetic cry for help.

Robbie Mullen recalls:

"We were all actually friends with the NF away from what those up the top were doing. The problem was that we kept antagonising them all the time. They'd not let the [Ryan] Fleming thing die or the fact that Ben [Raymond] claimed we could one day become a political party. The NF knew what we were doing. They were no longer important. Half their organisers were

smack heads and smack dealers – that is how the NWI controlled their members and organisers. If they could poison a young girl they'd have no worries poisoning one of them!

"The thing about [Shane] Calvert [leader of the NWI] was that he understood where we were coming from. But things weren't as simple as the way HOPE not hate reported them. NA, NWI and drugs were only half the NF's problem and although HNH were adding to the fuel, the NF were also trying to throw out one section of their leadership at the same time. The NF were terrified we'd finish them off."

In effect, the NF wanted the drug dealers gone but this was antagonising the NWI who fed much of their drug money into the NF. In March 2016, Michael Kearns, an NF/NWI organiser in the North West, was jailed for five years for his role in a major drug gang. The NF could no longer associate with the NWI drug gang, or the mad, bad alleged paedophiles of the NA, but this was hardly a wholly shared view in an organisation that had some 2-250 members. Aware this was going on, HOPE not hate reported, respectfully, the whole disgusting spectacle. Fascists across the UK and Europe were up in arms; not so much about what was happening, but that we had so much inside knowledge about it.

To put a stop to HOPE not hate reporting the internal difficulties of Nazis in the North West, Christopher Lythgoe sent Mullen and the taxi driver Chris McCartney to the home of someone they thought was directing our intelligence gathering in the North West. Dressed like workmen, the two were to force their way into her home and terrorise her, grab her computers and cameras and if she put up a fight, knock her around "just a bit."

Luckily for the person in question, she saw McCartney's taxi circling her neighbourhood on her way home from work, even driving past the pair as they put ski masks over their heads as they searched for her door number. McCartney was excited about confronting the woman, as was Mullen, and they were both prepared to invade her house and ransack it. She moved out that night.

National Action's international reputation continued to grow as it persistently fed its online fanbase with exaggerated updates of its prowess. The Americans even had a similar group to NA up and running, Atomwaffen Division. More about them later.

In March, National Action sent a delegation to Lithuania for a parade by neo-Nazis. The Lithuanians greeted NA like conquering heroes, waving NA flags when they arrived. Wearing expensive and unnecessary sunglasses, Raymond, leading the delegation, gave a short speech while Hickman, by now increasingly estranged from the group, recorded the whole event for for a video presentation later. During discussions, Raymond tried to present an alternative plan for NA to Hickman, offering him the chance to join him and Davies in taking it back from

Lythgoe. The two had never got along; Hickman had seen through Raymond very early in their relationship and was actually more drawn to Lythgoe's vision, if only to liven things up. Hickman was chronically depressed about the state and condition of his own life, most of which Raymond ignored.

CHAPTER 14: THE POLICE HEARD NOTHING OF THIS

*"That disease is international Jewry. In World War Two
we took the wrong side…"*

Jack Renshaw addressing a rally in Blackpool, March 2016

As winter gave way to a frosty early spring in 2016, Jack Renshaw, the troublesome and troubled former British National Party (BNP) member and now, ex-student, was about to make a short speech that was to have huge repercussions both for himself and for National Action.

On March 12, shouting into a megaphone in the seaside resort of Blackpool, flanked by a tiny group of fellow neo-Nazis from National Action and the North West Infidels (NWI), Renshaw railed against Europe's unfurling refugee crisis, talking about a "wider disease" at work. "That disease is international Jewry," he said. "In World War Two we took the wrong side…"

Warming to his disturbed theme, he went on to describe Jews as "[the] parasite who live among us" and called for people to "deal with the disease". He also claimed there was a "Jewish master race" running Europe and only when "(we) identify our Jewish problem will we win…. the major issue is Jewry."

Looking for a non-existent antifascist threat, Renshaw added: "When the time comes, they'll [antifascists] be in the chambers…. and we'll execute them."

He finished his four-minute rant by accepting he was a Nazi and was proud to be so. He also warned there were "hard times" ahead as the government "force these inferior people [refugees] onto us." He called white people the "superior race", but there was very little superior-looking about the foul-mouthed group he was addressing.

He finished by calling on people to focus on the "real enemy, and the real enemy is the Jew".

It was a horrific speech. Yet before launching into his tirade against immigrants and Jews, Renshaw had, without irony, chastised his fellow brethren for their foul language. Meanwhile, police stood by and let Renshaw call for what amounted to little more than the murder of Jews. Before his speech was uploaded to YouTube, Renshaw was asked by National

Action if he wanted his face pixilated or his voice distorted. He was offended by the suggestion.

***

Renshaw's tirades against Jews had started getting out of hand in 2014, after Nick Griffin had been kicked out of the British National Party. He spent hours writing some of the most insane and illegal anti-Semitic diatribes. There were constant calls for war against the Jewish community, missives that dripped with violence.

In December 2014, Renshaw wrote on his blog:

"World Jewry is the disease, whilst its product ideologies are just the symptoms. Beat the symptoms and they'll return or be replaced – but – beat the disease and you'll eradicate the symptoms."

He was so softly spoken, so middle-class sounding and so often dressed like a caricature of Harry Enfield's Tory Boy or perhaps Tim Nice but Dim, it was hard to imagine him genuinely wishing harm on anyone. Why was he so hellbent on these utterances? Utterances that would cause him so much harm? Having been thrown out of university, his family's dream of their son joining the Army for officer training was already in tatters.

That was the strange thing about National Action: the majority of members still had an almost distorted, angelic look about them, jarring and at odds with the violent words and choreography of the gang, plus the horrendous things they said and wished for in public and private.

When we published a picture of National Action supporters carrying a banner saying 'Only Bullets Will Stop Us' in Newcastle in 2015, the overwhelming reaction from those who saw it was humour. People ridiculed the group for its silly words and for looking like what many really were: kids. But it was concerning, too. We still had no-one deep inside the group; no-one who could give us a real indication of what was going on. It was the first time we'd never had anyone inside such a neo-Nazi organisation. In every far-right group there was usually someone who passed us information, but inside NA there was nobody. Skinny little boys with nasty banners aside, even with the group's disturbing penchant for violence and gross sexual deviancy, it was hard to judge what they might do or where their actions might lead.

Maybe the Jew-obsessed Jack Renshaw wanted to be leader, or to replace Ben Raymond as the group's Ayatollah, the person who eulogised the White Jihad. According to Robbie Mullen, Raymond had taken an extreme dislike to Renshaw. Maybe it was the intellectual competition between the two, or perhaps Raymond did actually see something in Renshaw that was unsettling, even by his own warped standards. For those of us who dealt daily with the drunken illiterate rantings of the English Defence League (EDL) or

Britain First supporters online, it wasn't necessarily what Renshaw said, but the jarring contrast with the rest of his appearance and personality. Wherever he went on social media, he called for people to rise up against Jews in the most violent terms, but when confronted with the man who held the pen that wrote such things, it was hard to marry the two. After all, this was a man who hated using profanity. Was this the sort of person who really called for Jews and immigrants to be done away with? Just what was really going on inside National Action?

Inserting someone into the group, even the periphery, was impossible. Those we knew operating in the far right didn't want to do it. National Action wanted to know everything about everyone who came near them. You had to run more than an inquisitive gauntlet in a poorly-lit pub somewhere to be a member of NA. The group had even refused members they couldn't control geographically, one in particular who was planning to carry out an attack in a gay bar and would later be sentenced indefinitely when his plot was discovered.

Late in March 2016, National Action produced a cartoon using the title "goals", depicting of one of its members firebombing our offices. Wayne Bell also issued a warning he was going to start "rounding up Jews," obvious hints that the group was more than prepared to up its ante.

Robbie Mullen said:

"Things were getting pretty dark, yeah. Angry, I think? But I can't put my finger on what the anger really was. Just real anger with everything and everyone and it was that in particular that Lythgoe liked.

"We took a lot of pleasure in hatred but I guess looking in from the outside you get a rather more disturbing picture because the people that were doing it were friends and so seemed to me pretty normal, kind of still human. I was still enjoying myself but the fun side to it was slowly evaporating. The fun had gone and it was like we were on an exhausting treadmill, if that makes sense?"

During March we had a stroke of luck. We met with a former member of the group, a young person I'll call 'A'. 'A' was desperate to leave the country, saying they felt threatened. Surrounded (as was almost the entire hotel) by 'bagmen' we used to provide security, 'A' methodically dumped a couple of years of radicalisation at me over a glass of Coke.

'A' confessed to a whole number of things, mainly low-level irritants such as stickering, putting up posters and harassing political opponents online. Long before it dawned on them that National Action was really moving towards terrorism, they'd fallen foul of some rule or some individual and had ended up a nervous wreck.

'A' was meeting us under duress, having been forced to contact us by their mother, who wanted her child to apologise. What for, I asked? "They [National

The Police heard nothing of this

Action] are targeting you," the mother said. "These people are very dangerous and I'm sorry for that."

The mother nudged her child, who grunted an acknowledgement. "You know they tried to kill that dentist in Mold?" she asked. I said I did. "They fill their emails and messages with disgusting pornography and talk about killing...." she went silent. "Like that poor dentist."

'A' showed little emotion throughout the encounter. It was strange. The mother had originally thought National Action was like the BNP – a nasty party but involved in the democratic process. That was until the police kept calling and she saw her child recite a mantra like a member of a jihadi group, refusing to help or to cooperate with the authorities.

The next morning the youth had left the country. Off to the US I believe, in the care of a church. The email and phone number we had for them were both dead.

***

"Jihadists and white supremacists share the same apocalyptic vision, and both groups have attacked London." – Padraig Reidy, The Atom, March 2018.

My meeting with 'A' had given us concerns. We all know the stories about weird boys in their bedrooms with dark thoughts and motivations. 'A' had known the Mold attacker Zack Davies. As we already knew, he was far more plugged into National Action than anyone had admitted.

As we limped into April 2016 the police were raiding the homes of far-right activists all over the country for the fighting in Dover and Liverpool. As expected, the NWI was hit the hardest. Their leader, Shane Calvert, had been photographed while on the phone directing the violence at both locations. He'd ignored the advice of his fan boys in National Action and not used encryption when calling the Poles into battle with the police.

In the same month we also picked up the return of an infamous character to the scene: Darren Clifft, one of the first people in the country to receive the infamous CRASBO, a bit like a super-ASBO. Now known as Darren Fletcher, he had a mild form of autism and had changed his name several times, including to several extreme names linked to far-right mythology. As well as being a violent admirer of Hitler, he was prohibited from working with children. He'd also been sent to prison for threatening to blow up the office of his local newspaper office in the West Midlands.

In 2014, as Christopher Philips, the 24-year-old gained national notoriety when, dressed in the ceremonial robes of the Ku Klux Klan, he hung a golliwog from stage at a far-right function. He was jailed for twelve months – a huge relief to those who had to deal with his penchant for random acts of violence. A contact of ours who met him described him as "cold and terrifying".

Philips, now Fletcher, had moved to Devon after finishing his sentence, changing his name again. He'd met a woman and started a family, trying hard to distract himself from his obsession with racism, racist violence and Nazism. Things appeared to be going well, but eventually his past caught up with him. He moved from job to job with a young family in tow and despite the name changes, his employers always cottoned on he'd served time in prison for outrageous crimes.

He was withdrawn, he was angry, mostly with himself. Over a period of years he'd quenched his thirst for violence and Nazism by joining a number of groups, most notably the National Front and the EDL. In Devon, after a succession of driving jobs finished prematurely, he and his family were living off food banks, facing eviction. He fought bitterly with himself because he knew back home, in the Midlands, where he had friends still in the movement, the temptation to get involved again would be still there. But he genuinely thought he and his family were going to starve so they moved back home where at least there would be family to look after them. After only a few days back, he joined National Action. He immediately added some steel, some hardened backbone to the Midlands group.

In the Midlands, which had been the largest and most prolific of all National Action's groups, there was now a major power struggle. Paul Hickman, the dour but methodical Nazi, lost control of the Midlands group to younger members. 20-year-old student Alex Deakin took control of the local group.

Hickman had been fighting with Deakin and Raymond for months, even taking back control and the impetus in the Midlands for a few weeks, but it appeared the trip to Lithuania had sealed his fate. This hardly helped him while he battled depression.

Alex Deakin took over running the Midlands. He had a reputation for foolhardy stunts: he once drank the entire contents of a vinegar bottle at a motorway service station to terrify a fast food worker who wanted him and a few others to leave. He'd also once hidden a wrap of cocaine by swallowing it during a police search. In between, he'd threatened to commit suicide after losing out to a love rival.

Deakin had been prominent at National Action's Liverpool demonstration, on the steps of St George's Hall, giving Nazi salutes while the Poles fought with police. Unbeknown to us, he had posted a recording of Renshaw speaking at a secret meeting of the Yorkshire Forum that same month.

What Renshaw said would later see him convicted for 16 months for inciting racial hatred against Jewish people.

"I'm lucky that I have friends who own land, so I've actually had experience with hunting, and I do think it is something that should be encouraged amongst our people. And luckily for me I'm a very good shot. So, yeah, the killer instinct is very important. We do need to have

the killer instinct, because whether we win through political means or whether we win through violent means, either way there will be violence. If we won by political means, these people who run our country, these invaders, these parasites, they're not just going to roll over and let us remove them from our country. They will put up a fight and I do think we need the killer instinct.

"You know, Hitler, he had an excuse he had lack of hindsight. We have hindsight, we see what the Jew did. We see what he did when offered mercy. And he acted as the Jew will always act, pretends to be your friend, but puts a knife in your back. So as nationalists we need to learn from the mistakes of the National Socialists, and we need to realise that, no, you do not show the Jew mercy. The Jew does not deserve any mercy. The Jew is a merchant, a deceiver, he is a Jew. He's nature's financial parasite and nature's social vermin. He needs to be eradicated.

"But this is an eternal, a righteous and a holy war and we need to show the Jew that this time it's for real. They don't have to fake it. Hail victory for Albion and for Europe, thank you." – Jack Renshaw speaking in April 2016 at the Yorkshire Forum.

I'd read somewhere, before, that Richard Edmonds, a founding member of the BNP and one of Britain's foremost Jew-haters and Holocaust-deniers, had chastised Renshaw over a speech even *he* felt had gone too far. This must have been that speech. Edmonds, who was by now in his 70s, had made his mark by never actually mentioning Jews in his colourful rants. He just referred to "the Jews" by nods and winks: that was what Jew-haters traditionally did.

Edmonds had shared a platform with Renshaw sometime that month at a meeting of the Yorkshire Forum, an extension of the larger London Forum network. Renshaw had been given top billing and had opened his speech by criticising Edmonds and the offence, naturally, followed.

"He proposed that the nationalist movement needs more street action, but did admit that while he prefers street movements and isn't in particular in favour of elections, he agreed that all avenues should be explored to further the nationalist cause. Renshaw's powerful speech was extremely anti-Semitic and controversial prompting many questions from the floor, many of which disagreed with him." – New British Union report into Renshaw's speech at the Yorkshire Forum.

In his speech, Renshaw had criticised those neo-Nazis who'd been soft on Jews, in particular those that during the BNP's height had been willing to allow Jewish members into the party as part of an attempt to placate the voting public's concerns over the party's alleged Nazism. In his speech to the Yorkshire Forum, he even criticised Hitler for being "soft" on Jews.

Coming so soon on the back of his horrendous Blackpool rant, what sort of madness was this going to lead to, now he, Renshaw was embedded with the other young unhinged radicals of National Action?

***

The Brexit debate was also raging, following Prime Minister David Cameron's decision to call a referendum on Britain's membership of the European Union for June that year.

Inside National Action there was a minor debate about whether the group should have a position on Brexit. Their Polish counterparts in the NOP, domiciled in the UK, had taken it upon themselves to campaign for Britain to leave, handing out leaflets up and down the country – as good as encouraging the British to voters to send them back home. NA thought this was hilarious, but couldn't have an opinion themselves until Raymond and Davies had seen what the left was saying. Christopher Lythgoe showed no interest at all.

Some National Action members actively campaigned for a Leave vote. Mullen had never been on a plane, never left the country. He saw little benefit in being in the EU. He saw foreigners and cheap labour undercutting wages. He saw more and more jobs across his own industry ferried off to foreign ports. The EU was represented to him as a destructive influence on Britain's sovereignty and he also felt angry the way silly old white people were portrayed by the cosmopolitan elite as being out-of-date, thick and worthless. In Warrington, NA carried out "standover" tactics – so-called because people would stand over individuals they wished to intimidate – on the Remain campaign.

Fascists from every far-right grouping, party and grouplet, joined the campaign for Brexit, but they didn't dominate it. They simply assimilated themselves into the legitimate campaigns, but always in the hope of picking up new members and new contacts. Another highly controversial former BNP youth leader, Mark Collett, approached National Action members to campaign with him for Brexit. One of those who joined him was Jack Coulson, the young man from West Yorkshire, who was building a pipe bomb in his bedroom. Like Jack Renshaw, Coulson had cherubic features and a penchant for dressing like a bitter Ronnie Corbett. Coulson readily took up Collett's offer, as did NA's violent, psychotic Yorkshire organiser, Wayne Bell. Bell and a senior member of the NF would later be named in court papers as an influence on Coulson's activities.

For many National Action activists, Brexit was the first real political campaigning they had taken part in. It bored them, it was wholly unexciting, but they went ahead with it anyway, getting out of bed and standing in high streets and shopping centres with "JewKip types" because, as Mullen admitted, they realised it would have a destructive effect on the country and people's relations with one another. And it was already apparent to them that there were tensions with neighbour turning on neighbour. It was an excellent way, as they saw it, to wind people up more than anything.

For Mullen, it was no different. He'd been indifferent to the EU, but the longer the campaign went on, the more he found himself infuriated by Remainers. They were overly confident, southern posh kids (in Mullen's opinion), cosmopolitan and without patriotism. Remain was in effect, a campaign to protect and defend the very things that Mullen felt excluded from. During the campaign, Coulson joined one of the many National Action chat groups and began sending regular updates on the progress of his rocket launcher.

Mullen said: "There were about 65 people on the chat. Coulson was continually banging away about what his latest plans were for race war. I remember one or two of the people on the group chatting elsewhere about him, we were thinking to ourselves, 'I wonder how far he'll go with this?' but no, nobody on the groups ever told him not to do it or to desist. Not even did we tell him to be careful with all this showing off. I'm not even sure I actually believed he was building his little rocket launcher, to be honest."

In hindsight, did Mullen see a parallel between Coulson's stories and the boasting and bragging of the sex offender and paedophile Ryan Fleming?

Mullen thought long and hard before answering. "Well, no-one had any issues when Coulson's bragging and story-telling came to fruition, if that's of any use to you."

CHAPTER 15: ALL THAT WAS MISSING WAS SOMEBODY TO MISQUOTE GEORGE ORWELL

"As of late we have been storming the media with dozens of stories, more people now know about National Action than ever before. Serious raids have been carried out against leading members of the group in the dead of night, seizing everything we haven't nailed down - despite no clear charges being brought against the accused, only a 'pending investigation'. Isn't it so great living in a 'free democracy'? A year ago this might have caused problems, but now the cat is out of the bag and absolutely nothing is going to stop us – activity and releases will continue as normal."

– National Action activity report, May 2016.

National Action had certainly gone on an offensive to be offensive in 2016. Alex Davies, Person B from east London, and a member from Dundee, had photographed themselves giving Nazi salutes at the site of Buchenwald, one of the largest concentration camps built by the Nazis during the Second World War. The three had gone to Germany to meet up with neo-Nazis who formed part of an Anti-Kapitalist Kollective (AKK), autonomous German extremists who, like NA, had copied some of their modus operandi from opposition groups such as Antifa, even going as far as to hold anti-capitalist marches and protests on May Day. Part of AKK's raison d'etre was that by acting in the way they did, it made it harder for the ever-alert and nervous German authorities to crack down on them.

For Davies there was a threefold purpose to the trip. In Germany he was popular with the young neo-Nazis who made up the AKK (apparently Ben Raymond wasn't), and he tasked himself with seeing if there was anything National Action could learn from the Germans in the event the group was banned in the UK.

On a personal note, it allowed him to drink heavily and engage in debauchery away from the disapproving glare of Raymond, who as well as being a flat mate had become needy, a nag and was in a permanent state of panic about having lost control of their gang.

National Action rushed to release the pics of its guys Sieg Heiling at Buchenwald. Raymond was in such a hurry initially, he posted the picture before the boys had even left Germany.

Raymond had become an old hand at lying to the police or, when necessary, throwing away computers and materials that were quickly and easily replaced by National Action's funds. His room in the digs he shared with Davies were, according to Davies, "like a junk shop of broken hardware and dirty bedsheets." The group had survived on an almost strict internal anonymity, which could be upheld as long as they obeyed the 'rules' about dumping phone and identities regularly. But the expenses were mounting. Given so many senior members now had access to NA's money and none of them felt the need to explain to Raymond where it was going, he was often having to meet the shortfall for legal bills himself.

At a White Pride event in Swansea in March 2016, five National Action personnel, including Raymond and Davies, were stopped and held by the police after a brawl with members of Antifa.

"They had clocked us. Not expecting any resistance he asked "Are you leaving now!?", he didn't like my response and a fight broke out – immediately our guys ploughed into a dozen social rejects and drove them off. The antifa were so concerned with getting us out quietly that they hadn't bothered to inform any of their comrades. Completely surrounded by protestors and antifa they just stood there and gawped – many could not work out what just happened until stewards were screaming at them to do something after we had left. A young woman in black bloc began wildly screaming and laying into our guys in the hope that her low energy cuck comrades would come to defend her – it is sad that this litte [sic] girl had more balls than any of the other antifa who moments before were so tough behind the police line. Some of our guys left through the side, while a couple of antifa joined us as the main group left and would also be arrested – a flare was thrown into the crowd. A couple of antifa who had nothing to do with either group started having a punch up; confusion was total. In one beautiful moment the counter demonstration split and a hundred antifa who were protesting the white pride demonstration came streaming down the steps. As we left the police conducted a stop and search and were not particularly happy with the amount of pyrotechnics found on the group. We were all arrested and later bailed with no further action taken. This experience had not perturbed us and has built camaraderie in our group." – National Action report (1 June 2016) 'Action Report Swansea 26/03/2016'.

National Action members had tried to infiltrate Antifa demonstrators and demonstrations a number of times. It helped that both groups dressed similarly. In Swansea, once Antifa realised they'd been infiltrated and NA people were trying to steal their flags, a brawl broke out. Two MMA fighters with NA began throwing wild punches. Raymond ended up battered and cut when a young woman attacked him. In the middle of the brawl, NA's Person B set off a smoke bomb in the belief it would help them vanish.

Mullen later said:

"When the smoke cleared, the police were holding five of our members. Ben [Raymond] was tearful because his face had been scratched by a girl and he had basically lost the fight with her.

Everyone gave the police false, prepared names and even Person B who was arrested and fined, gave a false name and address. We were really surprised because we were meant to be this gang under heavy police surveillance and the police knew fuck all about us and didn't really even give a toss about drilling us for information etc. Anyway, we were well drilled on what to do in such circumstances, believe me. A tearful Ben [Raymond] immediately promised Person B he would pay any fine."

To the wider membership, the first signs of a near-open schism emerged in April. More than 100 black-clad National Action members descended on the group's secret conference in Crosby, Liverpool. At a meeting at The Holiday Inn hotel in Warrington the night before, NA's principal members had met to try to thrash out their differences, without actually talking about their differences. Andy Clarke, who had organised the conference, had angrily refused to attend because sex offender Ryan Fleming had indicated he would be there and speak, defending his crimes. Although everyone told Clarke this wasn't the case, Fleming delighted in telling people he was still in the group, in the hope of antagonising those in the camp against his sexual and Satanic exploits.

A dozen of National Action's top people met in the hotel bar, the first time they'd actually all been together in one place. As NA leader, Christopher Lythgoe packed the bar with his people, mindful that Raymond and Davies weren't universally disliked. Raymond and Davies had tried to lighten the mood, but it seemed almost impossible to keep up with Lythgoe's drinking. While they tried to stay on the pace, Lythgoe just stared at them. Most annoying for him, he was being shunted down the running order of proposed speakers the next day and almost an hour had been set aside for Jimmy Hey, the MMA instructor who ran the Misanthropic Division, to talk about fighting and training.

The Crosby conference wasn't notable just for Hey's speech, which gave encouragement to the group's pursuit of the perfect violence, but Davies' horrendous (as far as the group was concerned) pitch to moving onto political ground – an obvious affront to Lythgoe's direction. Davies had a habit of jumping ship and climbing back aboard. Hysterically and obviously, Davies' speech was taken from some sales mantra he'd learned on a course recently, talking about striking-up conversations with the public. He promised he'd show the group how easy it was to communicate with members of the public with a trip to Bath in a few weeks. Lythgoe, infuriated, would claim he only gave such a speech because he had been blinded "probably by some woman" who'd tried to teach him to cold-sell.

Davies had always seen himself as the popular leader – and he was, compared to the debatable attributes of Raymond and the scowls and monotone utterances of National Action's actual leader, Lythgoe. Davies' real weakness, other than his vanity and insecurities, was his obsession with money. Maybe they were all linked together? He'd certainly displayed issues at school and college around his social standing. Halfway through his squeaking address to conference about the proposed success of his sales pitches, he paused to admit his employment was commission-only work. Lythgoe, who appeared to have no job of his own, sneered. The title of Davies's address was *The 5 Steps to a Conversation. Applying the Sales Approach to Engage with the Public.* Lythgoe sneered about that too. Davies's voice didn't even sound like it had broken.

Raymond's speech was even less impressive. He waffled about a "higher level of consciousness" and again, having borrowed words and phrases from somewhere, managed to contradict himself. The conference ended with Lythgoe almost turning what Raymond and Davies had said on its head, talking about the need for *more* provocation and *greater* secrecy. The only person who really impressed the conference was its chair, "posh" Matthew Hankinson. Tall, intelligent and quick-witted, he kept things flowing and moving as egotist after egotist tried to impress their will upon the crowd.

Lythgoe desperately wanted to create a stunning publicity video, something that would send shivers down people's spines, to let them know National Action was more than just some fancy youth group saying horrendous things, which was exactly how Raymond and Davies' speeches made them sound.

Lythgoe wrote endlessly back in his bedroom at home about how to create a revolution. He drew inspiration from medieval kings and knights, placing himself in a regal role. There would be no more of the "officer class" Raymond had eulogised back in 2013 – he'd accepted National Action was only ever going to recruit "brutes". And they couldn't trust Hey either: alongside the white warriors he taught, he also trained black fighters which was completely unacceptable in Lythgoe's eyes.

Putting his much-vaunted sales pitch to the test, in May Davies was confronted by a mixed-race teenager in Bath city centre. The girl's mother filmed her daughter tearing strips off him for handing out National Action's vile material. The video of the confrontation went viral within hours, due in no small part to the *Daily Mail* and others putting it out online. It showed Davies whining, almost tearful, as the teenager kept asking him if she was non-white.

"You look white to me..." Davies kept repeating, uncertainly, as shoppers gathered around to watch the confrontation. Eventually a homeless man shouted: "Go on, fuck off!" to Davies and his retreating mates, capping a horrendous humiliation as Davies sped away.

On our way out we were harassed by a woman with her phone out who saw an opportunity [sic] to socially signal. The mother asking what the group advocated pointed to her lily white daughter and insisted she was mixed race. This was of course a lie – mixed race is a first generation phenomenon because we are different races and genes are dominant or recessive. If there is no subsequent mixing the kid is going to be either white or black, even if they are carriers for the gene – though the policy of how to deal with it is a different question and not important at the current time. The story became a five second wonder on social media with outlets having the audacity to mock us for not knowing what 'white is'. In doing this they proved their collective rock bottom stupidity."
– National Action's report on Davies's international humiliation.

***

In the wake of this humiliation, Raymond, desperate to be remembered for his (very few) acts of bravery, sent a message to Lythgoe and the North West group mocking Davies for his "intellectual laziness" and for not being able to tackle a teenage girl over something as simple as her being a mud-race "mulatto".

Continuing their obsession with trying to see as many young girls in their underwear as possible, National Action held a 'Miss Hitler' competition, encouraging girls to send them saucy pictures that were then passed around the group for outrageous and lecherous suggestions about how they should be raped. An outraged media duly obliged by writing about the competition, swelling the number of competitors to a few dozen. The media portrayed it as another sick stunt by the group – which it was – but paid very little attention to the underlying reasons for the exercise aside from more publicity for young men who always had sick motivations.

Our earlier meeting with 'A' reminded us how sinister this competition would play out inside the sick minds of the group. When we learned how many young women had sent pictures to National Action of themselves in their underwear or posing in their school uniforms, we were astounded.

National Action had no interest in recruiting the young Aryan princesses who sent provocative shots of themselves, including their personal details, to a hate group they read about on the internet. NA had no interest in recruiting them, they merely waited and watched gleefully as pictures arrived in their inboxes.

The competition was stitched-up well in advance so that Person B's partner and the partner of one of the men who accompanied Davies on the German trip, won the competition. The sickness and true nature of the competition wasn't lost on others either. It was simply a hunt by paedophiles for wanking material.

To attempt to atone for the Fleming paedophile affair and further accusations that National Action were perverts, members in the South West of England made a suggestion. They'd been impressed by a series of stunts pulled by other fascists, who'd gone online to track predatory paedophiles. The North West Infidels drug gang had pulled their own series of stunts, getting men to meet them and, instead of exposing them, demanding payment for silence. In one case NWI robbed a person who, in turn, went to the police to complain that instead of having sex with a child as he was promised, he was robbed by Nazis. A member of NWI was sent to prison as a result.

Needless to say, National Action used pictures of their own supporters, sent as part of the Miss Hitler competition, to set up a paedophile stunt. One member even used pictures of his own sibling. The idea was to lure a potential paedophile to a place where the group could descend on him, either arresting him and handing him over to the police, or film themselves beating him up. Still seething at having his friendship with Fleming frowned upon, Raymond described the exercise as "Occupy Paedophilia". It was a phrase which was lost on the others.

The project was beset with problems. Firstly, almost all of those hitting the online bait were white, and the gang members didn't want to catch a white paedophile. Then, when they eventually found an Asian suspect, nobody wanted to hand him over to the police, nor did they want to be filmed killing him. The further problem was defining the actual purpose of the exercise. Much of the anger over the Fleming affair was that he'd committed his offence against a man. There were plenty of National Action members who lusted over underage girls, and those same people were more outraged that Fleming had been some kind of "homosexual", forcing a young male into a homosexual act. Some even suggested attempting to lure Fleming into a trap.

"Unlike Stinson Hunter we will not be providing the full names or personal information of the accused we are simply giving visibility to a social issue, and free from red tape – putting the fear of god into those who would hurt our children. Investigators will confront paedophiles in a public place, they will film, socially shame, and are allowed to give chase, but that is all anyone will ever know." – National Action, #occupypaedophilia, May 2016.

After one amateur disaster after another, Tom Collett from the South West group, a mixed martial arts fighter and instructor, finally confronted an Asian man in a secluded area. Despite Collett shouting warnings at the man, the individual fled to his car while pursued by a small group of National Action activists armed with martial art weapons. In his haste to escape, the alleged paedophile ran Collett over.

"I just want the Jews too lad. There's enough who'll purge the niggers. The Jew always get away scott [sic] free, nit this time though. Their woman and kids need to die this time." – Andy Clarke, in discussion with Wayne Bell and Garron Helm, 18 May 2017.

National Action chose the historic city of York for its next mass mobilisation in May. It was selected for the same reason the BNP targeted it: in 1190 Jews were burnt during an anti-Semitic pogrom in the city. One hundred years later Jews were then ordered to be expelled from England by King Edward I, "Longshanks", which was a popular user name for NA members in on line chat groups.

Arriving unannounced, 25 National Action members assembled at York Minster and the nearby St Michael le Belfrey church. They unfurled a banner proclaiming 'Hitler Was Right' and began Nazi saluting and chanting "Sieg Heil." Horrified locals and tourists began confronting the group; fights broke out. Masked and menacing, NA members laid into members of the public before the arrival of an enormous police presence who, with batons drawn, entered the fray. NA fought back, throwing punches and kicking until more officers arrived in riot gear to snatch the worst offenders. Most of the NA members were forced face-down to the floor. Throughout the confrontation, Wayne Bell gave instructions to the group to stand firm and fight back. Lythgoe timed his appearance to arrive after the fight had finished.

Four National Action members were arrested for public order offences. Chad Williams from West Bromwich, sporting a long beard, was arrested after a confrontation with an Asian police officer. He was later fined in court, but found his place in the group threatened because he refused to see the solicitor NA sent to the police station to act on his behalf. Williams later pleaded guilty and apologised for his behaviour.

"As far as we were concerned, that meant he had rolled over to the police and wasn't to be trusted any more," Mullen said. In 2018, Williams would receive a prison sentence for inciting racial hatred, for putting up National Action stickers around Aston University in Birmingham in 2016.

The actions in York also led to a first home visit from the police for Robbie Mullen. Early one morning he opened his door to a uniformed officer who said he wanted to talk. Bizarrely, although they had his address they were using the fake name he had assigned himself (along with many others in the group):

"I just slammed the door on him. They [the police] came back another time in plain clothes, thinking I may let them in, but I wouldn't and they

didn't force it, really. Word had gone around the message groups that police were trying to find out whose the 'Hitler was right' banner was. The police wanted someone to take ownership of it so they, they reckoned, could return it to them."

The publicity was rolling in. Where no action was going on, members of the group would simply ring a local media outlet to report one of their own stickers had been put up in the area, and the outrage would follow. Davies and Tom Collett (the MMA fighter who'd been run over), coaxed the local newspaper in Swindon to run a number of stories claiming National Action was active in the town. Raymond was even arrested over one of the offensive stickers. Despite his fingerprints being on the sticker, he simply claimed he had seen it and touched it but had nothing to do with it. Others made similar claims. Another member from Stockport was arrested for a disastrous smoke bomb and graffiti attack on a mosque, where the smoke bomb came back and hit him. He was re-arrested leaving a police station on another charge.

There seemed to be National Action members out and doing stuff everywhere. In London, despite having abandoned the city, they still had 20 young men out in the parks training on the weekends with Polish neo-Nazis. Up to 150 at a time were attending other training camps around the UK, watching Islamic State videos and beating each other up under the watchful eye of instructors.

"It was hectic, it was exciting, it was…..I don't know really. Like the run up to Christmas, I guess. Something was going to happen, you could feel it. I just wondered what exactly would be under the tree on Christmas Day," Mullen recalls.

"After York and the police coming to the house, I felt like I'd taken another step. We could parade around the country with Hitler banners, have fights, give false names to the police and even slam the door in their faces. Straight after that police visit I went into town on my bike and bought another phone. The Manchester Ship Canal must be full of my old phones. But yeah, I guess, something was definitely coming. We felt fit to burst. So did the country. Yeah, yeah, I remember Brexit. It was going to be the first time I ever voted."

***

In June, something happened to change everything: Labour MP Jo Cox was murdered outside her constituency surgery by neo-Nazi and loner Thomas Mair. The nation was shocked; there was an outpouring of grief by most decent people.

In the almost immediate aftermath, Bell, who had been out leafletting with the Leave campaign would tweet on behalf of NA:

#voteleave Don't let this man's sacrifice go in vain. #jocox would have filled Yorkshire with more subhumans.

Mair's statement in court just a couple of days later – "Death to traitors, freedom for Britain" – was adopted and became part of the group's landing page on its website. Mair was their hero.

With even more extremism and derogatory publicity came more pressure on National Action's increasingly ostracised spokesman, Ben Raymond. Other Nazis, "grief monkeys" as they were portrayed, even began threatening NA, and in particular the reclusive Raymond who was still assumed to be NA's leader. Although they appeared to revel in the attention and regularly bragged about it, the increasing number of visits by counter-terrorism officers was expensive. Raymond had agreed to foot any legal bills the group incurred and kept that promise when the arrests and house searches increased. It kept him just about popular, just about involved. Pressure was mounting, but he desperately wanted to be useful even if he was unloved. Him being the centre of the authorities's attention was keeping the gaze, public or otherwise, well away from Lythgoe and others who were beginning to engage in serious discussions about their time to act out their terrorist fantasies.

Lythgoe's long sessions in the pub, indoctrinating members in the ideals of jihad and jail, were a drain on resources. So too were the constant expense claims he made in order to foment the revolution. He either wouldn't or couldn't work, and was taking an increasing interest in the administration of the group. Revolution was a full time occupation. Did the IRA go stacking shelves at their local supermarket? No, they had lived off the generosity of the movement around them, they were even discouraged from signing on the dole. Aside from beer and books, Lythgoe had no extravagant tastes. He rarely changed his clothes, even after working out at the gym, he tried to keep the same clothes on most days.

After Jo Cox's murder, Raymond took to replying to inquisitive emails with abuse, calling journalists "cucks" (a weak, effeminate, unmanly, or inadequate man) among other insults. Mullen, tasked by Lythgoe to also oversee emails, followed Raymond's lead by responding "fuck off" to literally hundreds of requests from journalists for interviews.

"Do the IRA tell people to 'fuck off'? demanded Lythgoe when he saw the emails.

***

The group even jumped on the back of a project by Polish Nazis to feed homeless Poles in London, Manchester, Leeds and Glasgow. National Action claimed it was involved in the project to simply gain some more shock horror stories. Once the media picked up the story, horrified NA members found themselves

actually out on the streets handing out biscuits for the benefit of journalists
. Some took it further than others. Wayne Bell went to Leeds regularly with a
rucksack full of foodstuffs and sat with homeless soldiers late into the evening,
even buying them alcohol and cigarettes. In Scotland, NA member Nicholas
Waugh produced a video of gang members apparently feeding the homeless.
Davies once more brought up the idea of NA actually morphing into a political
project, telling the *Daily Record* newspaper:

*"We want to replicate what Golden Dawn were doing in Greece.
That's exactly what we want to do. Their charity work, activism and social
work has brought them a respect in the eyes of the Greek people. That's what
gained them those seats in parliament."*

Feeding homeless people a diet of biscuits and white supremacy outraged
and shocked the media. The more the shock and outrage continued, the
more biscuits and out-of-date bread rolls National Action was forced to buy.
In fairness, although many NA members were genuinely moved by contact
with the homeless, they had their own narrative about the causes of the
homeless problem. Judaism, mostly. During one session of offering biscuits
to the homeless on Manchester's Market Street, Renshaw, who travelled from
Blackpool, gave an impromptu speech to late night shoppers and revellers
hurrying past with their heads bowed. Standing on the tram platform,
looking down at people, he began shouting that Jews were killing white,
British people and flinging their dead bodies outside the very big shops they
owned. The theme caught on. The EDL began delivering sleeping bags to
homeless people in Newcastle who, they claimed, were out on the streets
and homeless due to Islam.

Post-Brexit, we were told, the government's anti-extremism Prevent
programme was apparently filling up with neo-Nazis, an increase of something
like 40%, according to reports.

CHAPTER 16: YOU CANNOT BAN THE ACTUAL REVOLUTIONARY, HIMSELF

*"The following constitutes the fundamental starting point.
Everything we do is to be done with this in mind.
What we want is a revolution. A revolution is primarily a
mental phenomenon – it takes place in the minds of men
first and foremost.*
*"We want a long-term transfer of power out of the hands
of the representatives of opposing ideologies (liberal democracy,
post-Marxism, etc.), and into the hands of representatives
of our ideology – National Socialism."*

**– 'Starting Point' document by Christopher Lythgoe,
December 2016/January 2017.**

O n June 25 2016, 52% of more than thirty three million people who voted
in the referendum, voted that the United Kingdom should withdraw
from the European Union.

A female MP, Jo Cox, who campaigned for Britain to remain in the EU, was
murdered in the street of her constituency by a man obsessed with Nazism.
The man, Thomas Mair, had taken inspiration from murder manuals he'd
bought from a tatty Nazi catalogue distributed years before. For most of the
referendum campaign, the media had run amok with horrendous stories about
foreigners and an apparent imminent invasion by brown people in boats.
National Action had played their part, too.

Jack Coulson, the teenager building a rocket launcher in his bedroom in
Bradford, was beside himself with joy with not just the referendum result, but
also with the actions of Mair a couple of weeks before. He filled his social media
with glorifications and memes exalting Mair's actions. It's not even worth
repeating the absolute vulgarity of most of his messages which were in line
with NA's attitudes towards her murder and her gender. Coulson wanted more
murders of more women. Out campaigning for Leave, Coulson had played his
part, he felt, in Cox's murder and he wanted more.

Coulson had come to our attention in video footage of National Action at York Minster. Whilst filling social media with the glorification of terrorism, he'd been at York telling others about the rocket launcher he was planning to fire into one of Bradford's mosques. It was only a matter of time before his social media profile came to the attention of the authorities. Eventually, a month after Jo Cox was murdered, Coulson plastered his college with NA stickers and posters. There were all kinds of excuses made in his defence, including NA's favourite condition, autism, though this doesn't appear to have been used in mitigation. He'd eventually avoid jail when it came to trial in 2017 because of his relative youth and because, one assumes, his rocket launcher, although viable, was more like a rudimentary pipe bomb he apparently tried to copy from a diagram used by the IRA in the 1970s.

Despite the supposed keen interest in National Action and the wider far-right terrorism threat, little other action appears to have been taken to investigate NA, despite Coulson having spent hours online talking to an alleged former member of the British Army's ordinance corps. Other than a note made in court papers about two well-known far-right activists, little also appears to have been done or noticed in relation to the chat groups he used to communicate with 65 other NA activists. Coulson's conviction was under the Explosive Substances Act of 1883.

The Jo Cox murder made others in National Action also think the time to begin terrorism was imminent but, surprisingly secret leader Christopher Lythgoe, stopped any suggestion of it. NA believed (rightly or wrongly) that Big Brother in its entirety was now upon them. Late in June the order went out for everyone to dump their telephones and online identities. Everyone could feel the pressure upon them and Lythgoe was more guarded than ever before to ensure he kept his anonymity. He went off the radar for a good few days, which added to the sense of urgency and immanency within NA.

Robbie Mullen said:

"Lythgoe, [Alex] Davies and Ben [Raymond] all thought we were about to get banned. Initially the scrutiny had been on Britain First for the threats and actions they did in the run up to Cox's murder – and also Mair's rant when killing Cox being 'Britain First,' but the tweet in support of Mair followed by us adopting his [Mair's] slogan on our website, made it pretty clear, I think, who Mair's fans were."

And were you fans?

"There was a culture in NA of when something bad or terrible happened, of gluing yourself to the television and enjoying it. Before the order to dump phones came in from Lythgoe, it was mad. Yep, everyone loved that she had been murdered. Mair may not have been a member of NA or even known to us, but everyone loved what he had done."

Was this the present under the Christmas tree that you had been expecting?

"I dunno. It certainly felt like an early Christmas present to NA. I know it sounds wrong, sounds terrible. But that was the way we were. If the order had gone out there and then, some of the younger, really weird kids would probably have followed it up with something similar or at least deadly. I was lucky, when the order to dump the phones came, I saw Lythgoe the same day and he said 'now isn't the time' or something similar. So I kind of allowed myself to think we were still only pretending to be terrorists. I thought it, but I less and less felt it."

Some National Action members temporarily decamped to Poland and Ukraine to escape the heat, and also to glorify what had happened to Jo Cox. They headed to Poland and the rifle ranges where they could pose like hard men with military hardware. Their hosts were the Polish Nazi group NOP, with whom they had an excellent, but competitive, relationship at home. The front group for the Azov Battalion in Ukraine, the Misanthropic Division (MD), was where the two groups met.

In September 2016, National Action sent a small team to see if they could disrupt a pro-EU march through the centre of London led by comedian Eddie Izzard. Just before the group could grab the headlines once more, a Polish chef living in west London, David Czerwonko, launched himself at Izzard and grabbed his trademark pink beret. Alex Davies, NA's co-founder, was furious. Czerwonko was well known to National Action: he had a reputation for unhinged violence, as well as being an international link-man for the Misanthropic Division. He'd upstaged NA and received a warm welcome from the Tory press for stealing the comedian's French-style headgear.

Worse still, the far-right networking group London Forum, was lauding the Polish Nazi for making the often-frocked Izzard look stupid.

Despite the fury, there was little Davies or National Action could do about the Polish chef stealing the headlines. The NOP (to which Czerwonko was also attached) was far more physically capable than NA. They were often, in fact, the muscle for NA, who eventually swallowed their pride and agreed to interview Czerwonka for their website. In the course of the interview, while police were raiding his home for his part in the violence at Dover earlier in the year, the NOP uncovered a Polish security service agent in their midst. The London Forum even paid Czerwonko's £300 fine.

***

National Action's secret leader Christopher Lythgoe had been keen to break ties with the Poles, NOP and the Misanthropic Division for some time. Despite being a member of MD, he was furious the group's UK leader, Jimmy Hey, was trying to recruit his members. Since taking over the leadership,

Lythgoe swung between bouts of trusting Ben Raymond and Davies, and hating them. He lurched between wanting to keep Raymond at arm's length, and keeping him close when he thought NA would need a fall guy. He also suspected (and wasn't wrong) that Raymond and Davies thought it was only a matter of time before the group fell back under their control.

***

"I don't recall anyone among us ever discussing openly or even contemplating a ban on NA. I know the leadership discussed it, but as so little was known about us, really, it had to be based on what people thought we were doing.

"Lythgoe was still obsessed with a big statement, a big video or declaration of war to the people watching at home, but we were not breaking the law any more than other far-right or far-left groups who engaged in violence and publicity stunts. But there was also an inevitably about it (the ban) I guess. The tweet by Wayne [Bell] after her murder [Jo Cox's] and Jack's [Renshaw's] speeches really did not help. Had they been listening into what Lythgoe and the rest of the 'gang' were obsessed with, I guess we would've been banned sooner.

"I think after Jo Cox's murder Chris [Lythgoe] saw some kind of green light. We were pushing at an open door. If Thomas Mair could go and murder an MP, why couldn't lots of people? Yeah, yeah, it was seen as a victory. But not Chris [Lythoge] doing it, something like that himself. I never saw Chris as seeing himself carrying out terror attacks. It didn't take long, I guess, until it sank in that it would be us, the members, (that) he saw killing people at his instruction." – Robbie Mullen, speaking in March 2019.

Nicholas Waugh, National Action's Aberdeenshire-based Scottish organiser, agreed with Lythgoe's dark and dramatic views. Between the two of them, they discussed the opportunity to put together the sort of video that Lythgoe had been wishing for: something that would shock and disgust liberals and the government and also send potentially hundreds of angry young white men headfirst into White Jihad. The idea was to make the never-ending NA publicity machine really explosive. Raymond was good at publicity, great at self-promotion, and making and editing videos, but they had to give him something to take the viewer's breath away.

Yes, National Action had to look stunning, impressive, but it also had to put the fear of God into people. It needed to combine its already impressive aesthetics and choreography with something that really would make them look like a terrorist outfit.

From Jo Cox's murder onwards there was an uncomfortable feeling about National Action. It seemed almost liberated from its shackles. But even before her killing the mood had darkened in the country, with hate crimes rising, along with tensions in the run-up to Brexit, and an increasingly active and violent far right. Anti-immigrant, anti-European sentiment dominated much of social media. The Labour Party was squabbling about its new leader, Jeremy Corbyn, and even NA had joined in with the Brexit campaign.

Raymond may have written some of the (often confused) musings on NA's obsession with violence, but since the murder of Jo Cox he wanted the group to slow down. Yet he ran the website that lauded Mair and wrote endless streams of antagonising abuse that encouraged members to act out the way they did. Of course, much of this inconsistency was down to his absolute belief that he really was the officer class and also that he would do almost anything to try and fit in, even if he was a coward.

Arrested again in early June 2016, Raymond had threatened to claim – in some sort of mitigation – he was gay, thinking it would allow him to work behind the scenes in National Action without being arrested again. The NA website had by then disappeared – an old trick used many a time by the BNP – with NA claiming 'hackers' had taken it down, thus allowing it an opportunity to fundraise further before putting the site back up.

Jo Cox's murder had ruined many of Raymond's plans which swung, on a bad day, from extricating himself and setting himself up as some kind independent politician, to a good day, when he'd tested his own popularity by attempting to force Lythgoe out and return National Action to some kind of arthouse, situationist project.

In the meantime, while Lythgoe was making his grand plans, his members started up their own porn page on the Russian social media network, VK, mainly showing young women topless. The obsession with sex, terrorism and violence would continue while they assumed the world awaited National Action's next big move.

Although there was more scrutiny, the group was able to continue small and low-level stunts to keep themselves in the headlines. Wayne Bell filled page after VK page with insults and threats to British Jews and antifascists. He even tweeted he would cut my throat as soon as he had a chance.

The explosion of racism and racist violence post-Brexit, and the increasing, unrelenting police pursuit of those behind the violence at Dover and Liverpool, showed no sign of abating. Dozens of far-right activists were being sent to prison for activities that had less to do with Brexit and the hatred it had unlocked, and more to do with an emerging sense of failure and desperation on their part. The race war so many National Action and other far-right members desperately predicted and wanted, appeared to be close, some thought: close enough to feel and taste. Obviously, much of the British far-right activist base was heavily dependent on drugs and alcohol, so the sobering reality of jail and heavy fines handed out during 2015-2016 was debilitating. But many in the wider world persisted with the idea that, despite NA's very small numbers, the far right was a big player in what was fast becoming a hostile environment in the UK.

Ben Raymond (left) on one of his many visits to Europe (Facebook)

Lythgoe (second right) with other NA members. © Robbie Mullen

Lythgoe (Centre) Holds meeting to unite NW and Yorkshire after the ban pic July 2017.
© unknown

Jeremy "Jez" Turner of the London Forum confronted at Lime Street station,
August 2015. © HOPE not hate

Naughty National Action Memes
1 hr ·

goals

NA held a special
hatred for
HOPE not hate
(Facebook)

The proud father, Adam Thomas. November 2017. (BBC News)

Paul Hickman. Would later take his own life rather than return to prison. © HOPE not hate

Rare footage Mullen
smuggled from
the gym of NA
members training.
© Robbie Mullen/
HOPE not hate

The secret headquarters and gym in Warrington. © HOPE not hate

Michal Trubini: The Slovak whose name the gym's lease was in (Facebook)

Claudia Patatas, the Matriarch of West Midlands NA. She was not considered white enough by the rest of the gang (Facebook)

Ben Raymond looking confused and disheveled outside the NA trial of Renshaw, Lythgoe and others the Old Bailey, June 2018. © HOPE not hate

Liam Pinkham (3rd from left) found his ideological home in NA (Facebook)

'Rad the Pole' Polish Nazi with a knife and gun obsession (Facebook)

Renshaw with NA members forced into delivering food. Manchester, 2016.
© Robbie Mullen/HOPE not hate

Jack Coulson
16 Jun 2016

Absolute fucking legend. He's a hero, we need more people like him to butcher the race traitors.

Young NA member Jack Coulson admiring Thomas Mair,
the killer of MP Jo Cox (Facebook)

Nick Griffin: Former BNP leader who radicalised but lost control of the party's youth wing. © Robbie Mullen/HOPE not hate

Nick Griffin British Unity added 4 new photos.

22 January 2015 · 🌐

Controlled UK media cover up a Muslim terrorist attack on UK soil
North Wales "racist attacker" was a MUSLIM CONVERT!

Last week Zack Davies brutally attacked a Sikh, Sarandev Brahambr with a machete and hammer, in a Tesco in North Wales.

The serious assault in Mold was rightly given wide media coverage. Much attention was paid to the fact that, according to witnesses, Davies was shouting 'white power',

But what the Lying MSM have totally failed to report is that it has emerged that Zack Davies is a Muslim convert who now calls himself "Zack Ali".

Ali warned on his Facebook page on the morning of his attack in Tesco:

"The wrath of Allah is about to come down upon the kaffir, I will have my revenge." He also posted four Qur'an verses (identifying the suras as "books") that call for violence against unbelievers:

Book of Al-Anfal, verse 12 (8:12) – "I (Allah) will instill terror into the hearts of the unbelievers: smite ye above their necks and smite all their finger-tips off."

5- Book of Al-Baqara, verse 191 (2:191) – "Kill them wherever you find them, and drive them out from wherever they drove you out."

6- Book of Al-Baqara, verse 193 (2:193) – "Fight them on until there is no more tumult and religion becomes that of Allah"

Nick Griffin writes about the Zack Davies attack (Facebook)

Mullen (left) leaving a
pub in Rochdale with
'Redwatch' webmaster
Kevin Watmough (far right),
Rochdale 2015.
© HOPE not hate

Garron Helm: Desperate for publicity. © HOPE not hate

Garron Helm's mantle piece. Adolf Hitler and Order of Nine Angles together (Facebook)

Combat 18 leader Wilf Browning guarded by Polish minders, Liverpool,
Febraury 2016. © HOPE not hate

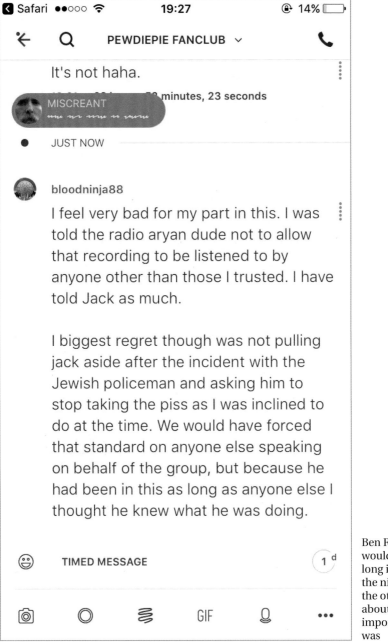

It's not haha.

MISCREANT   minutes, 23 seconds

JUST NOW

bloodninja88

I feel very bad for my part in this. I was told the radio aryan dude not to allow that recording to be listened to by anyone other than those I trusted. I have told Jack as much.

I biggest regret though was not pulling jack aside after the incident with the Jewish policeman and asking him to stop taking the piss as I was inclined to do at the time. We would have forced that standard on anyone else speaking on behalf of the group, but because he had been in this as long as anyone else I thought he knew what he was doing.

TIMED MESSAGE   1 d

Ben Raymond would waffle long into the night to the others about how important he was

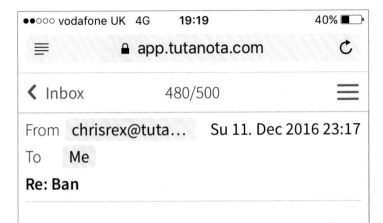

●●○○○ vodafone UK 4G   19:19   40% ▪

🔒 app.tutanota.com   ↻

❮ Inbox   480/500   ≡

From chrisrex@tuta…   Su 11. Dec 2016 23:17
To   Me
Re: Ban

Anything COULD happen, no matter how unlikely or illogical. Long-term we'll keep moving forward just as we have been. But the primary objective short-term is to make sure people further down the NA hierarchy don't lose their heads. Some people have overactive imaginations. Some people like to talk pure shit. So if we see any hint of pessimism or hysteria within our ranks, we stamp it out pronto. Assure everyone that a) nothing's likely to happen, and that b) even if it did we've got plans in place ready. Also reassure people that any ban would NOT be retroactive (it baffles me that some people think it would be, but there you go...)

Christopher Lythgoe worrying that people are losing their bottle

Ashley Bell delivers
Newcastle speech flanked
by Wayne Bell (left)
and Matthew Hankinson
(centre), March 2015.
© HOPE not hate

MMA instructor Jimmy Hey (centre) outside Liverpool Lime Street station, August 2015.
© HOPE not hate

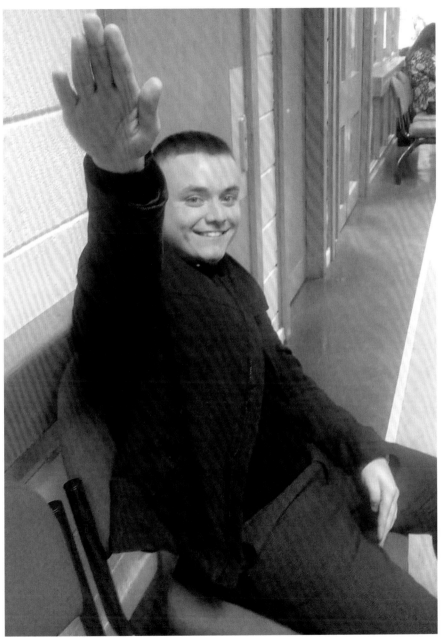

Renshaw attending a plea hearing for Garron Helm 2017 (Facebook)

The Dover riot in early 2016 saw hundreds of fascist and Antifascist protestors clash.
© HOPE not hate

In 2016 new far-right groups with fancy names such as Right Wing Resistance would appear on social with great self-fanfare, before splitting and folding within days. There was a plethora of groups, such as National Action, that had no interest in engaging in the electoral or political process. As always, in either style or poor content, theirs was a wink at NA's militarism and militancy. This would continue long after NA had finally exited the stage. People who worked for HOPE not hate inside the far-right spoke often of a sudden drive by small gangs of disenfranchised Nazis to be the 'significant body' once there was a conflict to exploit. Most of these groups rarely made it off Facebook: the numbers were so small and the individuals behind them so flawed and chaotic that wheel after wheel was reinvented week after week much to NA's delight, who saw nobody and nothing coming close to what they'd created. Someone, somewhere was making a small fortune churning out flags and banners that were obsolete by the time they were delivered.

Britain First was a model for how British fascist groups experienced peaks and troughs and would learn to ride one disaster after another with very little or real public political support. The British National Party (BNP) and the English Defence League (EDL) – limbering in permanent paralysis – were blissfully ignored. Nobody saw any point in reinvigorating old parties. We were entering into the 'DIY' era where everyone was their own Führer. Having ridden great waves of popularity, National Action was also becoming an outcast to those who had encouraged their growth.

"It [2016] was a bad year for arrests. Dover and Liverpool aside – which we all viewed as great success because there had been so much violence directed at Reds – caused real problems. The problem was our numbers were also going down, people even going on the run if they were not already caught for stuff they did. I remember feeling a bit flat about it. I also think National Action contributed to the mood that something bad was coming. Yeah, it was infectious a bit but I don't think it was solely us [the far-right] creating the climate people could see or feel.

"Once Jo Cox was murdered the majority of us knew we would get the blame, but in the main we only read mainstream newspapers on line and shared the content. Even we could feel the pressure building in the newspapers, on twitter and Facebook about race and immigration. There certainly was a mood that year. People were literally lining up to throw themselves in nick if they thought something would happen.

"Once Cox died and National Action sent that fucking tweet even we thought that was too much. I had a feeling they [the government/ establishment] just wouldn't stop until we were all in prison. And also, after they [National Action] sent that tweet [about Cox], a lot of people around the London Forum were even saying some of these [National Action] kids needed a fucking slap. None of them were going to prison." –'Maurice', a London Forum member, on National Action.

***

The same month Jo Cox was murdered, swastikas and National Action stickers appeared on walls in Stamford Hill, north London, home to a large Orthodox Jewish community. Sean Creighton, a man with links to NA as well as the NF – and an alleged supplier of materials to both groups – was arrested in possession of a terrorist manual. He'd later be sentenced to five years in prison. What with this and Coulson also due soon before the courts for his pipe bomb, a change would have to come soon.

In August 2016, the largest 'Legion' summer camp was held. 'Legion' and 'Sigrund' were the names of the two camps run to prepare fascists for a race war under the guise of keeping fit and healthy. Writing gushingly about the event, Larry Nunn of Western Spring (his personal website) and London Forum infamy, the man National Action believed would be their spiritual guide and funder from the outset, wrote of the event:

"Last weekend a great many nationalist [sic] from a great many locations met for the most enjoyable weekend of camping, archery, field craft and martial arts training at a location in Yorkshire of outstanding natural beauty. During the martial arts training and after they had been shown how to keep their knives sharp by an ex-army instructor, there were two "minor" injuries. We had taken young and not so young nationalists to a physically challenging environment and had provided an educational itinerary that will prepare them for the privations that we will all one day face if the socio political trends continue."

CHAPTER 17: HITLER IS NOT ENOUGH

"We want to make it clear that stickers of this nature are not welcome in Cambridge, or in fact any part of our county. We welcome any information from members of the public who may know who is responsible. Please call 101."
"Cambridge has resettled 14 Syrian refugees under the Government's Syrian Vulnerable Persons Resettlement scheme."

– 'Go home to Africa' Anti-refugee stickers spotted on lampposts in Cambridge, *Daily Express*, September 29 2016

In his late sixties, financial guru Larry Nunn was one of the few people in the wider movement that National Action's founders looked to when they were starting out. His patronage of the group had drawn some sharp criticism, even from those within the London Forum, who ostensibly shared his and NA's analysis that the electoral path was pointless. By the time NA came into being, Nunn had placed himself and Western Spring at the forefront of spreading new ideas about the perennially-busted flush of British fascism. On most of his writings he hid behind a nom de guerre: Max Musson.

Nunn's notorious chequebook had first attracted National Action founders Ben Raymond and Alex Davies back in 2013. Nunn had even handed over cash to Garron Helm on at least one occasion.

As National Action became more and more of an embarrassing nuisance, Nunn remained a stalwart defender of them, even during the dark hours when the Ryan Fleming sex abuse scandal broke. But the young neo-Nazis were also his Achilles heel. While he defended NA to others in the white supremacist world over the Fleming affair, NA members seemed to positively revel in the notoriety. Nunn and Jeremy Bedford Turner, the ostensible head of the London Forum, invited Davies to address the Forum during 2016. At another London Forum event, Davies and Raymond got so drunk they ended up soiling themselves.

Determined that National Action should succeed, Nunn nominated Davies for the London Forum's award for "good speakers". But the reality was, as even

Nunn must have been able to see by this point, NA's increasing extremism and vulgarity wasn't like the intellectual youth group he'd so admired back in 2013.

Nunn proposed a conference for all the UK's far-right's tin-pot leaders to come together and endorse such an idea:

"Following the controversy of Nick Griffin's ultimately disastrous stewardship of the British National Party, that party has shed most of its former members and the nationalist movement in this country has become fragmented and disoriented. Today our movement is composed of a number of comparatively small organisations, many of them tiny, and all of them largely impotent in terms of being able to effect political change either now or within the foreseeable future." – Larry Nunn, on the need for a Leaders Conference: Quest For Unity and Direction, 29 July 2016.

Aware as we were of the schisms within National Action, but unaware of how drastic they had become, it was interesting that Davies made it onto the list of invitees to this conference. There were none of the "leaders" present that Nunn so enthused about when describing his audience as "twenty of the most experienced and influential people in British nationalism." It was just a collection of low-level former BNP personnel who fell on their swords during the party's demise. All were associated with Nunn's other obsession, the London Forum, where as we said in HOPE not hate magazine (Nov-Dec 2016) "far right relics meet to gather dust."

Nunn railed throughout the two days about the futility of both the electoral process and democracy in general. Only Davies was afforded a place at the top table. When he spoke, others shook their heads in confused and insulted disapproval of his fraught, squeaky analysis. Nunn realised Raymond and Davies were no longer in control of National Action.

***

Nunn now approached Christopher Lythgoe directly, opening a series of email exchanges with the secretive National Action leader. Eventually Nunn drove to the Angel pub in Knutsford, on a Sunday morning in September to meet with Lythgoe and his new NA leadership team.

Robbie Mullen recalled:

"He spoke for hours about his plans, that he would be the leader of the NF [National Front] and we [National Action] would be like his cutting-edge Stormtroopers- or as he called it 'army'. Chris [Lythgoe] just sat there giving him his 'death stare.' I don't know if Chris was insulted or not by Larry's [Nunn] suggestions, but he rarely even grunted. Larry had it all

*planned out and even said he would fund National Action if we would
just come on board.*

*"I guess Larry was thinking that if he could get 200 NA members to
join the NF, it would be a simple case of us moving against the NF
leadership and putting him in charge. He had quite wild, extravagant
ideas about himself."*

Lythgoe arrived at the meeting seething that the older man had been too
busy to read a document he'd carefully prepared and emailed before the
negotiations could begin. To punish Nunn, Lythgoe drank heavily, staring
through the older man as he sat talking in hushed tones. Inspired by Lythgoe's
insolence, Mullen demanded a board position on Nunn's Western Spring.
Nunn apparently said "Yes", enthusing it would be a democratic arrangement
between the two organisations until such a time as the political opportunity
arose to form a political party.

Lythgoe kept barking "How much?" every time there was mention of an
opportunity of putting more cash in his pockets. He also rebuked Nunn for
suggesting a democratic arrangement. Tapping Mullen to respond, Mullen told
Nunn: "This isn't a democracy. People will do what the fuck they are told to do
or nothing will ever get done." He was enjoying himself now, watching Nunn
squirm.

Nunn claimed he'd previously held very fruitful discussions with Davies and
Raymond. Lythgoe laughed, telling Nunn that Raymond was now not only no
longer a leader of National Action, but that he was barely important, merely a
trusted member who looked after the administration.

The meeting went on for nearly four hours, with Lythgoe stringing out gruff
responses and arguments for as long as Nunn would keep putting his hands
in his pocket. Michal Trubini, a six-foot-four Slovakian neo-Nazi, sat behind
Nunn the whole time, attempting to menace him.

Tired and wanting to go home for dinner, Lythgoe eventually put a price
on the collusion: £3,000 per month, which would include a full-time salary
for himself. According to Mullen, Nunn didn't entirely baulk at the idea, but
when the others at the meeting burst into laughter, Nunn took the blue folder
containing his plans and put it in his car.

It was one of the few times Lythgoe earned Mullen's respect. Despite
making Mullen his number two, Mullen had still not really taken to Lythgoe.
Now, not only had he taken him along as the joint brains of the non-venture,
he'd allowed Mullen to ridicule someone that the new National Action boss held
in very low esteem. Raymond and Davies, "arse lickers", would have thrown
themselves at Nunn's feet – but Lythgoe wanted NA to have no masters.

According to Mullen, when Larry Nunn left, Lythgoe shouted at him
"You drive a woman's car" and that was the last they ever heard of his plan.

Lythgoe's pressing obsession had been outlined at the April conference
and during a series of exchanges with the leadership group. The last thing

he wanted was to be a rich man's plaything and lapdog. A statement about National Action's intentions had to be made and, in keeping with the group's artistic and dramatic obsession, it had to be explosive as well as impressive.

The 'Warrington sessions' where Lythgoe held court sometimes two or three times a week, upstairs in the Friar Penketh pub, began to resemble a proper council of war. Mullen, Matthew Hankinson and Lythgoe would sit at a table and wait for any number of members from around the country to come and pay homage to the leader. What didn't strike Mullen until much later was how Raymond and Davies acquiesced to all of Lythgoe's demands. Despite their very real angst at having their formidable founding double-act demoted, and Lythgoe ridiculing and bad-mouthing Raymond for his stupidity and weaknesses, at no time did either of the two early leaders (except for an argument over who should lead the West Midlands unit) raise any objections or doubts about Lythgoe's stern, austere leadership. Nor did they raise any objection to the group quite obviously heading closer and closer towards terrorism. The pair wanted Lythgoe gone and NA back under their control, but it was a surprising maturity of them both that instead of arguing or splitting away, they went out of their way to ensure NA stayed intact and the organisation survived under Lythgoe's leadership.

In every British far-right organisation splits occurred when leaderships changed. It was the quintessential nature of British fascism, and something that Raymond and Davies, students of the British far right's disastrous past, desperately wanted to avoid. Although we're fairly certain Lythgoe was the terror-obsessive, in July 2018, giving evidence at the Old Bailey, Lythgoe claimed it was Raymond, not himself, who kept pushing for race war. That may also be the case, but in fairness, Raymond had absolutely no desire to be involved in one.

> *"I didn't really see it as a schism. It was presented as such by HOPE not hate but they didn't really know what had happened or who it was happening with or to. Lythgoe was just a name among hundreds, nobody knew he was the leader outside of NA. I think that's an achievement.*
>
> *"There was a notable change and things were changing rapidly after the murder of Jo Cox and he [Lythgoe] asserted himself more. Ben [Raymond] and Alex [Davies] never complained, though you could see Ben was needy and desperate. Those were the rules, you did as the leader told you, no matter what it was. To the rest of the organisation they just kept pushing internally as much as anybody else for the group to harden up, to toughen up like Chris wanted."* – Robbie Mullen, March 2019

***

Throughout National Action's legal existence, Mullen gave little thought about the effect of the group's behaviour on others. He saw no reason for

Jews, for instance, to be horrified by 'Hitler was Right' banners. He was living inside a bubble. It never crossed his mind that talk about murdering people might crystallise into hardened plans; he never thought for one moment that more than a dozen of his compatriots would receive long sentences simply for membership of the group, or for plots to kill others.

In one sense, Mullen could be described as a simple lost soul who wandered into a group dynamic that was infectious and violent, like a cult. But that would be too simple, a cop-out which would let him off the hook. He went into National Action as an avowed racist but he readily admits that growing up in and around Widnes, he'd never met any non-white people. He took what were, for him, eye-opening trips into Lancashire with his brother to install Sky satellite dishes and it was there, in towns such as Burnley and Blackburn, that he witnessed immigration or, as he felt it, "colonisation". Like a lot of far-right activists, he would say that he came from a solid Labour-voting family, but not one that was fully engaged with the Labour movement.

Watching on television when the Nick Griffin was elected as his region's MEP, a young Mullen could see no reason why the BNP was any worse or any different to Labour.

> "They voted Labour at home, but we wasn't tied to the party. What I saw in Nick Griffin's BNP and then, I suppose to some degree, the National Front, were people who were speaking for me. I came from a working class family and I felt we were ignored. What loyalty did I owe to the modern Labour Party? When grooming gangs started and there was like the deafening silence from them. We all felt the same. I had very little [empathy] with non-white people."

And so Mullen's disaffection took him from immigration concerns and anger about grooming gangs into the orbit of people who wanted to murder Jews, people who called immigrants "parasites" and "vermin".

> "Well yeah, that [articulated] I guess an opinion. I'm not a great thinker on deep issues, sadly. But I just never saw it [National Action's behaviour] as a real issue. At the time I just felt we were fucking about on issues we had no say about. That was my bubble and I thought we were being allowed to do and say the things we were getting away with because it kept us occupied."

Their own political obsessions were minuscule, however. They looked (only) at the ultra-left's response to everything, because it affirmed not just their most fervent prejudices, but kept them within their bubble. Davies and Raymond pored over left-wing websites believing the left was failing, was torn over Brexit and immigration, and that the great collapse was imminent. They believed it was the left holding together the will of the rancid multicultural society, protecting its Jewish masters. Perhaps this was another reason to keep National Action together, despite the antagonism between Lythgoe, Raymond and Davies. NA had to remain regimented and united because similar ideas were spreading throughout the group, throughout the regions where it was training and engaging. Jo Cox had been murdered and the state and its agents now claimed it feared NA as much as it feared the Islamists. The government feared Jihad.

"I knew it was coming, could sense it was coming, but I never believed it would. Does that make sense? I knew we needed/wanted more Zack Davies's (the Mold attacker) and more Thomas Mairs." – Robbie Mullen, March 2019

Lythgoe firmly believed if Thomas Mair could go out and kill his local MP, a 'treacherous multicultural liberal', there would be others who would follow. He graded those who came to visit him in the pub on their loyalty and the likelihood they could withstand the pressures of a race war, with him leading – as he wrote down – like some medieval king. The killer piece of propaganda was so important. The neo-Nazis began downloading images and footage of people they hated, turning it into a collage of hate – pictures of people, traitors, they hoped would signal who was to be taken out either when the race war began, or in the hope of starting a race war.

Lythgoe had called for better speakers to step forward to communicate for the group. He needed a new voice to front what he believed would be the most brilliant piece of Nazi propaganda anyone in Britain had ever produced. Instead of just marching on demonstrations, Lythgoe demanded National Action members should advance as if they were an army, like the IRA with faces covered for dramatic effect and propaganda.

Raymond and Davies weren't to deliver his masterpiece for a number of reasons: Davies' voice was squeaky and a habit of stuttering mid-sentence would mean, even if disguised, that he'd be recognised. Raymond would be charged with producing the footage, but would have no say in its content. Any speech by Raymond would more than likely embarrass the group.

The first example of this new direction was in Berwick, close to the English/Scottish border. The town had been the focus of a number of demonstrations by both Scottish and English fascists over the years, a place where they could meet, drink and terrorise locals. By this point, October 2016, Lythgoe had been the leader of National Action for more than a year and was now recognised as such by all the membership. He'd overseen a dramatic internal upsurge in the thirst for violence, had sidelined the group's founder and 'owner' Ben Raymond – silenced him almost – and made plain to members that Raymond's revolutionary cowardice had held the group back.

Lythgoe kept things in line through fear, paranoia and secrecy. On numerous occasions he sent masked men to intimidate people. One trade unionist came home from work to find eight masked men at her front gate delivering, IRA style, a message they actually read to her. She had young children cowering in the house. Her crime had been living too close to one of Lythgoe's men in Liverpool and having gone on an antifascist demonstration. Each and every action he called for was a test, a test of his members' commitment and a test of the adrenaline it generated. Mullen took part in more than the odd intimidation on Lythgoe's behalf. They were the 'punishment squad'.

"Every month has been like a new beginning; new members, new developments, new boundaries crossed, October has been no exception. The start of the month began with our march in Berwick which marked a new watershed for our movement. The myth of Lime Street has taken a severe battering in 2016, and this was the final nail." – October Report, National Action website, 31 October 2016.

The Berwick demonstration was primarily organised by the North East Infidels (NEI) and the Scottish Defence League (SDL). The SDL had begun life as a mirror of the English Defence League, but had slowly and surely boiled down to little more than a neo-Nazi group which the EDL very quickly wanted little to do with. There had been antagonism between the SDL and National Action over a period of time, in the main over Garron Helm's outspoken support for the IRA. But as the original Scottish leadership melted away from the gang, a bizarre transition occurred. A series of young men, with Celtic and Irish names, came to the forefront of the SDL and then joined with NA, espousing hardline Nazism that was neither pro-Republican or pro-Loyalist. An early member of the SDL said in January 2017:

"In the early days, when we were close to the EDL it was about 50 lads doing the anti-Islam thing, but when they [the EDL] began to fracture so did we. We were all Unionists, Rangers supporting protestants, pro the union etc. Then suddenly about half a dozen kids with Irish heritage came in to the group and it became all about Jews and making friends with Nazi groups. It wasn't what we expected, as we always thought they [Catholics] were Fenian lefties."

The NEI didn't want National Action on their protest. Warren Faulkner, the convicted football hooligan and drug dealer who led the gang, had made it clear he wanted no Nazi saluting or to have NA anywhere near the march. NA tried to open a discussion but Faulkner held firm behind his own fearsome reputation for violence.

"We decided to fuck him," said Mullen. "Who the fuck was he anyway? Just another coke head and dealer. Lythgoe said if Faulkner got in our way we were to simply put him on his arse and get on with it."

On October 1, National Action arrived en masse in cars and a minibus in Berwick at the designated pub by the train station. Faulkner approached the first car, only to be confronted by the six-foot amateur boxer Hankinson, along with Chris McCartney, Lythgoe's chauffeur and heavily-tattooed bodyguard.

Faulkner knew to be wary of Hankinson, who earlier in the year had attacked a member of the racist gang Yorkshire Casuals on a train from Rotherham. The Casuals member had taken issue with a National Action Nazi saluting at a protest against child grooming that day, and then found himself confronted on the train by Hankinson, who knocked him out, laughing as he stood posing with a foot on his victim's prostate body for pictures.

"Faulkner suddenly realised there was about forty of us in total. He approached Hankinson and said 'I don't want any face masks today' and he was told we would fuck him and his firm over there and then on the spot," said Mullen. Confronted by a group itching for a fight, Faulkner backed down. Eventually the march, which was against the proposed housing of refugees in the town, moved off. National Action marched in threes behind the main body of 50 assorted neo-Nazis, marching in columns, carrying black flags in silence. By the time former leader Ashley Bell had delivered the group's speech, there was a sense of awe at the way the organisation had conducted itself.

Even Faulkner, used to parading around with scruffy racists holding cans of beer, offered NA the hand of friendship. They responded with a distinctly limp wrist.

Back in Warrington the gang held a little party above the Friar Penketh pub, then went to a night club. Things were darker, but Mullen also felt like they could take on the world. It was a feeling unmatched at any time in his life.

"One group which has been causing concern is the neo-Nazi group National Action, which though consisting of only around 100 activists has a large presence on the internet.

On the weekend of Remembrance Sunday, the group stuck up posters in south Liverpool declaring the area a "Nazi-controlled zone" The group has held marches in support of Adolf Hitler and hailed the election of Donald Trump – as did "alt-right" groups in the US and the KKK." – 'Neo-nazi youth movement as big a threat as militant Islam says UK security minister; IB Times, November 2016.

CHAPTER 18: THE BOYS IN BLACK

"We need to get rid of the random flag effect. Lots of nationalists just bring out random flags like Combat 18 flags for example and the effect is it looks awful. We need to have just one flag or two flags coordinated in a way that shows that they are meant to go together. Whenever we have numbers we should try and use flagpoles with our flags and only in small numbers does it work holding the flags. We will dress all in black, no exceptions. We need to make a real visual impact on people. We will use our own bandanas which we are in the process of designing. We will use pyrotechnics, flares with our provocative banner. In front of that we will use a fiery speaker, a real orator, someone who can set the crowd alight with their words and with that we are going to set up our own internal school for the development of public speakers. ...we can take our demos wherever we want, whenever we want. The left like to say no platform for the right, but we will make our own platform and defend it with violence, so we can speak to the people directly wherever they are. .....We need to split our activists up into cells....

"What we are fighting is a war of ideas, a mental war. We are trying to convince people that the ideology of national socialism is the correct ideology while discrediting all rival ideologies."

Christopher Lythgoe's address to the National Action conference, 2016.

To deliver the killer piece of propaganda, for only the second time in National Action's history, the leadership cracked a three-line whip.

Bishop Auckland Against Islam (another front group for the North East Infidels) was to hold an anti-Islam march through Darlington on November 5. Having offered the hand of friendship to National Action in a humbling climb-down the previous month, Warren Faulkner was falling over himself to see another military-style parade by the young and dedicated neo-Nazis. And even if they had to beg, borrow or steal, every NA activist had to be in Darlington.

Alex Davies, still officially Lythgoe's number two, was charged with finding a base for the group. On the Friday night some 20 National Action members descended on Newcastle, staying at a series of AirBnB locations and hostels. From Newcastle, further pressure was applied to wavering members to come and join the demonstration. Mullen was among ten people with jobs who put in a £50 solidarity donation to help those who wanted to be there.

Person B, the talented but troubled former YBNP member, arranged for half a dozen of his activists to take an exhausting route by coach from London. Flags and poles (martial art kali sticks) arrived in the afternoon and were assembled in a flat rented by Davies for the weekend. The North West group hired a minibus, and transport was arranged from the Midlands. Secure chat and messaging groups on Signal, Wire, Telegram and Tutanota were used to spread word of the operation with utmost secrecy. Pictures were sent out to convince people to come, set to delete after they were accessed.

A café was chosen in Darlington where everyone would assemble on the Saturday of the demo and where they'd receive their special National Action masks and bandanas. Thousands of bundles of stickers, freshly arrived from Poland, were ready to be handed out, as were instructions about what they should do if the police tried to interfere. It would be a full paramilitary parade. If members could also wear sunglasses that would be even better, they were told.

Robbie Mullen travelled by taxi that morning, driven by Lythgoe's driver-cum-chauffeur, Chris McCartney. With them was Matthew Hankinson, who Mullen constantly trailed. Christopher Lythgoe chose to travel by minibus because he feared cars belonging to members of the group would be known to the authorities.

As Mullen's ride approached Darlington city centre, McCartney began to panic. Before them was a police roadblock and a dozen or more black-clad NA members lying in front of it in the road. Police officers in navy jumpsuits and baseball caps had their firearms trained on them. Each member lying on the ground had their hands on their heads and was being lifted up so they could be photographed by Counter Terrorism officers. Among the West Midlands group on the road was Corporal Mikko Vehvilainen, a 31-year-old soldier in the British Army. A Finnish national, Vehvilainen was known as the "quartermaster" in the Midlands National Action network because he stockpiled (and encouraged others to do similarly) weaponry.

A dedicated neo-Nazi, Vehavilainen was a supporter of various Finnish militias who followed avowed Nazism. He was also known as the "driver", because he was one of the only members in the Midlands who could drive, let alone own a car. McCartney began to panic and tried to swerve his licensed taxi to the other side of the road to make an escape. The police officers raised their weapons towards him, quickly putting an end to that idea. He pulled over. Forced facedown into the road Mullen and Hankinson obeyed 'the rules'. Both refused to give their names, and refused to be photographed. Astonishingly, the police accepted their refusals.

"Me and Matt [Hankinson] kept turning our faces away from the photographer," Mullen recalls. Not many of the gang from the Midlands were co-operating, but the Finn [Vehilainen] seemed confused. "I'm pretty sure he told the police he was a member of the military."

McCartney, who would go on to make a name for himself later as the internal enforcer inside National Action, gave his full name and details to the police, despite Hankinson and Mullen's example. There was little alternative for McCartney: he was driving a licensed taxi registered to a particular authority.

After a 30-minute facedown on the floor arguing with police, Mullen and a few others won the day and were neither (knowingly) photographed by the police nor gave their names. The police were from London, a long way from home.

"We've got our fucking eyes on you boys," one of the cockney coppers' warned Mullen. "You ain't doing a very good job of it," he replied.

***

Allowed to proceed, by the time National Action had changed into their masks and bandanas, there were more than 70 of them gathered in Darlington. It was fewer than Lythgoe expected; there'd been more than 100 at the Crosby conference earlier in the year. As he surveyed his troops, he couldn't help but comment how many of the assembled seemed pretty weird. Mullen and Hankinson felt the same. These weird kids, in the main, were the white jihadis Lythgoe wanted to go out and fight his race war.

Neo-Nazi portrayal of race war is often that of strong, Aryan-looking men of action, 'heroes' imagined in the pages of William Pierce's *The Turner Diaries*, fighting for race and nation. In this fantasy of flesh and fury, they're outgoing alpha males, and sex gods to boot. The reality is it's always sad young men like Zack Davies, who maimed the Sikh dentist in the attack on a supermarket in Wales, or the London bomber David Copeland, who killed three including a pregnant woman, who attempt to carry out this "war". Just because they're lonesome, loners and "pretty weird" doesn't make them any less dangerous. Any lonesome idiot can plant a bomb or, armed with a machete or sword, attack a defenceless woman. When Lythgoe saw a lot of weirdoes, he wasn't complaining that the race war had been slowed down in anyway.

The choreography of the march was quite spectacular. With faces covered and the marchers dressed all in black, National Action's young men marched behind the collective mess that was the rest of the British far right. There were members of the Infidels gangs swigging cans of lager, other Nazis with bizarre tattoos on their faces, morons wrapped in the national flag, a Nazi with a

Chinese wife, drug dealers, drug users, thieves, drunks, toothless and gormless racists. McCartney led the NA section, right at the front with his large, lardy frame, giving photographers the finger.

Wayne Bell, the only member without his scarred face covered, had a whole row in the march to himself. Enjoying his growing infamy, occasionally he would break rank to threaten photographers, pushing his scarred face into faces and issuing curdling threats as to what he would do to them when the time came. Ben Raymond marched too, trying to look important. He enjoyed the choreography. That, for him, was what National Action was really about. At the end of the march the group held its own rally. Surrounded by masked boys and men and with flags flying, Nicholas Waugh from Aberdeenshire delivered the killer speech, underscoring that this was an angry group and it was ready to fight. His speech had a chilling effect. Maybe it was his Scottish accent; maybe it was the rage and desperate anger in his voice; perhaps it was because it was unfaltering and almost anonymous.

> *"I've seen them all speak; Tyndall, Edmonds, Griffin and a few others of note. It was the way he delivered it, it was astonishing. And yeah, I felt threatened, I think everybody there did. Right at the front filming it for National Action was the man I now know to be Robbie Mullen. A lot of their stuff was choreographed, but I remember thinking 'where did this bloke come from?' It was some speech. Normally with the 'fash' someone half-pissed gets up and rants on about a load of bollocks for hours. This time, the NA speaker, I felt, delivered what I felt was a death threat."*
> – Peter Faith, HOPE not hate's photographer, talking about Nicholas Waugh's speech at Darlington.

Afterwards there was a jubilant, carnival atmosphere among the group. Davies suggested they go back en masse to Newcastle and confront a "red" activity in the city. Late in the afternoon, 40 National Action members did descend on the city and again marched in formation, this time shouting "Jews Out!" and raising their right arms in the air – but they could find nobody to confront.

At Davies' AirBnB flat in Newcastle some of the group snorted lines of cocaine in the kitchen, while white power rock music blared out, intermingled with industrial techno. Beers flowed until the group became overly rowdy. Mullen picks up the story:

> *"Somebody kicked a door in and then someone else pulled the radiator off the wall. It was a really cheap, ugly flat so everybody joined in. We flooded the bathroom and people pissed and shat on the floor of the toilet, shit in the bath, that kind of stuff. We ransacked the entire flat, everything we found we destroyed."*

Quite understandably, Davies became upset and burst into tears. He screamed at the looters: "This all goes on my fucking credit card", but then decided to join in the carnage. Raymond, who had enjoyed his day so far and had been looking forward to a night out with chums, was sitting in the corner of the living room while the furnishings and content of the flat flew around his head, trying to edit the video of the speech. He was under strict instructions from Lythgoe that it had to be better than anything NA had produced before. Seeing the carnage unfold he tried to assert his leadership on the rest of the pack:

"Ben got up and said 'C'mon everyone, this isn't the way to behave' and I think it was then he realised how out of sorts with the group he was."

"People turned on him and it went dead silent. Me, Person B [the London organiser] and Ashley Bell [the group's once-temporary leader] laid into him verbally. He was called a 'queer', a 'virgin' and a 'lightweight' and we took the piss out of him for trying to shag Ryan Fleming's old flat mate. He responded with a smile at first, but then others in the flat joined in. People started shouting 'queer cunt' at him and I realised just how far he had fallen from grace and how Lythgoe had built this group now to have absolutely no respect for its founders.

"I didn't mind, you know, he kind of deserved a verbal assault because he had been shown up for cowardice so many times and he was an awful snob with it. People were screaming at him 'cowardly wanker, posh cunt, virgin' and he actually began to cry, sobbing. I've seen stuff like this in cults, you know documentaries, where they bully people into submission. It was really cruel but actually, I found I had very little [empathy] for him. Others accused him of wanting to shag little kids and he curled up into a little ball. I guess you would if you had, I dunno, maybe 20 people screaming abuse at you. But what it was really, was people telling him to fuck off and man up for a change.

"Some of the really young members there, the weirdoes who thought he was some kind of visionary, went to console him. He was sobbing and crying like somebody had died.

"About 20 of us then went out on the town and the rest stayed indoors. We went out on the town looking for trouble, looking for a fight. I messaged Lythgoe and told him, 'Ben situation has been sorted' and he knew exactly what was meant by that."

***

Despite all this, Raymond later delivered a masterpiece of propaganda. To accompany the very sort of speech Lythgoe had demanded came a video to drum home the threat National Action now claimed to be. With Nicholas Waugh's speech as a commentary, film footage showed masked NA members marching into Darlington city centre interceded with images of Asian youths rioting, burning buildings, whites being beaten, liberals marching, gays demanding their rights, Parliament and pictures of old Britain underscored with both subtitles and atmospheric music for just over four minutes. The flavour of the speech can be captured from its commentary:

> *"We are here because it is necessary, because no men of conscience may turn a blind eye. The battle has come to us. It rages in our towns, our cities, on our very own doorsteps.*
>
> *"A dark cloud looms over this land, and we must now fight (so) that the generations who succeed us will not wake up one day as a despised and persecuted minority on the very land that is their birth right and which is soaked with the blood of their ancestors.*
>
> *"Pushed aside to make way for those encouraged to come here seeking entitlement at the expense of those who have been taught to wallow in self-hate and shame for the glorious deeds of our forefathers.*
>
> *"Well we say 'no', we will not be shamed and we will not be cowed. We will take back what is rightfully ours by birth and by the will of God.*
>
> *"The time has come where mere words must give way to action and you the individual must take up this struggle or be condemned to history or else risk being condemned to history as a traitor to your nation, your race and your very own children!*
>
> *"The time has come my brothers to make a stand... Hail Victory!"*

It was a terrifyingly brilliant propaganda video. The leader had demanded it and the group had delivered it. It was Lythgoe's declaration of war and the YouTube hits ran into their thousands very quickly. Always flashy, always competent, this time National Action had produced something quite exceptional. Raymond, almost recovered from his "hazing", excitedly pushed the video as far and wide as he could. The American market, always a good cash cow, duly obliged and by the end of December around £10k had flown into the group's PayPal account.

The police were belatedly catching up with some National Action members at last. Lawrence Burns from Cambridge was arrested and charged for putting up hate stickers late in November 2016. Another supporter, from Bethnal Green in east London, was arrested for encouraging others to "Jo Cox" another MP, early in December 2016.

Burns would later go to court, with the evidence against him revealing he would lie in his bedroom for hours dreaming of another Holocaust for Jews and non-whites. One NF activist told us that Burns "wanked himself off to the movie Schindler's List." He'd been a regular figure on National Action activities for two years but had made few friends. He had a series of YouTube and Facebook accounts that called for Jews and other "sub-humans" to be exterminated. He was defended in court by the barrister Adrian Davies, a long time far-right activist and attendee of the London Forum. Davies had only recently seen another client, a man from Northern Ireland with alleged links to paramilitaries, sentenced to prison for attempting to intimidate former BNP leader Nick Griffin and his daughter over an unpaid debt.

So extreme was Burns's internet output that he was sentenced to four years' imprisonment in the New Year, which was later slightly reduced on appeal. Despite the horrific nature and extreme hatred in his output, the London Forum, the intellectual beast of the British far right, threw its entire weight behind him.

The anticipated but feared change approached, at last. The word was coming. The government was going to ban National Action.

CHAPTER 19: WE'RE GOING UNDERGROUND

"National Action have also received an enormous amount of free coverage in wake of the Prevent controversy and the sentencing of 'Brexit gunman' Tommy Mair. A group of crusty academics at the university of Birmingham have produced a document which has convinced dopey Sunday Times journalist Dipesh Gadher to state that National Action 'is likely to be proscribed as a terrorist organisation' - a comment that is below discussion on grounds of extreme ignorance and retardation, and all likelihood printed for sensationalism."

National Action, November Report, 30 November 2016.

Christopher Lythgoe sent out an order in November 2016 that rather forcibly reaffirmed him as leader, with Alex Davies as his deputy and Ben Raymond as the group's spokesman. Lythgoe even attached two pyramid graphs that showed how information was to flow up to the top of the organisation and orders were to flow down from his lofty perch. Raymond and Davies were also on bail at the time for allegedly putting up offensive stickers. Both would deny the charges and escape prosecution.

Having been humiliated and 'hazed' by the members, the confirmation that he was still "officer class" delighted the oddball Raymond. Lythgoe was certain a ban was coming and was already preparing the organisation for life underground. Maintaining Raymond in a public position was also an insurance that if a ban did come, and if there were any slip ups, groups such as HOPE not hate and the authorities would chase Raymond. As bold as his email was, sent to the nine members of the leadership (including Robbie Mullen), Lythgoe was now certain National Action was impenetrable and that nobody outside the organisation would have even heard of him.

Raymond however wasn't going to take talk about the banning of the group lying down. He pushed back against a lot of what Lythgoe was instructing others to do. Lythgoe may have been the leader, but NA was Raymond's baby.

On December 12 2016 it was announced National Action would be the first far-right organisation to be banned in the UK since the Second World War.

It was a considerable feat, considering that groups such as Combat 18 had avoided proscription in the 1990s, when those involved with that group had been behind at least two murders and an offshoot organisation had provided a home to the 1999 London nail bomber, David Copeland. When the polite email came from the Home Office giving advance notice of the proscription, and instructing NA how to disband, Raymond was crestfallen. There were tears and temper tantrums. Despite all the praise for genocide, Zack Davies' hammer and knife attack in Mould in 2015, rampant anti-Semitism and damage caused to Jewish monuments, as well as openly celebrating the death of Jo Cox MP and the constant preparations for a race war, it just seemed grossly unfair to ban Raymond's dandy youth project.

"The banning of National Action will not drive it "underground". The group already operates as such. Already the group's members are saying they will continue to organise and march en bloc together at other demonstrations, as like most people, they are still unclear as to how draconian the policing of the ban will be. Yesterday they were still encouraging people to get involved with them." – Duncan Cahill, 'A Look Behind The Scenes of National Action', HOPE not hate, 13 December 2016.

***

Raymond was bitter at Lythgoe's apparent happiness with the new ban. He insisted that National Action should seek a judicial review of the decision. He was laughed at. Again. The rest of the organisation was only notified on December 9, before the Home Office's decision was made public. Nothing was to be kept for posterity: no flags, masks, t-shirts (even the special ones NA sold claiming they'd "get girls wet"); no stickers, business cards... everything was to be dumped. Thousands of pounds was emptied from the group's PayPal account.

On December 10 Lythgoe and the rest of National Action in the north west of England headed to St Helens for one last public outing. Mullen recalled that day:

"There was something quite ceremonial about it. We were all there; Oggy (Oliver Ashton) even wore a massive swastika patch on his jumper for the world to see. We had loads of NA leaflets left so went out into St Helens to fly the flag, hand out leaflets and terrify a few people. I remember thinking, 'this time next week, this'll be a terrorist act. We'll all be terrorists!'"

In St Helens, Andy Clarke did most of the speaking through a loudhailer outside the Poundland store, shouting abuse about immigrants and Jews.

Footage of National Action's action from that day was later shown in court. Clarke implored shoppers to rise up against Merseyside's Jewish MPs, describing Jews and immigrants as vermin. NA had a good day out: no arrests were made and few people even bothered to listen to Clarke's homicidal and highly illegal rant:

***

"The primary objective short-term is to make sure people further down the NA hierarchy don't lose their heads. Some people have overactive imaginations. Some people like to talk pure shit. So if we see any hint of pessimism or hysteria in our ranks, we stamp it out pronto. Assure everyone that a) nothing's likely to happen and that, b) even if it did, we've got plans in place ready. Also reassure people that any ban will not be retroactive (it baffles me that some people think it would, but there you go...)"
– Christopher Lythgoe talking about Ben Raymond (among others) and the National Action ban, in an email to Robbie Mullen.

By mid-December, Raymond was becoming hysterical. As he would later claim in a bizarre lecture he recorded and distributed for the masses he believed he, and only he, had the intellectual capacity to go head-to-head with the Home Secretary over the issue of National Action's proscription. He implored the rest of the group to allow him to challenge the ban. The more they denied his requests, the more hysterical he became. On December 11, for some bizarre reason, he even wrote on the American Nazi site *Daily Stormer* denying claims NA was about to be banned as "totally fabricated." He pleaded with Lythgoe to form a political party, pleaded with Davies to talk to Lythgoe, pleaded with them all to fight the ban. Lythgoe and Davies both worried that Raymond's hysteria might become infectious. Lythgoe also knew a judicial review would mean he would himself come under scrutiny: and he never wanted to lead a political party. Raymond had to silenced.

Lythgoe wrote to the group:

"Make sure you maintain contact with ALL your members. Reassure them they will be personally OK as long as they don't promote NA from Friday on. Make sure they understand that the SUBSTANCE of NA is the people, our talents, the bonds between us, our ideas and our sustained force of will. All of that will continue into the future. We're just shedding one skin for another. All genuinely revolutionary movements in the past have needed to exist partly underground. These are exciting times."

Lythgoe's excitement about going underground was compounded by the thought of opening a headquarters in Warrington. Ban or no ban, every great terrorist organisation had to have a headquarters of some sort. Davies and

Raymond had visited a series of far-right 'social centres' during their visits to meet with other fascists in Europe and had reported back to Lythgoe about their potential. National Action's leader dreamed of having a little office where he could oversee the group train, encourage and instruct members. In that respect he was no different to Raymond: they both had great self-belief. Lythgoe wanted somewhere he could hold lectures, training seminars and where members could go to train under his guidance. More importantly, it would help break the tie with Jimmy Hey and his gym of black fighters.

Davies transferred £1,500 to Lythgoe in early January 2017 once it was confirmed he'd found the perfect property. Slovakian neo-Nazi Michal Trubini, based in Warrington, agreed to front the lease to protect Lythgoe from scrutiny. Listed as a workshop and office, the property sat in Warrington's Wellington Street, 668 x 62 feet, with a kitchen and toilet, for £380 per month. It was also approximately one mile from Warrington town centre and train station, making it easy for members to get to and from wherever they were travelling. A whole host of training materials arrived soon after they signed the lease: weights, crash mats, boxing gloves and kali sticks, along with benches, protective gloves and a small fridge. Everyone was expected to chip in for the costs. Money was guaranteed to arrive from the Spanish call centre run by a supporter the group now believe to have been an MI5 officer, and if the remaining 60 or so members could all chip in £5 a week each, the gym would be easily maintained.

National Action groups around the country were told to keep meeting but to change venues and locations. Its London branch was instructed to completely cease operations and not engage with supporters still keen on carrying out activities. Person B made plans to move himself and his girlfriend, the Miss Hitler competition runner-up, to a property in Sowerby Bridge in West Yorkshire, in preparation for the white homeland project.

Everybody would have to visit the gym if they wanted to remain a member of National Action. Only now, like in the movie *Fight Club*, the first rule of National Action was that nobody talked about National Action. Lythgoe made it clear that once you had been and trained in the gym, there was absolutely no leaving the group.

Raymond went back to work, busily trying to suggest new names for the group so that it could continue operating legally. He ran a host of ideas past the rest, as well as potential new logos. 'Thule Society' and 'Thule Society of Albion' were his unwelcome suggestions. Nobody was interested in reforming the group legally. From around the country members came. By bus, train and car, every Saturday morning up to a dozen National Action members would arrive, ferried to the gym by McCartney's taxi. The training became more intense and more violent, the urgency for race war becoming more immediate. McCartney's taxi also doubled up as an ambulance, ferrying blooded and injured recruits to the hospital and walk-in centres after a hard training session. There was no protective headgear; everyone was to hit and be hit hard. Mullen was training two to three times a week before retiring to the Friar Penketh pub for drinks. At these sessions, which had always been ideological seminars centred on Lythgoe's theories, it wasn't just the training that had hardened. Lythgoe, who kept a massive personal library of books on terror groups, now laid out the plans for the race war to everyone. And it wasn't just talk. On Saturdays NA activists and members dominated the upstairs of the pub, ferrying themselves and their leader's drinks up the stairs. Some only came once, could only afford to make the one pilgrimage, but for them that was enough. They met Lythgoe, got battered at the gym and then got pissed at the pub afterwards.

According to Lythgoe the war was imminent and the group had to be ready to fight it. In January 2017 Jack Coulson was in court. He'd built himself a pipe bomb, under instruction from National Action. Once he appeared in court Lythgoe sent word that everybody was to dump phones again, and immediately.

***

Under the conditions of the ban, just three people associated with National Action could constitute a meeting, as far as the Home Secretary's ban was concerned, which in turn could lead to up to ten years in prison. Some NA members still attended National Front or North West Infidel (NWI) activities, or those held by the London Forum or its Welsh offshoot, the South Wales Forum. Raymond in particular seemed desperate not to vanish from sight and began appearing all over the country, offering lectures on his NA experiences.

The National Action group in Scotland had a secret change of leader, wanting to take the group in an 'identitarian' direction (the identitarians were part of a European-wide network inspired by French far-right philosophers, which believed that a "great replacement" of whites was underway and argued for separating out racial groups). Raymond gladly designed their banners and flags: Scottish Dawn was born. It was a collection of NF, Scottish Defence League (SDL) and New British Union (NBU) rejects and misfits. HOPE not hate exposed the organisation along with ITN News, who we helped infiltrate a number of Scottish Dawn activities in Edinburgh and Alloa, as well as a training camp in England where Larry Nunn and Garron Helm spoke to an undercover reporter.

At HOPE not hate we'd always been aware of a schism in the group. We found more evidence and proof of it with Raymond's plans to launch a National Socialist Network with the same views and similar "cutting edge" designs and humour as the now-banned NA. We knew National Action had never stopped, despite the ban.

The first group to form and fall under this umbrella was to be Scottish Dawn. This wasn't approved of by Lythgoe and the others. In mid-January 2017 we were given access to an online folder containing thousands of sick and disturbing images Raymond had collected. We monitored the file as Raymond added more and more pictures, memes and designs, many of them creations of his evidently disturbed mind, frequently depicting acts of sexual violence against political opponents. Later that month, Raymond registered a domain name for 'National Socialist Network' with his details hidden behind a Panamanian front company. He also added new flag designs for the Scottish group in his secret files, and despite relative and deliberate silence from former other NA members online, we were directed to online chatter that seemed to confirm that NA was up and running again.

In early March 2017, Raymond added a series of designs to his files that he made for two protests to take place in Scotland. One was an anti-refugee protest along with the North East Infidels (from Sunderland), plus the NF, SDL and NBU on March 11 in Alloa. The other was the now annual White Pride demonstration that moves around the UK, having formerly been held in Manchester and Swansea and, this year, was going to be held on March 23 in Edinburgh.

While this was ongoing, ITN secured a ticket to a top secret training camp run by Legion, the martial arts and training group used by National Action in its early days. The ticket came from a source who'd agreed to pass information to HOPE not hate. The object of the operation was to catch National Action and its secret backers together in defiance of the government's proscription. There was an urgency to the operation and a belief that it was imperative to get ITN's man into the camp. Larry Nunn, acting as gatekeeper, wasn't convinced of our figure's authenticity and only satisfied his paranoia through a series of strained email exchanges right up till the 11th hour.

Confusingly, the Legion camp was also planned for the same day as the Alloa demonstration and, adding to a full diary of events and confusion, Raymond flew out to Lithuania for a far-right march through Vilnius the evening beforehand. National Action was spreading itself very thin.

In Bakewell, Derbyshire, fewer than a dozen people bothered to show up for the much vaunted "Legion martial arts club" camp. This was despite a rejuvenated and almost reinvented Mark Collett (a former BNP press officer who'd once been the ludicrous star of Channel 4's *Young, Nazi and Proud* documentary) being billed as a major contributor to the weekend. Former National Action deputy boss Alex Davies was supposed to attend but was believed to have gone to Lithuania instead of having to face Collett, and also, it transpires, being in the same room as Helm (whose high profile and belief that he was under constant surveillance had made him a pariah within the group).

When Helm arrived in Bakewell he was no longer the clean-shaven Nazi-saluting yob who once made national news. Instead, he shuffled around with long greasy hair and a wispy beard, looking unkempt. In almost every conversation, he exhibited a twisted appreciation of both political and domestic violence. Davies obviously thought the jail term of up to ten years if the group was caught meeting again wasn't worth serving for a bedraggled and increasingly paranoid former comrade.

Helm was later recorded talking about Jo Cox's murder, saying: "It's not our fault she was killed. I mean, she did have it coming." He later went on to say, unchallenged by others in the group: "I do think if you're committing an act of treason against, you know, your own ethnic group then by right you should be put to death." He also spoke of parts of the country being "infested" and, further, how some people in National Action no longer had any "tolerance of it."

In Alloa, meanwhile, Raymond's shiny new flags were flying high as masked former National Action members cockily mingled with fellow Nazis from the Scottish Defence League, the NEI and NF, unaware their ruse was about to be blown by HOPE not hate and ITN. When challenged by an ITN journalist if they were from NA, the masked individuals reacted violently.

After the weekend, ITN decided to pay Helm a home visit in Liverpool and put some of his comments about Cox's murder to him. Firstly, he demanded money. But when ITN refused payment, another man with him became agitated and threatened violence while Helm watched through a gap in the curtains from an upstairs bedroom. James Mac, a self-appointed "reverend" from the racist and bizarre 'Church of the Creator' later issued a video excusing Helm's comments and blaming them on his "immaturity".

It was clear that National Action was still active, but grievously split and disorganised. In HOPE not hate's April 2017 magazine, I wrote:

"But we know never to judge the danger of the far right and its violent adherents simply by size. Helm, for instance, who once wrote of dying for the cause in a bloody and violent sacrifice, is a resigned and shabby-looking former shadow of himself. Deserted by his friends and those who radicalised him, he's left sitting scruffy and desperate in an armchair looking resigned to another violent act."

***

Helm's exposure by ITN, talking about the murder of Jo Cox as well as making threatening noises about violence, upset Lythgoe. When we reported that he'd been willing to tell ITN everything for a few hundred pounds, things became increasingly difficult and dangerous for Helm inside National Action.

In March, Helm also tried to arrange a meeting with HOPE not hate. He wanted money for his story, about how he was the biggest Nazi in Britain. He demanded a double spread in our magazine and a feature story in a national newspaper, plus £400 for his time and a hotel in London for the night. For some reason he got cold feet and the meeting never happened. According to Mullen, £400 was what Helm had bragged to National Action that police had offered him to grass them all up. That, and the promise of a leg-up on the housing list. When the deal fell through, we were both relieved, concerned and determined to continue investigating NA, even though everybody else appeared to have stopped. More than anything, there was something particularly needy and desperate about Helm. And dangerous.

Raymond was also left more than a bit humiliated when his sick fantasies about raping and defecating on opponents were revealed by a HOPE not hate investigation published at the same time as ITN's programme. Yet he still tried to maintain his tenuous grip on events. In a tiresome and contradictory vlog he clearly believed that his new 'National Socialist Network', which he'd registered as a domain name in January, would be able to avoid the government's ban and act as an inspiration to National Action members.

"We had no property, membership lists, constitution, banks accounts… and copyright," he wrote. Yet despite contributing to the fund for the gym in Warrington, he had very little to do any more with the ideas and intentions of the organisation. He'd started this merry dance in helping to found National Action, but whether he liked it or not, he'd also set the course for a terrorist organisation that wanted little or nothing to do with him any more. Davies had even broke off their friendship and moved away from the digs he shared with Raymond. He simply could no longer think straight in the environment he shared with Raymond. Raymond, already a panicked night owl, paced the floor waiting for Davies to entertain him in what he knew would be long and arduous conversations. Davies, it seemed, threw all caution to the wind and decided to throw his lot in with Warrington.

Davies travelled to Warrington once the stories had broken about Raymond's new groups and that National Action members were still active, to discuss and show off that he and Raymond could still form organisations and that although there'd been obvious distractions, Davies remained cutting-edge and a paid-up member of the neo-Nazi elite.

Lythgoe was unimpressed. Raymond and Davies had behaved like amateurs and had been caught out. In Scotland, they'd been preparing to launch Scottish Dawn, and Davies had launched another offshoot, 'NS131', the 131 depicting the initials 'Anti-Capitalist Action' in the alphabet. Lythgoe questioned why Raymond still persisted with his silly arguments about the banning order; why had he helped the Scottish "traitors" start what had been a watered down version of National Action?

Davies bragged how he had joined in with hunt saboteurs who were oblivious to his history and politics. He also boasted he was dating a rich woman who wanted to fulfil his every desire, sexually and financially. As he told his wild stories about sex and champagne, the rest of National Action simply raised their eyebrows. When someone suggested the rich woman was actually a pensioner from the National Front, Davies flew into a rage, stammering and raising his squeaky voice. To Davies, popularity and revolutionary posture were everything but his fellow gang members were simply not interested any longer.

To keep in with Lythgoe, Davies handed over £500 in the pub when they met as part of a salary Lythgoe demanded.

***

Ostracised and increasingly regarded as untrustworthy, Raymond and Helm found solace and a listening post in the Midlands group, which was firmly now run by Alex Deakin, the man Raymond had forced the now chronically depressed Paul Hickman out for. This group, which included the jail bird Darren Fletcher, acted, according to evidence in court, with a "ruthlessness with which they were prepared to spread terror." Deakin was a comical figure at times, a man of self-deprecating stunts and humour, tall and gangly with thick glasses, but absolutely and completely dedicated to the group and its founder, Raymond. Nobody who survived the ban on the group could be anything other than completely and utterly dedicated from now on. Many had left, walked away – including former leader Ashley Bell. Those who remained behind, to continue the fight, knew what they were doing and where this was heading.

In building National Action secretly in the Midlands, Deakin reached out to Raymond and Helm who he saw as part of the 'originals' who'd first founded and promoted NA.

Operating on secret forums which included the North West members and Mullen, Deakin's group shed its skin for a series of names including 'Thule Combat League', 'Vanguard' and 'The Triple K Mafia', the triple K in homage to the Ku Klux Klan, and one assumes that group's most ardent admirer of that group, Darren Fletcher.

The Midlands group stockpiled weapons; shotguns, assault rifles, knives, ice picks, crossbows and longbows. It had a particular fetish for machetes and bomb-making manuals. Members included serving soldiers, most prominently the towering and intimidating Fin, Mikko Vehvilainen, a corporal in the British Army. Vehvilainen was so obsessed with stockpiling and recruiting members of the British Army into the group, he was nicknamed the 'Quartermaster'.

The Midlands group also recruited Adam Thomas from Banbury in Oxfordshire. Still only twenty when National Action was banned, he'd helped Fletcher and his wife settle back into the far right after his failure to make his life work away from it. Fletcher and Thomas went back years, despite their relative youth. They'd been a fixture on EDL and NF activities until Fletcher was sentenced to prison for his horrendous 'act' of lynching a golliwog on stage dressed in Ku Klux Klan robes. After that, still in his teens, Thomas, with his tiny frame and protruding teeth, had felt lost on his own. His head often seemed too large for his small, thin body, and he'd often been the target for bullies in the far right. At some stage he had a religious epiphany, that despite his Nazism, had sent him to live in Israel for a year.

Having left for Israel as a hardline Protestant, while there Thomas apparently went as far as to consider converting to Judaism. Whatever went wrong is not clear, but upon returning to England he quickly met a Portugese national nearly twice his age, Claudia Patatas, and fell in love with her. Unable to believe his good luck, Thomas suggested the pair move in together and start a family.

Thomas was introduced to Patatas by Garron Helm, who she would later tell police, she met doing "Pagan stuff." Using the name 'Sigrun', a Norse Goddess, Patatas dominated the Midlands' group's internal conversations and plans. Like a maternal hate preacher to the rest of the group, she'd often send directives or loaded suggestions they carry out attacks on random individuals. Some say she made sexually suggestive remarks, but Mullen claimed the rest of North West National Action excluded her from their chat groups because of her skin tone and a penchant for dressing in 1930s garb.

The home Patatas would make with Thomas in Banbury was like something out of a time warp. It had doilies on the table and neat, handmade swastika cushion covers. Dressed in long, 1930s style dresses and sensible shoes, Patatas hung pictures of Adolf Hitler from the walls of their home and they'd throw tea parties where Patatas would entertain their bemused guests by singing songs of the Hitler Youth whilst pouring tea from their finest bone china.

Patatas would claim to make her living as a photographer whilst she waited for Thomas to impregnate her with a child they both longed to name Adolf. Wanting to be the masculine figure Patatas wanted in her life, waif-like Thomas would apply to join the military. Despite a glowing reference from Corporal Vehvilainen, that he had an "exceptional display of patriotism which will positively influence his performance," Thomas was rejected.

Despite being turned down by the Army, he carried on his hardman bravado, dressing up in Ku Klux Klan robes and burning crosses.

Others in the group can for the moment only be identified by their chat group names, including 'Grandaddy terror'. Deakin directed the group by using the name 'Charles Garrison.' Despite the strict rules Lythgoe had laid down, Deakin would report to Raymond before he reported anything to Lythoge. As for London, that was abandoned.

***

It was at a meeting above the Friar Penkrith pub in late March when, wholly satisfied the bruising and battering being meted out to recruits was having the desired effect, Lythgoe, the self-proclaimed 'medieval king' finally set a timeline for terrorism. It wasn't without a small amount of fanfare.

Lythgoe was a lot of things; hygiene challenged, dour, gruff and angry, but he was no idiot. He'd studied and adored terrorism, mastered anonymity and secrecy. He recruited well, dominated others with weaker personalities, encouraged those who waivered or had self-doubts. Most of all he had an extremely hardened self-belief in his own leadership; he'd won a battle of wills with the founders of National Action, a hard battle but one that eventually saw them fall in behind him. He had enormous belief in his leadership qualities and also in his methodical way of driving NA further toward his dystopian vision. He'd been self-taught, done his A-Levels again, studied studiously, kept himself fit and aggressive. He now unveiled a three-step plan for terrorism.

CHAPTER 20: MEETING THE DEVIL, HIMSELF

"We should be blaming the Jewish vermin, the Jewish parasite, for coming to our country. They infest our country and worm their way into our government …
"They come into our country and worm their way into the media, the banking, foreign policy. They make us go and back the terrorist state of Israel against the Muslim state, trying to make the white man hate the Muslim. I say 'send the Muslims back to the Muslim states' and take our British soldiers out of the Middle East. We spend our times hating things that are only symptoms, let's go for the disease; let's go for the Jewish vermin.
"Yesterday we celebrated 70 years since the end of World War Two. What were we celebrating? Europeans killing Europeans for Jewish gain. What's that to celebrate? The Jewish vermin still infest our country, they still have over proportional influence.
0.5% of the population and look at how they turn up. Look at Simon Danczuk, the local MP. He's a Jew! He's a Jew! We spend our time looking at the little things, you know, we're against feminism, we're against Islam. You know, we're against the bankers. What's the common thing that comes up? It's run by Jews and everybody's scared to say it because as soon as you mention the Jews the Jews come forward and go 'what about the Holocaust?'
"In Nazi occupied Europe there were only five million Jews, but six million Jews died and the population increased! Do your bloody maths!! The Jews weren't killed, they were put in camps where they belonged so they can work and pay back the Europeans that were robbed by the Jewish bankers.
"It's about time we started pointing the finger at the real enemy. It's not the Muslims, it's not the ethnics, it is the bankers and the bankers are JEWS!"

Jack Renshaw on the loudhailer in Rochdale, June 2015.

J ack Renshaw had been arrested in January 2017 for his speeches on the beach at Blackpool and the Yorkshire Forum in March 2016. HOPE not hate had campaigned to have him prosecuted for inciting racial hatred.

It was seen, not as a silly lad being prosecuted for horrendous speeches, but as more evidence, that apparently, a secretive coven of Jews at the direction of HOPE not hate were directing the government to clamp down on National Action. We'd only "cautiously" welcomed their banning, but it didn't matter.

Robbie Mullen was about to commit the far right's cardinal sin. He was thinking about contacting HOPE not hate with some information. He'd been weighing it up and it had been gnawing away at him for some while.

HOPE not hate makes no secret that we have people operating inside these networks. Some who pass us information even pre-dated the official formation of our organisation.

Liverpool's notorious fascist Joe Owens dedicated hours of his laborious YouTube lectures issuing warnings about HOPE not hate spies. He seemed to suspect everybody but himself of this 'heinous' crime. Many of our revelations were carried, usually just in part, in our *Insider's Blog*. The *really* good information we often hold back.

The reasons people "turn" or pass information are always hotly debated and discussed by the far-right. Do people turn for money? Are they corrupted or compromised by HOPE not hate operatives? The theories and the realities varied. In truth, some people came to us just once; others returned for a while. Some wanted help getting out and away from a life of hate, while others, in a state of confusion, stay for years. There's rarely a Damascus moment so many people long to hear about.

Some of those who pass information are decent people with interesting lives and horrendous problems and issues. Others would sell their grandmothers for fifty quid. Passing information to us is worse than grassing to the cops in the eyes of many fascists. If caught in the act, it could be a potentially deadly mistake to make. But these people are vitally important, too, for the antifascist effort. Moles inside the far right played a huge role in disrupting the BNP's electoral push in 2009-2010, and a wholly destructive final role in mortally wounding the NF. There was no serious group, frustratingly aside from National Action, where we had nobody giving us information. We'd had bits and bobs, 'flings' and 'clinches' if you will, but nothing and nobody of substance inside NA.

We're not easily frustrated people so we knew, well hoped, it'd be a matter of it happening eventually. Mullen saw HOPE not hate as a huge part of that "bubble" in which he operated. We were a worthy enemy, we were the people everyone hated.

Arrested in January 2017, for his notorious speeches in Blackpool and Leeds the previous year, Renshaw claimed HOPE not hate had run a "vicious campaign stirring up the Jews to pressure their friends in the government to persecute" him. We were also the people Ben Raymond constantly complained about, frustrating him time and again, and mocking him and disrupting his and National Action's plans.

To Mullen we represented everything he hated and feared: confidence, operating in secrecy, proud of multicultural Britain and completely dedicated to the destruction of fascism. But he also saw in us an escape route: away from National Action and away from the constant buzz of hatred. His phone was constantly coughing out notifications of new messages, new instructions and new conversations as NA moved further and further into the wilderness. He had to keep dumping one phone for another as the mantra demanded. He also had to keep training and attending the sessions in the Friar Penketh pub with NA leader Christopher Lythgoe. It was just like a cult. The fun had gone, the game of cat and mouse with the rest of the world was now tiresome and dangerous. His body ached from the constant pounding of fists, the constant head jam of the group's murderous desires.

More than anything was the worry that someone in National Action was actually going to kill somebody. There's little point raking over the endless signs that this was inevitable; Mullen had felt and known it, had ignored it, and hung in long enough with that constant reality from day one, from the moment he had first tuned in to NA and dropped out of his wholly unrewarding previous existence. He'd sat in and listened to, contributed to, the inner thoughts of NA. The darkness of the internet where they hid undetected or the disgusting desires of his comrade who wanted to rape and murder just about anyone they disagreed with. He'd stomached the debauchery, the lusting and the disgusting. Mullen had held on in there, because that's where he wanted to belong. "Have you ever just wished your friends were a little bit more normal?" he once asked.

At the time Mullen was unknown to anyone outside the very small circle inside the gang. Few inside the group even knew his real name, such was the secrecy they encouraged. He was known to Lythgoe and Raymond and maybe a couple of others, but to others inside the group he was the North West Organiser, 'North West Robbie'. Even the police didn't know his real name. The hits HOPE not hate had made against NA post-proscription had shaken many of them. Maybe Raymond was to blame for his own stupidity – and Renshaw most certainly was – but we'd got close enough to cause a panic by highlighting their ongoing endeavours. Mullen had seen a hurried, maddening and desperate edge creeping in to the small circle.

Terrorism now felt imminent. Lythgoe had revealed his plans in the pub in Warrington. National Action was gearing up to do something "spectacular". Theories became plans, plans were sketched, scenarios discussed upstairs at the Friar Penketh. Small groups of people, often the minority of a movement, get to take power through violence. Lythgoe could cite the examples – the Bolsheviks who took control of the Soviet Union, were a prime example. They murdered friends, enemies and even allies until they took the control.

***

"A student will admit making and then planting a ball bearing bomb on a London tube train, a court heard. Damon Smith, 19, left a 'viable improvised explosive device' on a Jubilee Line Underground train at North Greenwich Tube station on 20 October. The black Adidas bag containing the bomb was left on the train between Southwark and London Bridge.

"Two concerned members of the public spotted it and alerted the driver at North Greenwich station. Both the train and platform at North Greenwich were evacuated and the device was then made safe by a snipping a wire."
– Court News, 1 March 2017.

With the Warrington gym up and running, Lythgoe was there every day sitting in the office and admiring the operation. Some of Warrington's more unhinged types, those who used to be dissuaded, were encouraged to join the group, or at least take advantage of the gym. Two notorious getaway drivers for Cheshire drug dealers regularly began appearing at the gym. "They'll be useful...," said Lythgoe mysteriously. "They'll do just about fucking anything we ask them."

Lythgoe believed that now National Action was illegal, 2017 would be the year when it set in motion the great fightback: the beginning of the race war. The state was as good as promising more Islamist terror attacks were to come. When, not if, the attacks started, NA would throw one back into the mix. Based on NA's size, Lythgoe believed they could answer every three Jihadist bombs with an action of their own, inspiring the desperate and dateless to follow their lead.

The Jihadists were not classical terrorists. Anyone could just go and carry out a Jihadi attack, he believed. The same could be said of National Action, with its White Jihad. The stunning, startling video of last year had been as good as any ISIS propaganda video. Obviously NA couldn't put beheadings and bombings on their recruitment video, but as a call to arms to all the sad little boys who watched, it was emotive and brilliant. The great words, the narrative, the urgent tones of Nicholas Waugh's speech set to the vision of Britain's immigrant crisis, was going to inspire people, somewhere, to strike back. And it wasn't a war against Muslims or Islam. They'd be casualties, for sure, but this race war would be against the state and those who owned it. As Renshaw had laid out in another wholly illegal speech in Rochdale in 2015, when the White Jihad theory was developing, "It's not the Muslims, it's not the ethnics, it *is* the bankers and the bankers are JEWS!"

On March 19 the Midlands group hosted a social in Sutton Coldfield which was listed for all regions to attend. Although the idea was to bury the hatchet and any differences between National Action's two biggest groups, there was a fall out over the presence of Patatas who the North West group had decided was non-white.

The Midlands group discussed between them whether they wanted Helm, ostracised as he was from the North West group, to join them. In the ensuing debate about Garron Helm's associations with the occult and the sex-offending Satanist Ryan Fleming, the consensus was best summed up with the line "age is just a number." Alex Deakin, who led the Midlands group, created some half a dozen different chat rooms and groups for his members to communicate to each other at varying degrees of rank and hierarchy. The big decisions were taken in the 'Vanguard' group for the most dedicated.

The first terror attack of 2017 took place on March 22. Six people, including the attacker, died and 50 more injured on Westminster Bridge and outside the Houses of Parliament in London. Khalid Masood mounted the pavement in a hired car and drove into pedestrians. He then ran towards Parliament and stabbed a police officer to death, before being shot dead by other police officers. For Mullen, it was the straw that broke the camel's back:

> *"I remember the real excitement when it happened. Internally we mocked those mourning and the dead. It was just another dead cop and a few tourists. There was already so much going on, the gym was so busy with people coming in and out, and what with the HOPE not hate exposés, it was almost breathless. We knew more was to come: it was as if the timer had been set for our own foray into the game.*
>
> *"I had to get the fuck out. I was surrounded. It felt like I was drowning and I could not breathe. We had a meeting that night [after the Westminster Bridge attack] at the gym and everyone just seemed to be so happy."*

An email arrived in my inbox in April. It was claiming National Action had a new leader and were operating out of a gym in Warrington. The email was from someone calling themselves Lucas Harrison. I'd never heard of him. Still, it was a bit more interesting than the Flat Earth conspiracy emails and death threats I usually receive. I got on the phone to Manchester with the details, which included a link to the advert NA had themselves answered to rent the property. A 'bagman' was despatched to Warrington to check out the gym and sure enough, shortly before 3pm, Lythgoe was seen entering the building with a large box.

"Looks like fash, but I've never seen him before," the bagman reported. Of course not, these fuckers always wear masks. Lucas Harrison was now going to be my best friend. I just had to win his or her trust.

There'd been so much excitement in National Action, so much mistrust and suspicion that an encrypted email to the leadership from Deakin (who signed himself off as 'Charles Garrison') early in May was ignored. It was both a warning and an apology, that he'd been arrested in relation to putting up some stickers at Aston University the year before, when NA was still legal. He'd also deleted none of his messages. For some reason, Lythgoe chose to ignore it, possibly to punish Deakin for insolence, possibly because he did not accurately realise just how much information Deakin hadn't deleted and possibly further, how much terrorism the Midlands group was invested in. Or, maybe because it was so strangely worded:

> *"On the morning of May 4th at 7:30 West Mids CTU came to my parents house with a warrant and seized the following; my computer, hard-drive, various forms of ID and some leaflets I forgot were in my book box. That night I was staying at a friends house and at 9:45 they let themselves into his apartment. I was intoxicated at the time and so acted irrationally by hiding in an airing cupboard where they found me, along with my phone and wallet concealed below floorboards, along with my coat and bag which I matches with the items I was wearing the CCTV footage. As I wasn't at home during the raid they were able to seize the computer and hard-drive with everything therein (includes photos of activism as well as some deep buried and forgotten pdfs on revolutionary warfare that got downloaded as part of a large folder that I haven't looked through). I've deleted my wire insta and fb accounts though I can't delete my telegram (anyone who has been in my region chat knows how fucking thick they are), seized phone is full of texts that will mark me as an organiser. I was found due to undeleted texts that were on Garry's phone. I'd advise you to tell everyone in the region to get new sim cards and block me on all platforms. Andy Malek called me yesterday and said he'll look over the case and get back to me on Monday, bail conditions are as follows: Excluded for bham city centre, required to live and sleep at my parents house till bail date, can't talk to following people: Chad, Dean, Garry Paul Hickman. Bail date is June 1st at 7pm after which I will almost certainly be charged. I need to call Ben if you have his phone number just to talk over this. There's probably stuff I missed and will go over at a later point. I can understand if you despise me for this sloppiness (it really couldn't have been any worse if I tried) but I really need you to get back to me as soon as possible and advise me on what to do. Charles"*

***

As painful and painstaking as it was, Robbie Mullen – who'd been the mysterious Lucas Harrison – was on the first train out of Liverpool after rush hour on May 18. I told him he could sit anywhere on the train, but it would be busy and I'd booked him a nice window seat and a table. Watching him were a bagman and bagwoman, supposed young lovers on a day trip to London. He took the seat booked for him and played with his phone for the whole journey. HOPE not hate's intelligence budget for the month of May was already out the window, but this was important.

In building trust over the previous few weeks I'd got to like Mullen, but there was absolutely no record or trace of him anywhere. He seemed to have vanished after being born.

According to the defence team at a trial of alleged National Action members and Jack Renshaw at the Old Bailey in June 2018, Mullen and I had exchanged more than 50 text messages the day before he arrived in London. They found that suspicious, but they'd never had to convince a young man he'd be safe in their care and neither did they have the worry he might be leading a team of knife-wielding fascists into a meeting.

From Euston station in London, Mullen was picked up and monitored until he was directed into a waiting taxi and off for lunch with me. Over four hours he told me everything he knew about National Action. We'd been closer than most, but we were still a long way off the proverbial cigar. Aside from a few names that were public, there was a whole army of bedroom-dwelling perverts and wannabe terrorists preparing for race war. Some of the information was extreme. In person, Mullen was large, about six foot with a round face and wispy hairs spouting from his chin and rosy cheeks. He spoke softy, grinned occasionally but seemed, well, a little dead inside. I remembered the feeling myself from a similar meeting I'd had over 25 years before, when I exited the far right.

Having told us what was going on and warning about the potential for terrorism, there was no way we were going to let Mullen go off into the night. "I ain't going to the police," he insisted in a high-pitched Scouse accent. "If you involve the police, I'll fucking walk. I'm not a police grass!"

National Action had a whole team in their bedrooms at home attempting to hack our emails, hack our websites, find out where we lived and who our partners, mothers and fathers were. They'd even enlisted help from those on the forum 4Chan and jihadi hackers. "Everyone hates you," Mullen told us matter of factly. But I liked the kid. He was 23 and very smart. He had opinions – not all of them particularly great ones – but the one thing that stuck in my mind from that meeting was that he didn't want anybody to get murdered and he certainly didn't want to do the murdering himself.

"It'll be the Jews" he said. "If it happens, NA will probably target a synagogue, somewhere that gets blown up, probably in Manchester or Liverpool. That way you'll all think the Muslims did it and then the race war will start."

It just seemed as simple to him as that and it was going to happen some day soon. "We're just waiting for another bomb or two from the other side. I want the fuck out. I want the fuck out of this group."

I scheduled our next meeting for late May, in Manchester. Between the two meetings I got a flavour as to just how furious and constant the exchanges were on the messaging groups National Action used. Mullen relayed message after message as he could find them and access them before they'd self-delete. Some of the messages were just so banal; we were dealing after all, with a generation that recorded for posterity with their friends every bowel movement and daft thought via social media and apps. The North West's internal messages were the most intense and angry. The leadership operated under the name of a children's entertainer made famous by YouTube. They called it the 'PewDiePie fanclub' in his honour. Because Raymond was on the group (as 'Bloodninja 88') the messages wouldn't stop even in the very early hours of the morning. There I got a real flavour just how childish and insecure Raymond was. He'd write long, monotonous messages, thoughts and instructions that rarely got replied to. To circumvent Raymond's constant distractions, the leadership operated also on a number of other chat groups.

What Mullen wanted seemed very simple –to him. If HOPE not hate could expose the group, maybe fit some cameras in the gym, it would all collapse. It would be as easy as that, he thought. Then, he could just go about his everyday life unscathed. Maybe there would be some arrests, sure, but HOPE not hate were smart and National Action paranoid, so between the two groups, it should be enough to halt everything. I remember thinking, "some of those people could get ten years under the law" but Mullen didn't seem so sure. He also firmly believed that any terrorist plot or plans would simply be thwarted because the police would catch them at it, would discover any preparations being made. He didn't want his friends locked up; he just wanted them to stop planning to kill people. Was that too much to ask?

Mullen felt he couldn't just walk away from National Action, either. I'd seen that and even felt it, before. NA had become the most dominating feature in his life, more important than work to him. He'd entered into a bond and an arrangement that wouldn't let him go. It scared him. Attendance at each and every meeting wasn't expected; it was demanded. Every member could be and was when necessary, picked up from and dropped back at home. Mullen's little house was also used for sleepovers by trusted members visiting from elsewhere. Every part of his life, his confidence, his friends and even his isolation, he owed to them.

Just after our meal and a walk in the warm evening, I made my way back to the hotel. I was thinking we could get Mullen out of the group and totally destroy National Action while doing it. We could write one of those great exposés before "handing a dossier over to the police" in *News of the World* style. While I was having my evening daydream, Salman Abedi was walking into the Manchester Arena to detonate an explosive at an Ariana Grande concert, killing 22 people. It was a fucking horrendous night. National Action were delighted.

The next Saturday, May 27, National Action organised a get-together. It was a special occasion. Lythgoe instructed a dozen of the group to travel into Manchester to admire the handiwork of the jihadi bomber who'd torn such a hole in the lives of ordinary Mancunians. By now, I was receiving every communication that Mullen was party to. The most active was the 'Pewdepie Fanclub' maintaining their liking for children and the childish. The messages were endless, day and night.

Mountains of flowers and press photographers crowded Manchester Arena and the surrounding city centre as Lythgoe, Mullen, Hankinson, Rekki and a few others strolled along with grins etched on their faces. For many of them, it was a brilliant spectacle: this was what a bomb did. The whole group took great delight in the misery and tears. Lythgoe said nothing, just gave a cold stare.

When they returned to their headquarters in Warrington, Lythgoe was strangely quiet for the rest of day.

***

For the next few weeks I concentrated on building a relationship with Mullen, regularly staying in Manchester or Liverpool as we went long into the night poring over photographs, videos and other outpourings from the group.

The constant buzzing of his phone never stopped as emails and messages from National Action continued to mount. The challenge was to capture them before they disappeared into the ether. The group shared everything, from what they had for breakfast to who they wanted to rape and murder.

Mullen was always honest as far as I could tell but not in the slightest introspective. He was protective of his posh friend, Matthew Hankinson, but Hankinson shared none of his doubts about murder and terrorism. It was a familiar situation. When trying to leave the far right myself years before, I tried to cling onto a friendship with a man who was intent on shipping guns to Northern Ireland.

The same month, Wayne Bell from Castleford, 36, was sent to appear at the Old Bailey on two offences of stirring racial hatred and three counts of criminal damage. Mullen was crest fallen; as psychopathic neo-Nazis go, Bell had been one of the 'nicer' ones. In the same month, Helm was also to face court over comments he had made about a person on Twitter. There was a mood, that with the arrests of National Action personnel and the terror attacks, the crisis that so worried Mullen, was coming together. But by the same respect, there were no concrete plans, either. And anyway, all indications were that Helm was so out of favour with the group, they were hoping quite openly he would top himself.

And then the unexpected happened: as National Action was concerned with its own watching and waiting game, their American friends, Atomwaffen Division (AWD), suffered the humiliation of one of their number shooting and killing two other members.

AWD had formed on the Nazi web forum 'Iron March' around the same time Raymond was bombarding the forum with inflated updates on the early progress of National Action. In many ways, AWD formed in homage to NA and the idea they could bend every starched and conservative rule dominating the higher echelons of both the American and UK far-right movement. The shooter had apparently converted to Islam as part of their shared White Jihad idealism. Having converted to Islam, something obviously went wrong. As they were polishing their firearms one evening, 18-year-old convert Devon Arthurs murdered the other two neo-Nazis for making anti-Muslim comments.

And it wasn't just jihadism they shared an interest in with National Action. One of AWD's leaders used the username 'Rape' on internet forums and similarly as they, too, thrashed around with religion and spiritualism, they found themselves heavily into the idea of occult rituals and child abuse. Although there was plenty already in the American Nazi movement's annuals about such, the group studied books by the British Satanic organisation, Order of Nine Angles (O9A) which also influenced both Helm and the sex offender Fleming.

Like everything else, the Americans took National Action's fixations and interests to the next level. AWD encouraged its members – believed to be fewer than 100 – to read the book *Iron Gates,* which is part of the underground gore porn genre. Among other things, the book's been accused of fixating on murdering a child in front of its mother, and other sexual violence and rape scenarios. Whether it was to dehumanise its adherents for the future race war isn't clear, but it certainly wasn't occupying the genre for the good of the white race. Atomwaffen Divison's leader, Brandon Russell, who was Devon Arthurs' roommate, was later found in possession of multiple materials meant to build explosives, including a lethal bomb-making chemical, hexamethylene triperoxide diamine which FBI and Tampa Police Department officers found in the garage. Despite this, Russell would be released on bail, allowing him to attempt firing a mortar at a nuclear power plant.

National Action and AWD had been more than internet buddies. Their members had shared emails and been web friends. Brandon Russell had visited NA two years previously, in July 2015. He was meant to meet just Person B, who it appears unbeknown to Raymond, was a moderator on Iron March. Person B bitterly complained that Raymond gatecrashed the meeting to get a 'selfie' of themselves together. They too were fans of self-fulfilling genocide.

National Action links to AWD had been far deeper than we'd imagined. Neither Raymond nor Person B were interviewed by the British police or the FBI about what exactly they'd discussed on Russell's trip to London.

AWD had, obviously, been more extreme than National Action. They had more guns for a start, but like NA, made no secret of their murderous desires and their interest in rape and child abuse. Rather than hide the fact he had met with Russell in London, Raymond advertised it on his Facebook page. He was, apparently, keenly anticipating a visit from the FBI, but nothing happened. Infuriatingly for Raymond it went ignored other than by HOPE not hate with the story running on our website. With so much tension and excitement, nobody paid enough attention to a short email from Alex Deakin from the

Midlands, informing them he'd been arrested for stickers he'd put out around Aston University the year before.

On June 3, seven people were killed and 48 injured when a white van was driven into pedestrians on London Bridge allowing three men to get out and begin randomly attacking shoppers, pedestrians and diners in a busy, cosmopolitan part of London. Mullen and I rung each other immediately the news broke. There'd been no word from Lythgoe yet, but people inside the group were growing excited and expectant.

***

"Police are appealing for information after two arson attacks at restaurants in Sedgley, Prestwich. The first incident happened at Taam Restaurant on Bury New Road shortly before midnight on Friday 2 June 2017 when two offenders approached and threw a milk carton filled with petrol and a lit rag at the premises.The makeshift petrol container failed to ignite before one of the offenders threw a large stone at the front window, smashing it in the process.

"The second happened at around 3:30am on Tuesday 6 June when the offenders approached J S Restaurant on Kings Road and forced open a window before pouring accelerant inside and lighting it. "The fire service was called and was able to put the fire out before any serious damage could be done to the property. On both occasions the restaurants were closed and no-one was injured in either of the attacks. Police in Bury have launched an investigation and initial enquiries suggest the attacks are linked; however, the motive for the attacks isn't clear." – Police appeal for information after two arsons in Sedgley, Greater Manchester Police, 6 June 2017.

With Mullen's help, we were really beginning to upset National Action. Our objective was to increase suspicion and ramp up their already-high levels of paranoia. Small, subtle remarks about the group and the individuals within it were fed into our blogs, making some of their members suddenly sit up and take notice. The finger of suspicion immediately fell on the loud-mouthed Helm. In normal circumstances that would suit us immensely, but National Action had the very real potential to kill him. We had to cool it a bit.

Lythgoe had worried about a story we did about a National Action member joining the army, way before Mullen came to work for HOPE not hate earlier in the year. Unbeknown to Mullen, the idea to recruit into or recruit from the army was already afoot in the (in)capable hands of NA's people in the Midlands. The story was written after we came across the information by chance. It was the first time Lythgoe had ever been worried, but as nothing else failed and the recruit was again, not accepted, he saw it for what it was: a coincidence.

Mullen and I were now meeting two or three times a week. His mood had lightened dramatically. Our conversations and exchanges between meetings were done almost completely by encryption. No-one would ever know we'd met, were meeting or were in communication. By June, Mullen could even order a fairly decent Indian banquet in Liverpool, London and Manchester. But still we met in strict secrecy, jumping in and out of taxis and leaving places by separate doors. We had contingency plans were someone he knew to walk into a restaurant, park, library, pub or bar where we were meeting. It involved discreetly leaving, or pretending not to know each other, right through to fighting to the death over a hot plate of chicken Madras.

We kept the secret Warrington gym/headquarters story under wraps, mainly because it was good to keep the proverbial gunpowder dry. I planned that the headquarters would one day form the crux of our major exposé. The only mildly troubling thing about Mullen was that he'd made no plans for the future, didn't want to move on or away. He didn't even have ungodly or unearthly desires. "You're about the one normal person I know," he said once. "And I ain't too certain you're all *that* normal, either."

We waited and waited for Lythgoe to give the order or even the intention for a terrorist style reprisal for the three Islamist attacks. According to Mullen, Lythgoe had taken to sitting in silence, stewing in the pub with the others, who appeared to be sitting in anticipation of a big announcement. Nothing was forthcoming. Then, on June 19, Darren Osborne, 47, from Cardiff, drove to Finsbury Park Mosque in north London in a hired van, mounted the pavement and drove into worshippers close to the Muslim Welfare House as several people gathered to help a man who had earlier collapsed. The man, Makram Ali, died after he was run over by Osborne's van; several others were severely injured.

Met Police Commissioner Cressida Dick said the incident in north London was "quite clearly an attack on Muslims", and the community would now see more police, including armed officers, in the area, "particularly around religious establishments".

Osborne had been rapidly radicalised, having gorged on extremist material over the internet, particularly from EDL founder and serial criminal Stephen Lennon (known to most as 'Tommy Robinson') and the anti-Muslim fanatics of Britain First. A violent drunk and increasingly a loner, ostracised by family and friends due to his behaviour, Osborne wanted to kill either the Labour leader Jeremy Corbyn or Muslims. It was a terrorist attack, and he handed himself in similarly to Zack Davies, saying "job done" as police took him into custody.

Osborne was giving what he thought was pay back for Islamic grooming gangs and Islamist terror attacks. The man he killed, Makram Ali, 51, was involved in neither grooming nor terrorism. It took Osborne just three weeks on the internet, distressed and confused, to convince himself that a Muslim or Muslims had to die. He was also quite prepared to die himself if need be.

There was never any evidence to suggest Osborne had accessed National Action materials online, but his actions were predicted it would seem, by Lythgoe. This is the dream. This is the reason for all the propaganda violent fascists send out into the world. Either spoken, written or simply by suggestion, it's a violent ideology that encourages panic and the panicked to then act out on it.

Maybe Lythgoe had a time limit where he was waiting for someone like Osborne to appear? Osborne may not have accessed National Action materials, but the same couldn't be said of Ethan Stables, 19, who appeared at court the same month after he planned a massacre at an LGBT event at the New Empire bar, in Barrow-in-Furness, Cumbria. Finally given an indefinite hospital order in 2018, his trial heard he made "awful and disgusting" posts on neo-Nazi chat rooms, revealing his "deep-seated hatred of black, Jewish, Muslim and especially gay people". Stables lived like most NA members. In his filthy rented flat, police found weapons including an axe, three knives, a machete and a kendo stick (a wooden practice sword), plus materials to make a pipe bomb.

According to Mullen, Stables fitted exactly the profile of a young man the group had been in contact with during 2016, but had rejected his full membership because he was "too rural" for their tastes and they feared they could not control him.

"With both Osborne and Stables the group were part delighted and part disappointed. I think the feeling was with Stables he had been a bit too daft, like Zack Davies, and it was another missed opportunity. But with Osborne, whether NA influenced him or not, it proved like with Thomas Mair, there were people who would do the killing if they were just pushed in the right direction. I know it's sick. Osborne driving into the crowd outside the mosque gave everyone a lift and it also meant we could 'stand down' for the moment.". – Robbie Mullen

At the end of June 2017, I took a long deserved holiday.

CHAPTER 21: "DON'T FUCK IT UP"

"The Gladius Machete features the classic guard and ball shaped pommel of years gone by, but with the added strength and durability found with full-tang construction and modern materials. We use high-impact Polypropylene for our handle, making it almost impervious to the elements and rugged beyond belief. The Gladius Machete comes complete with a sturdy Cor-Ex^a sheath and belt loop for easy of carry and use."

– coldsteel.com advertisement.

J ack Renshaw had been arrested in January 2017 for his two speeches in Blackpool and Leeds in 2016, in which he called for violence against Jews and immigrants.

Unbeknownst to his comrades, he'd also been reported to police for grooming children by an unnamed relative in February. In the course of the police investigation evidence was found on four different phones that he'd been attempting to persuade young boys to spend the night with him. Renshaw had offered two boys cash and pizza to perform a variety of sexual acts. In February 2017 he was informed that he was under investigation for child exploitation, as well as his race-hate charges.

His friends in National Action were aware Renshaw had been forbidden from contact with children, but misunderstood it to mean he was regarded as a radicalisation danger. Yet his lust for boys was extreme. Using the name Randy Marsh ("because you make me randy") his internet search interests centred around finding young boys who liked to be or were forced to be penetrated. As well as sending pictures of himself to two youngsters he met online, his internet searches were for terms like "young boys being bummed."

In May 2017, Renshaw was formally notified he was likely be charged on two counts of grooming. Trying to play for time, he told NA the police investigation into his speeches was trying to make him look like a paedophile. Everyone sympathised with him, but he was becoming awfully morbid on his Facebook account. "It will soon all be over," he wrote. Later in the same month, a meeting was held in the Midlands about "moving people".

Renshaw was stewing over what life would be like with a conviction for child grooming. His reputation for tough speeches and advocating the hunting down of Jews and immigrants would be all but forgotten. He'd be a friendless pariah and would spend years stuck in prison on the 'nonces' wing, with no visitors to bring him fan mail from fellow Nazis on the outside.

As I flew off on holiday in late June, I told Robbie Mullen I'd bring him back a stick of rock and 200 Benson & Hedges. He seemed rather under-impressed by the idea of toothache and lung cancer. I asked him and the others who passed information to try not to call me unless it was an absolute emergency. My other half had even stipulated, given the recent intensity and days away because of work, there were to be no phone calls from HOPE not hate, Nick Lowles "or any Nazis who have run out of bog roll at 2am" while we took a rare holiday together.

On Saturday July 1, just after 10pm, my phone pinged. It was Mullen. "Call me ASAP," the message read. Shamefully, I collapsed on my bed thinking it could wait until morning.

At 6am I rang Mullen and our lives changed on the spot.

The previous day Jack Renshaw had met with three people in Liverpool. From there he travelled to Warrington for the evening, ringing an assembled cast and crew to make sure they were in their usual spot at the Friar Penketh pub, where National Action lead Christopher Lythgoe held his briefings. Renshaw had been trying to initiate this meeting for a week.

Renshaw joined Mullen, Lythgoe, Matthew Hankinson, Andrew Clarke and Garron Helm, who arrived on Renshaw's invitation. It would transpire that Renshaw's Liverpool meeting had been with Claudia Patatas, Adam Thomas, and Helm.

There was little messing about. Flashing his credit cards (he'd used a taxi to transport him from Liverpool to Warrington) Renshaw told the group he had bought a machete – an 18-inch near-sword – and was going to murder his local MP Rosie Cooper, a British Labour Party politician who was first elected as the Member of Parliament for West Lancashire in 2005.

He'd had enough, he said. He wanted to send a message that the "dog was going to bite back". He, the dog, had been poked too many times and Rosie Cooper would go the same way as Jo Cox. The group sat impassively as the small, almost delicate looking young man spoke. Jack Renshaw, the weird creature that had unleased some of the most vile tirades imaginable against Jews in his most recent past, told them that as well as killing Cooper, he would kill the female police officer investigating him for child sexual offences (though he omitted details of the charges he was facing).

He had it all planned out. He knew where to find Cooper, had even searched online how to kill her and how long it would take her to bleed to death. He would surprise and take her as a hostage, and after attacking her would then demand that his investigating officer, Victoria Henderson, should be sent in to negotiate with him. He would then kill Henderson before dying at the hands of other police officers, who he hoped would shoot him as he ran at them wearing a fake suicide vest.

Mullen claimed the group quibbled why he would only wear a fake suicide vest. They could discuss it later, he said, but, Mullen claims they were they up for it. He even offered to do a Jihadi-style video for the occasion of murder, murder, death by cop.

Rather than voice outrage or tell him not to go ahead, Mullen would tell the Old Bailey the group discussed whether it would not be better to kill Amber Rudd, the Home Secretary, who'd banned National Action. Renshaw rejected the idea. For one, as a former Home Secretary Rudd would have too much security around her, plus his heart was set on Cooper, whose movements he could easily monitor and access as early as the next few days.

Hankinson suggested instead of the laborious task of having to manually kill two women, wouldn't it be better for Renshaw to carry out an attack in a synagogue? At this point Mullen interjected, protesting there would most likely be children inside. Renshaw turned sharply. "Their kids are still vermin," he said. "You don't say 'oh look, it's just baby vermin, do you?' Vermin is vermin and has to die."

Renshaw's 18-inch Gladius machete was specifically chosen for the task of cutting through human bone and flesh. He'd even seen an example of the machete's prowess when it was used to cut through a pig at a trade show when he worked in a DIY shop. For three hours the group discussed Renshaw's incredible plot. Once he had convinced them he could carry out the murders and explained how much effort he had put into researching them, it seemed like the job was done. No choreography, no Raymond demanding an edgy backdrop, no face masks.

Renshaw had prepared everything needed to carry out the murder and as Mullen and the Crown Prosecution Service saw it, he wanted permission to do it in the name of National Action. It was at this point Mullen claimed Lythgoe uttered the immortal words "Don't fuck it up."

Having learned of his murderous plans, the group decided to go to a nightclub to get Renshaw laid and cheer him up. At the club, Renshaw even approached a woman and introduced himself as a terrorist, but as he would tell Preston Crown Court the following June, he really had little interest in women.

For Mullen the moment was surreal. The calmness over three hours during which all of his fears and the others' dreams seemed to be playing out in front of him, made him spin. Many of the group would later claim in court that it was drunken talk, but between them they had only 15 drinks in three hours, while Mullen drank just coke. Andy Clarke, the barrack-room lawyer, visited the toilets on numerous occasions during those three hours to powder his nose. Helm, who was working with the government's Prevent programme, said nothing about the plot until he was arrested for alleged membership of National Action in September 2017.

Mullen, as per our rules and instructions, extricated himself from the situation once the others were set on nightclubbing. He made his way home nervous, confused and panicked. He didn't ring 999: what was the point? The lads would all be pissed by now and the local police would pay no real attention to a bunch of drunks – and that lack of understanding over what was at stake could prove as fatal to Mullen as to the MP and the police officer.

As we spoke I went over the information twice with Mullen. I was confused. For a start, I asked, "Who the fuck is Rosie Cooper?" We argued that maybe it was Yvette Cooper, the Labour front-bencher and head of the Home Affairs Select Committee, that Renshaw had meant. She'd been targeted by National Action twice before.

Mullen was now in deep trouble, bordering on trauma. "He's gonna kill the MP, really soon, immediately!" he shouted. "His local MP, Rosie Cooper from Skelmersdale." For a minute I was struck dumb and panicked. My missus wouldn't take well to a murder breaking out on her sunbed watch. I had to ring Nick Lowles, HOPE not hate's chief executive. For the rest of the day there were panicked and cautious phone calls. Lowles made me drill Mullen for more information, but a call had gone in to Ruth Smeeth, the Stoke North MP to get the Parliamentary police to contact Cooper immediately. We all bit our lips and nails; the tension was horrendous. Lowles had never met Mullen but we both agreed whatever happened, we would look after him come what may.

We all spent the whole day, the three of us, on the phone in dazed conversations. We'd sort of expected an act of terrorism, we'd seen so much evidence that it was likely imminent, but little Jack Renshaw?

The last call of the day was late in the evening. Mullen was walking his dog, feeling miserable alongside the canal. The whole weight of the world was on his shoulders. We now had to discuss the inevitable. Other than Lythgoe's "Don't fuck it up", the words I remember the most, is having to tell Mullen that it was all over. If someone's going to kill an MP and a police officer, there's no way those revealing it can simply disappear. We were all going to end up in court.

"I know" he said, "Just look after me."

"A man has been charged by North West Counter Terrorism Unit and Lancashire Constabulary.

"Jack Renshaw (03/06/95) of Bearncroft, Skelmersdale, has been charged with two offences contrary to Section 18 of the Public Order Act 1986 – using threatening/abusive/insulting words or behaviour or displaying written material with intent/likely to stir up racial hatred.

"He was bailed to appear at Preston Magistrates' Court on Thursday 27 July 2017.

"This relates to comments made at an event in Yorkshire in February 2016 and Blackpool in March 2016 and comments made on social media."
– Man charged by North West Counter Terrorism Unit', Greater Manchester Police website, 3 July 2017.

***

On Tuesday, July 4 Nick Lowles made a statement containing information from myself and Robbie Mullen in the police offices in the House of Commons. Ruth Smeeth, the MP for Stoke North who Lowles had first notified of the threat, accompanied him. As per our agreement, Robbie Mullen wasn't named. My holiday was over. My missus packed in an angry silence.

Rosie Cooper had changed her planned routine and been given security. Jack Renshaw was meant to report to police on both July 3 and 4 to answer bail for inciting racial hatred and for child grooming. He didn't show up and the police didn't know where he was. On July 4 the police started kicking down doors in the hunt for the potential murderer.

Renshaw was eventually found at an address in Skelmersdale on July 5, along with his machete. His father's doors were put through; he later complained it cost £204 for a locksmith to repair the damage.

After leaving Parliament, still not knowing what lay in store for all of us, Lowles rang me. "I've just been told by the police that Jack Renshaw is also up for child grooming." It all made sense to us now.

Back in Runcorn, Mullen was in a state of confusion and fear. We had no idea of knowing what the police were going to do next. For Lowles, the problems were just beginning. On July 5 he attended a meeting at the Home Office. Presenting to the group, the police assured the meeting National Action was finished, was no longer active and was no longer a threat. Lowles bit his lip, but people were going to be angry with us. What an absolute humiliation that Lowles had sat through the presentation in silence without saying a word. What could he say?

Almost immediately we came under huge pressure from the police's Counter Terrorism Command (CTC) in London. It was as if they resented us having the information ahead of them. We had somebody active in a group they'd assured themselves, and now the Home Secretary, had disbanded. Understandably, the police wanted to talk to Mullen so he could help them prosecute Renshaw. However, HOPE not hate had a duty of care to our source and we insisted on an immunity agreement, whereby he wouldn't get prosecuted for what he told them. The police were none to discreet when it came to letting us know they were pissed off with us, either.

We knew the establishment had reacted because Rosie Cooper was safe and Renshaw had been arrested. We wanted Mullen to be part of the process. We'd been resolute in believing that. But was it too much for us to want some kind of assurances he wouldn't be prosecuted too? The police initially rejected this offer and insisted we pass him over to be interviewed immediately:

"In mid-July I received a call from a Detective Sergeant at Counter Terrorism Command who told me we were "out of our depth" and we needed to pass our source over to them. He also added, in what I took was a threat, "Of

course, as I'm sure you know, by handling a source from within a proscribed terrorist group you've broken the law under the Terrorism Act."

When I asked him for a contact number, he replied he wasn't allowed to talk to journalists and he had no interest in speaking to me again – unless it was for me to hand over the name of our source." – Nick Lowles, HOPE not hate

HOPE not hate took legal opinion and the news wasn't good. We were informed that under the Terrorism Act there was no protection for journalists and their sources. With no cover, we were advised it was only a matter of time before we had to hand over the name of our source or leave ourselves open to potential prosecution.

***

Rather disturbingly, Mullen took the news that Lowles and I were facing going to go to prison as a good thing. He seemed positively delighted at the thought that "Lord Lowles", as he called him, would be taking art classes at the Scrubs. Mullen had grown up thinking entering prison was an inevitable rite of passage for young men. We spent a long time dissuading him it had to be inevitable.

Mullen was resigned to the fact he might have had to go to prison for membership of National Action, but rather darkly and understandably queried: "I saved two lives, right?"

The reality was now hitting home with Mullen. As a precaution we gave him money and instructions to get himself a passport. He'd never been on a plane in his life, but I didn't really give a toss what anybody thought about that. Mullen had to continue inside National Action while all this took place. Worse was, of course, the police knew it would be somebody close to Renshaw in the North West. The light relief was they knew who none of them were. We had to get Mullen into negotiations and get the rest of the gang off the street. As far as they knew, Renshaw had simply been arrested for his speeches again, but how long would that remain a secret?

Only a week after the murder plot, the group met in the Piccadilly Tavern in Manchester, where Mullen saw, among others, Person B and Radoslav Rekke. To compound things and make them even more confusing and stressful, Alex Davies – who'd been anointed Lythgoe's deputy – launched a secret bid for the National Action's leadership, asking Mullen and Hankinson to help unseat Lythgoe. Mullen feared there'd be a bloodbath. Since the Home Secretary's ban, Hankinson had taken a severe dislike to Lythgoe. We photographed them all meeting up outside the train station.

National Action had growing concerns about their own safety and liberty. On July 26, Renshaw's father, in response to a worried query from NA about both his son's state of mind and the safety of the group, told McCartney, Lythgoe's chauffer and bodyguard, that one of the group inside NA "was plod [police]." Terror broke out inside the gang. At this point, nobody knew about Renshaw's other charges, related to child sex grooming. Raymond encouraged the rest of the group to disassociate themselves from Renshaw, telling the 'Pewdiepie Fanclub' secret chat group on 29 July 2017:

> *"I hate to say it but I really am finding it hard to sympathise as he has done absolutely nothing to help himself from start to finish, it is almost like watching suicide by cop. However I don't think he would be the type to rat or to go on some counter-extremism program. He already did everything conceivable (sic) to become a normal human, to ask him to do that again when they took that away forever would be too much for anyone's pride. Besides he was never ever in the loop guy was basically independant (sic). He will either do his time or hang himself imho."*

By the end of July, Mullen had been to see a solicitor, paid for by HOPE not hate, who made an arrangement for him to be interviewed by Counter Terrorism Command at a secret location for two days. His case was hopeless. There was still no offer on the table and surprisingly, as well as being humiliated and shouted at during a two-day interview under caution, they asked very little about the Renshaw case. At times, it felt as if it was HOPE not hate that was being investigated, not National Action. The police said horrific things to Mullen, threatened him and bullied him throughout. When they returned him after two days, he was traumatised. So too was Mullen's solicitor. He told us he had never seen an interview like it.

Mullen, Lowles and I met and discussed the interview. The police were close to losing Mullen, who now had a passport and the names of people overseas who would put him up and look after him. Our own doors were potentially hours from being put through by the police.

On August 1, after much arguing with Lowles, he agreed to us firing a shot across the bows; we ran a story that hit the international headlines. *"Exclusive: Nazi Terror Group Back on The Scene"* with pictures of National Action's Warrington gym, naming and shaming Lythgoe for being the gang's leader, along with other juicy bits of gossip. Now every fucker went into a panic.

It was a huge risk and that's what Lowles didn't like about it. But rather than argue about it any more, we went shopping for ties to wear in court for our own potential sentences (code for getting drunk). Lowles and I were picking out ties when news came through that there was an offer of limited immunity on the table for Mullen if he made a full disclosure to the counter-terrorist police. But the harassment didn't end there. Mullen refused to go into police protection and just about everything that could be plugged in was taken away from his house. The house itself was turned upside down and once more he was dragged away for two days. This time his solicitor put his foot down. He was certain the police were trying to recruit Mullen, while Mullen steadfastly refused. Despite the whole world now knowing where the gang's headquarters was, the police in Warrington carried out a raid on the wrong location, instead raiding a keep fit place National Action had used once or twice the year before.

Inside National Action there was real horror at the thought of a mole, worse still, potentially two moles – an HOPE not hate mole and a police mole – in their midst. Mullen was now juggling police harassment, our expectations and the increasing paranoia inside the gang. NA's leaders thought they were looking for two different people. If they found the HOPE not hate source, they decided, they'd murder him. They had a plan to take the person out to the woods and set fire to the body and bury it in acid. They were potentially very thorough. The police mole was just to be beaten up. Worryingly, Lythgoe had gone into a trance, wracked by revulsion and anger, barely able to speak.

Raymond, now almost an unpopular joke, offered advice on what to do about the leaks, writing as 'bloodnija88' to the group he wrote the day after our Warrington story:

"Consider this warning a grace. These HNH idiots really are morons. Until Jack's trial they'd have had somebody in the group who could continue to watch from the inside. The trial will probably demoralise people and provide quotes – but sending an email weeks before you can publish allows everyone to prepare for the worst and prevent further damage. Plus, it also spoils the big reveal. If you're HNH surely you want as much exposure as possible – door step someone, turn-up at the gym, do a world in action; something a bit more jucier (sic) than the previous ITV piece. Rather than write a story their aim is more to break up the north and shut down operations, sow distrust, etc."

Things really took a queer turn very quickly. Hankinson decided at possibly the worst juncture in proceedings to replace Lythgoe as leader. With there having been no terror attacks as yet by National Action, he was certain Lythgoe was the police grass and Helm was the HOPE not hate mole. Alex Davies' plan to oust Lythgoe in his own favour was also rubbished. Davies's first act was to completely cut off all funding to Lythgoe and the gym.

We watched aghast as the previously impenetrable gang turned on themselves, splitting into microcosms. For a brief moment it appeared that everyone had decided they wanted Helm, the Satanist clown, dead. It didn't help that Helm was suddenly telling people we'd offered him £400.

His timing was almost suicidal as well as inaccurate. Person B, Hankinson, Davies and Mullen agreed to meet in Manchester to see what was the best course of action. In the meantime, Lythgoe suggested his laptop had been hacked by HOPE not hate and that all of the information leaking out was done by HOPE not hate staff entering his home at night while he slept. Just what fucking planet were these people on?

Mullen and the others agreed to stop meeting at the gym and installed Hankinson as temporary leader. Lythgoe went into a massive panic and began issuing threats. Time was running out for everyone.

**

On August 10, Clarke threatened to rape my mother after we published another blog revealing information about the group. Person B sent a dire warning of what would happen to the person leaking information. He also issued a warning to Raymond that if his cowardice continued he'd be the last person left in National Action. The group was finally crashing. Now we just had a waiting game.

It appeared that London's Counter Terrorism Command wasn't interested in the Renshaw case and was being shadowed by Lancashire Police, who were handling the Renshaw investigation. In all, Mullen would be interviewed for more than 70 hours. Now we had to worry about the safety of the complete idiot and Satanist, Helm. Lythgoe emailed Mullen on August 27 with his suspicions:

> "Yes. I'm pretty certain it's Garron. No-one else had access to all the info passed over to HnH, or the personality to even contemplate doing something like this (as manifested with his Satanist(sic) and insight roles shit.). Plus there are screenshots of him saying he was considering doing an 'interview' with HnH in exchange for money. But what possible angle could HnH have had with an 'interview.' Clearly if they were wiling (sic) to pay him cash it would have been in exchange for info, and he's on record as considering it. It's vital however, that Garron does not believe that we suspect him, as that will make it next to impossible to smoke him out. The official story should be that we believe antifa got access to the info through hacking my laptop."

On September 5 everyone was rocked when police carried out raids across the Midlands against Deakin's crew. We had to check among ourselves that it wasn't the Warrington lot. It would appear it was only after information gleaned from Mullen's interviews that Deakin's phone was given a proper forensic examination. On doing so, the police felt they'd hit the jackpot. The group had been stockpiling bomb manuals as well as weapons. The police hadn't tipped off Lancashire police, either. Their greatest worry was that a number of serving soldiers involved with National Action in the Midlands were about to be shipped out the country, so they had to act.

Other raids followed in the region, causing a massive dumping and burning of materials across the country, particularly in Warrington, where Lythgoe was still meeting with a few old and new National Action recruits at the gym, awaiting the next move by Hankinson's faction.

Lythgoe was no longer receiving a stipend from National Action and, in panic, he very quickly signed up to work at a warehouse around the corner from his home. He still kept on trying to persuade Mullen and Hankinson to come back to training and meetings, but they both refused, saying it was too dangerous. We genuinely feared Lythgoe and others would instigate violence against what was now a rival faction. Bizarrely, despite all the paranoia and threats, and the no small matter of the world knowing it was the headquarters and training centre of an outlawed terror group, when he wasn't working, Lythgoe kept the gym open and running. He just continued with it. A steady stream of people kept visiting for training and instruction. At the very least It didn't appear to dawn on any of them, that with Renshaw in prison, those party to his plot would soon be arrested in relation to the charge too. This was a heavy burden for Mullen.

The different police forces seemed to have made no co-ordinated efforts to inform each other about the raids; valuable evidence was probably lost as National Action members dumped as much as they could. What a chance was lost.

One of those arrested in the raids in the Midlands was Paul Hickman, the former BNP man and one of the very early voices in National Action. Hickman would take his own life in November 2017 rather than face trial.

On September 21, the heavily-pregnant Claudia Patatas, the Portuguese national living in Banbury, Oxfordshire with a penchant for swastika cushions, was googling for 'best crossbow for apocalypse.' Adam Thomas, her waif-like husband had been convinced the end was near, that it was the end for their little excursion into terrorism too. She'd been googling on the HOPE not hate website for news and updates about National Action. There were none. We'd removed the entire history of the group from our servers.

On September 26, officers from London's Counter Terrorism Command drove to Runcorn and picked up Mullen from his desk at work. He slunk in the back of a car with darkened windows and wished the world would swallow him up. Mullen was now without his solicitor. This was just never going to end. He cursed himself and me, he cursed National Action and most of all, the police.

In a nondescript room in a nondescript building that seemed to have no other occupants, he sat in a room with a man and a woman plainer than paper. They informed Mullen that if he went into police custody/protection, they'd pay his then current salary for two years. He refused. Mullen was exhausted, antagonised and confused. When would they ever arrest the people who plotted to murder an MP and a police officer? He was dropped off home in silence just after midnight. He wondered if he'd die. Later that morning, Warrington erupted. On the same day it was announced the mirror groups of NA, 'NS131' and 'Scottish Dawn' were now also proscribed organisations, the police finally hit the North West gang as part of operation Harplike.

"Counter terrorism police raided a property on Greymist Avenue at around 6am this morning, Wednesday, as part of a national investigation into banned far right group National Action. Two men from Warrington, aged 31 and 35, have subsequently been arrested on suspicion of preparing a terrorist act, funding terrorism and being a member of a banned organisation. Across the country, 11 people were arrested following searches of 11 properties as part of coordinated activity between police in the north west, north east, Wales and Wiltshire." – Two men arrested on suspicion of preparing a terrorist act after police raid house in Woolston, *Warrington Guardian*, 27 September 2017.

***

People in Warrington were almost relieved with the arrests. There'd been an air in the town that something had been going on under their noses, that terrorists and race-haters had been travelling to their neighbourhood to train. The odd bits of graffiti, the endless stickers, weird boys dressed in black hanging around the train station had all been explained when HOPE not hate had revealed the secret gym. It wasn't just for the money Lythgoe had rushed himself into a job, it would also give him cover.

The chat groups and messengers became silent. The pinging and buzzing ceased completely. One by one the groups were deleted as the entire leadership of National Action were having their doors kicked in. It was the sudden silence from the phone that proved so disturbing for Mullen. In the time he'd been passing information to us, some five months, he'd sent on thousands of messages from these group chats. By 8am on September 27, the groups had all vanished.

Mullen and I watched the police raids unfold, messaging each other when we could name another person we knew by their location. A helicopter was deployed for the raid on one home. It would take them three days to sift through Lythgoe's home, his mountain of note pads and endless books on the art of terrorism.

Neighbours of the arrested, taking to Twitter, made for the best reading. Mullen rang in sick for work. There'd be no more sick pay. As he quite clearly wasn't going to be raided, he felt at somewhat of a loose end. I said I'd come up and we'd go to Manchester and hide out in a hotel bar for the evening. I worried he'd take the names he had and fuck off to the airport if I left him on his own. It looked like the harassment of the day before had been his final invitation to jump onboard with the police.

Shortly after 10am Mullen's phone rang. He didn't know the number. It was Chris McCartney, Lythgoe's chauffeur and bodyguard. Two other members were on their way to Poland and Ukraine. McCartney mumbled and put the phone down.

The police entered Mullen's workplace after lunch looking for him. He'd been waiting at home for at least a pretend 'nicking'.

At 4pm the police went to his home and knocked impatiently. One of the team presented him with an Osman warning, meaning there was now a credible threat to his life. Having shown him the warning and him having acknowledged being shown it, they were gone. The minute I heard from Mullen, I headed for Euston train station.

By 8pm that evening, Mullen was switching cars in the pissing rain at Runcorn Station, all his worldly goods stuffed in a sports bag. His dog was taken care of. The rain was furious and the street lighting not the best. We'd blocked the road as he ran out of home into the back of the car. We drove through the deserted, dimly-lit streets until we found the second car, jumped into that and then we too were gone. The only words were everyone in agreement they'd never seen or experienced rain like it. It was just as it is in the movies.

Mullen lay in the back of the car, along the floor, in silence, not saying a word. It was a fucking awful drive. I had very little idea what I was going to do with him. For him, the world was ending.

"The past year has been stressful and even traumatic, not least for Robbie Mullen, who has had his whole life turned upside down. He had to walk out of his job, leave his home and go into hiding. He has not been able to get another job due to being flagged up on a terrorist watch list and has lived with the constant fear of being hunted down by his former National Action friends.

His situation wasn't helped by the attitude of the police, who initially tried to exert pressure on him to leave HOPE not hate and go into their custody. In front of a Thompson's solicitor, who we instructed to represent Robbie, police officers from London bad-mouthed HOPE not hate and told him not to trust us.

On the day of the National Action arrests a police officer from London arrived at Robbie's Runcorn home to issue him with an Osman warning, explaining that there was a credible and serious threat to his life. They then left. Disorientated and confused, it was left to HOPE not hate to pick him up within hours to move him to a safe location. He is still under our care, now.

Within weeks, we were given a personal apology for our treatment by the Counter Terrorism's Head of Operations North West and from then on all our contact with the police was directly with North West CTU and Lancashire Police. It was courteous, professional and good and the results of which has led directly to the imprisonment of leading National Action members and, more importantly, saving the lives of Rosie Cooper MP and DC Victoria Henderson." – Nick Lowles, writing in July 2018.

CHAPTER 22: I NAME THIS CHILD, ADOLF

"An alleged member of the banned neo-Nazi group National Action has admitted to plotting to kill a British MP for "white jihad" and making threats to kill a police officer. Jack Renshaw, 23, of Skelmersdale, Lancashire, bought a 48cm (19in) gladius machete to kill the West Lancashire Labour MP Rosie Cooper last summer. Afterwards, he planned to take hostages to lure a police officer, DC Victoria Henderson, to the scene so he could kill her too, jurors heard.

"On the opening day of his trial at the Old Bailey on Tuesday, Renshaw pleaded guilty to preparing acts of terrorism and making threats to kill a police officer. The judge, Mr Justice Robert Jay, directed the jury to deliver a formal guilty verdict on the two charges. Renshaw also faces a third charge of membership of National Action, which he denies."

'Alleged neo-Nazi admits plotting murder of MP Rosie Cooper'
– The Guardian Online, 12th June 2018

L ife in hiding wasn't easy on Robbie Mullen. In many respects, it was all over now and all we had to do was wait for the court proceedings to begin, but the terror arrests would continue and misunderstandings would also continue. We tried to settle him into a home life, moving him between hotels, taking him on holiday, but even getting him onto a plane was becoming difficult.

On a trip to visit my Uncle Gerry in Ireland, Robbie and he spent three hours together watching the football in a crowded pub while I sat feeling so absolutely empty that I had put him into a life of limbo. No amount of throwing credit cards at the problem would go away or that he was sinking into a massive depression.

Upon his return from Ireland he was questioned; who did you meet there? What did they say? Was it another extremist group Collins was introducing you to? In the three hours he and Uncle Gerry had sat together watching the football, chatting amiably about Manchester United, it transpires, as Mullen would tell the police, nether could understand a word the other was saying.

The same in Amsterdam: staring aimlessly at tits in a shop window, missing his dog and their long walks along the Manchester Shipping Canal, even smoking expensive cigars out of hotel windows whilst watching English tourists fight with drunken Germans did little to lift the gloom. The word was out at home in England and there would be people who would kill him. People were saying he and we had taken a drunken conversation in a pub and stitched up poor Jack Renshaw.

By Christmas we rectified one of his problems. We moved him across the country again to another new town and reunited him in a cottage with his dog. Unfortunately, we barely had enough money left to buy it biscuits. Between Lowles, HOPE not hate and I, we were exhausting all our monies. My hair was falling out in the shower and my partner barely spoke to me. None of us could sleep and now the police and the Crown Prosecution Service were beginning a forensic sweep of every conversation, ever biscuit and cup of tea we'd shared.

Every receipt, every bus fare was being checked. We had to stop spending money. Mullen volunteered to find a job. He applied for dozens, he received plenty of offers of work too. Each time it went to the reference agency for checking, he got knocked back. He had no criminal record, but his name was flagged up as a terrorist in some darkened room somewhere. He couldn't even get a new bank account. It was humiliating and degrading. He'd done nothing wrong but admit he was a terrorist, as he was told to by the police. He was punished for doing the right thing.

In desperation, we turned to our solicitors, the trade union firm Thompsons. Their partners agreed to pay Mullen's rent out of their own pockets. They even gave him legal aid. We came close to making redundancies. My partner found my credit card statement and took the scissors to my card. Nick Lowles went begging for money from donors without saying too much about what it was for. Like Kevin Maguire says in the foreword, they all had an idea that Robbie Mullen was our man. We gave him a job with us.

Whilst Mullen was struggling, there was good news for Claudia Patatas and Adam Thomas. Despite large swathes of their gang being incarcerated, baby Adolf was born in November. They donned Ku Klux Klan outfits along with their friend Darren Ferguson (formerly Stephens and Clifft), and posed with the baby. And with machetes and crossbows. Prevent had been to the home just before the baby was born because they were concerned Patatas may be an extremist. They were arrested for membership in January 2018. Their child, it was alleged, had never been bathed in water, instead the couple used babywipes to clean him. The reason being that they allegedly believed the water supply was poisoned (by Jews) with fluoride.

In January 2018, Jack Renshaw, still awaiting trial for the plot to murder Rosie Cooper and DC Victoria Henderson was convicted for his two speeches:

"A self-confessed Nazi who called for the genocide of Jewish people has been jailed for three years.

The 22-year-old Lancashire man, who cannot be named for legal reasons, was found guilty in January of two counts of stirring up racial hatred.

Preston Crown Court heard he committed the offences in speeches at far-right gatherings in 2015 and 2016. Judge Robert Altham said the defendant's comment had been "intended to mobilise others".

He said the intent of the man, who was involved with the now banned group National Action, was "clear". Judge Altham said: "He seeks to raise street armies, perpetrate violence against Jewish people and ultimately bring about genocide."

He said they were "not idle comments said in the heat of the moment" and he was "resolute in his original views and withdraws nothing".

'Shocking and inflammatory'
The judge described an apology submitted in mitigation as "meaningless" at best, and "dishonest" at worst.

He sentenced him to 18 months in prison for each offence, to be served consecutively.

The court heard the defendant had described Jewish people as "parasites" and called for them to be "eradicated" at an event in Yorkshire.

At another demonstration he claimed Britain "took the wrong side" in World War Two.

The court heard the defendant also said: "You can call me a Nazi, you can call me a fascist, that's what I am."

Judge Altham said material discovered by police at his home was "as shocking and inflammatory as it is misguided".

Wayne Jackson, defending, said his client wasn't making excuses for his behaviour and had been "impressionable in the past". – BBC News Online, 18th April 2018

Whilst his first trial drew lots of his supporters, Renshaw invited none of them back for his next visit to the Preston court. It was only a month before 'Lythgoe and others' were due before the world-famous Old Bailey in London.

The National Action conspirators were continually moved and shifted around the country in pairs to keep them apart. Renshaw was also constantly moved in and out of prison for a variety of other hearings. As he was an alleged terrorist, he was afforded some respect from prisoners who had to be locked down when they moved him. Despite all his previous bravado, Renshaw never once played up his long sought infamy. He would be leaving prison a dead man if those prisoners knew he was also going to hearings about his alleged obsession with young boys.

A gang of six: Christopher Lythgoe, Garron Helm, Andrew Clarke, Jack Renshaw, Matthew Hankinson and Michael Trubini (Lythgoe and others co-defendant and signatory on the lease of the gym) were set for trial in June both for membership of a proscribed organisation and the plot to murder Rosie Cooper. Other than Helm, the others had made very little comment in their statements worthy of note. Helm had made some twelve pages of comment.

Just days before Renshaw was due in Preston to face four charges on child sexual exploitation (CSE) at the end of May, Nick Lowles received a phone call. Renshaw was going to claim it was HOPE not hate that engaged online with young boys. HOPE not hate, as part of some massive Jewish plot, had managed to hack Renshaw's phone and ruin him and his political career. Lowles had to give a statement. Despite independent experts appearing as witnesses saying this was impossible, Renshaw was prepared to challenge their expertise with his own, based on a summer he spent working for a mobile phone retailer. There was also the threat of subjecting a young boy to cross-examination. We knew there wasn't anything Renshaw, who'd once called for paedophiles to be hung, wouldn't do to stop news of his crimes being found out. That included murdering Rosie Cooper MP and DC Victoria Henderson, investing him for CSE.

As Lowles was preparing to head to Preston to refute this nonsense, Renshaw backed down and changed his story again. He was found guilty on June 1 2017 of four offences, including encouraging or inciting boys aged under the age of sixteen to engage in sexual activity, between September 2016 and January 2017. Other charges related to the sending of pictures. As he was sentenced to a total of four years added onto the earlier convictions for inciting hatred, his father shouted across the courtroom "Love you, Jacko." His father had been convinced all and every charge against his son, in particular to murder the MP, formed a part of some greater conspiracy against him.

By the time Renshaw was to stand trial at the Old Bailey later that month, he was (not quite) officially, a "nonce." Mullen was delighted, but nobody could be told in case it prejudiced Renshaw's terror trial for the plot to murder Rose Cooper.

For Mullen it was vindication that despite all his hardships and understandable self-doubts as he languished in his own personal hell, that these people, these fascists, were a danger to all decent people. That had already been proved, the endless "banter" about raping and seducing children by National Action wasn't just bad taste jokes. As Renshaw was led into court later in the month, it was everything we could do to stop Mullen shouting "Nonce!" as he smirked at him from the defendants' glass box.

London was in the middle of a massive heatwave and the World Cup was upon us. We were all living with our phones switched permanently off.

Every newspaper in the country wanted to tell Robbie Mullen's sexy story for him. The three of us, Lowles and Mullen and I, weren't allowed to talk while we were still to give evidence. Internally the case was being billed by the police as National Action vs HOPE not hate. Having said that, Lancashire Police were gracious and helpful.

National Action were going to prove we were part of a massive Jewish conspiracy. Everyone one of the six pleaded not guilty to their charges, which, they protested, were part of the plot. It was daunting, some of the flashest and finest QCs in the land were going to prosecute and defend the case at the magnificent Old Bailey.

Renshaw and Lythgoe were shackled as they were driven into court and even when they sat in the dock. The jury weren't allowed to see the shackles. The police picked Mullen up every morning from a hotel to make his way into court whilst Lowles and I nervously took public transport. On his first day Mullen's car was surrounded by press and he hid behind a jacket the police placed over his head.

On the opening day of the trial, Renshaw, possibly still terrified he would be unmasked as sex offender while sitting with the other defendants, threw a lifeline to the other five; he changed his plea to guilty on charges of preparing acts of terrorism and making threats to kill a police officer. Everything went slightly crazy. His defence was more than a little stunned by the decision. He would deny, however, being a member of National Action after its proscription. He wanted to stay and fight with the others.

Renshaw would antagonise and shock the court with the great pleasure he took in revealing the intimate details of his plot and his sickening hatred of Jews. Bizarrely the case would continue, going over the evidence against Renshaw anyway, in an attempt to link him and the others together as members of National Action.

Mullen gave evidence for three and a half days. Lowles and I for half a day each, in a trial lasting six bruising weeks. Mullen was targeted mercilessly by the defence for his class, his education and upbringing. They certainly didn't hide how they felt about him. In one exchange he was as good as accused of being thick and unable to read. We all had our eyes open to just how brutal, dirty and bordering on dishonest insinuations made by learned friends could be. Certain newspapers took great delight in reporting every snarling exchange and one newspaper even twisted what Mullen said to make him sound like he was still a committed neo-Nazi and race-hater.

But he wasn't beaten down. He never wavered, never buckled and never did he falter. One QC continually mocked his accent, claiming he was too quiet or that they couldn't understand him. Mullen was visibly shaken by the experience. There wasn't anything sacrosanct or decent about it.

By the second week we had a sneaking feeling Lythgoe would get away with encouraging Renshaw to act. It was one prosecutor versus several defence barristers after all, but there were what we felt cruel omissions from the massive pile of evidence. Added to the confusion was the fact the prosecution and defence had prepared so much on Renshaw's now-admitted terror charge that it became a constant distraction and point of reference.

Of the defendants, Hankinson appeared every day beautifully turned-out. The others wore prison attire, Lythgoe's even with an egg stain on for two days. When Mullen gave evidence, Helm, who'd made much in his statement that Mullen had replaced him in the role of Liverpool organiser, appeared to be trying to summons some kind of wild beast to attack him. All would shoot Mullen 'death stares' except for Hankinson, who could barely bring himself to look at his former friend.

For Lowles and I it was similar. Renshaw smiled at us while both of us could sense Clarke trying to grab our attentions. From the corner of my eye on a number of occasions I spotted Helm's bizarre behaviour. One journalist told me "never mind the terrorism and the Jew baiting, I've never seen a more angry, disturbing bunch of people in my life."

Whether they looked like hardened wannabe terrorists or not, I couldn't decide. In our society we are told they have brown faces, anyway.

After given evidence we spent the rest of the trial in a series of cafes with free wifi and bottles of cool drinks. Small numbers of Nazis would appear in our eyeshot outside the court, including NA founder Ben Raymond, looking dazed, desperate and confused wandering the streets outside the 'Bailey with a rucksack, drawing on cigarettes and looking lonely. They were being humiliated.

"Jurors were told Lythgoe reacted to news of the ban by telling members that they'd "just shed one skin for another".

Mullen, who became disillusioned with the group, began leaking information to Hope Not Hate, and a significant amount of evidence came from him.

The defendants denied being members of National Action. Lythgoe's lawyer, Crispin Aylett QC, suggested Mullen had implicated National Action because he was "in the pocket of Hope Not Hate" and it was what they wanted to hear. Mullen denied this.

Renshaw was accused of being a member of National Action along with Lythgoe, Hankinson, Andrew Clarke, 33, Michal Trubini, 35, and Garron Helm, 24.

The Jury failed to reach verdicts on Renshaw, Clarke and Trubini.

In his sentencing, Mr Justice Jay said that, under Lythgoe's leadership, National Action meetings continued on a "modest" scale. They kept alive "an aspiration which was truly insidious and evil – the idea that this country should be purged of its ethnic minorities and its Jews, that the rule of law should be subverted, and that once the ideological revolution had taken place this national socialist worldview would triumph", he said.

"The idea that there could be such a triumph without violence is arrant nonsense, despite the weasel words to the contrary."

The judge added: *"Fortunately, and I can take this into account to some extent in the defendants' favour, the truly evil and dystopian vision I am describing could never have been achieved through the activities of National Action, a very small group operating at the very periphery of far-rightwing extremism.*

"The real risk to society inheres instead in the carrying out of isolated acts of terror inspired by the perverted ideology I have been describing."

Det Supt Will Chatterton, head of investigations for counter-terrorism policing for the north-west, said outside court that the verdict had enabled the spotlight to be shone on the activities of the group.

"Today's result is a body blow to extreme rightwing organisations such as National Action. It sends out a clear message that counter-terrorism officers and partner agencies will rigorously identify and investigate any violently extreme individual or group who seek to bring a reign of terror to our shores." – 'Two members of banned neo-Nazi group National Action jailed' – Guardian Online, 18th July 2018

Helm walked free. We'd have to go back and finish the job in February the next year.

EPILOGUE: THE FIGHT GOES ON

Robbie Mullen made his television debut the night after the first trial ended. Hastily filmed, still reeling from his ordeal at the Old Bailey, he equipped himself well for a thirty-minute Channel Four *Despatches* programme about the plot to kill Rosie Cooper.

Life went on and trials of National Action members continued to grab the headlines, none more so than the curious case of Adam Thomas and Claudia Patatas, who named their baby son after Adolf Hitler.

At their trial the judge said National Action's aims and objectives "are the overthrow of democracy in this country by serious violence and murder and the imposition of a Nazi-style state that would eradicate whole sections of society."

Addressing the media's obsession with the couple he told them: "You acted together in all you thought, said and did, in the naming of your son and the disturbing photographs of your child, surrounded by symbols of Nazism and the Ku Klux Klan."

Thomas, who'd been a security guard, and Patatas, who claimed she was a wedding photographer, held hands and wept as they were sentenced to six years and six months, and five years respectively for being members of a terrorist group.

Jurors saw images of Thomas wearing Ku Klux Klan robes while cradling his baby, which he claimed were "just play", but he admitted being a racist.

He was also found guilty of having bomb-making instructions for which he was given a two and a half year sentence to serve concurrently. A police search of the home he shared with Patatas uncovered machetes, knives and crossbows, one kept just a few feet from the baby's crib, swastika-shaped cutlery and swastika scatter cushions.

Earlier the court heard how Darren Fletcher, who'd moved back to the Midlands and into the neo-Nazi movement out of sheer desperation, had trained his infant daughter to perform Nazi salutes. In a desperate attempt to impress Patatas he sent her a message saying "Finally got her to do it".

In all, at the time of writing, there are thirteen people linked to National Action in prison and more still awaiting trial.

This hasn't allowed us to sleep easier or even take a break. Whilst awaiting the second trial for membership, Jack Renshaw, who wasn't sentenced for admitting the plot to kill Rosie Cooper, tried to vacate his plea – change his mind. He changed his mind on that too, though.

We kept digging to see where the next set of neo-Nazi terrorists would come from. The more we dug, the more we found. As with every group that came after National Action, the point at which NA had finally crumbled was the point at which another new generation would pick up the disturbing and distorted baton and run with it, further.

Unlike its alma mater, Sonnenkrieg Division (SKD) didn't develop a disturbing nihilist ideology like National Action, but was born with it. Tying themselves with the US-based group Atomwaffen SS (AWD) which surpassed National Action with its sicknesses for pornography, rape, violence and five murders, SKD had boiled itself down completely after splitting from the second generation National Action group, System Resistance Network (SRN).

The SKD had been followers of National Action and some had interacted with them online. It obsessed about Satanism, Nazism, paedophilia and rape. In fact, these were central, philosophical themes and ideology to SKD.

In National Action, much of the flirtation with the occult was driven by the search for spiritualism some felt would help them further develop the concept of a White Jihad, one assumes to counter the fear of dying. The court cases in Birmingham of NA activists also gave a slight insight into prevailing ideas around sex with minors that had developed in some members of NA overtime.

Whilst some of the early National Action statements were the products of a wholly unrealistic and underdeveloped sense of what was achievable legally in Britain, the AWD realised some of the potential in particular in arming itself and establishing cells of supporters directed by secretive internet discussions.

AWD, like NA, would also encourage Islamic conversion (or, most likely 'imitations') under the guise or form of 'Insight' as suggested or demanded by Satanic cults like Britain's Order of Nine Angles. AWD also explored the idea of encouraging its members and supporters to use rape and sexual violence against opponents, encouraging its followers to read up on and explore child rape. Aligning themselves with the US group which had completely surpassed NA's own objectives, the British group, SKD held rape, paedophilia and sexual violence as a central tenet of the group. A large selection of SKD's outpourings encourage rape, paedophilia and murder. Sodomy was also a disturbing and repetitive theme. SKD also adopted and mastered much of the communication apparatus and technique first experimented with by NA during both its legal and illegal carnations- most importantly in keeping a strict code of secrecy and anonymity.

When SKD was exposed by a brilliant BBC investigation and arrests of its members made in December 2018, the main headlines focused on the group's charge that Prince Harry, grandson of the Queen, should be murdered for marrying a woman of colour- race mixing. What was less re-reported was the group's fixation with rape and sexual violence. The BBC did report on the fixation members of the group had with self-mutilation and that they shared still images of one female supporter being scored with a knife by one of the group's male members. What the police and counter terrorist officers found when investigating SKD so disturbed investigators they apparently opened a parallel investigation into the activities of the Satanist group, Order of Nine Angles. During the course of our investigations into SKD, one associate of the group attempted to pass us information he hoped would incriminate an individual linked to the group and potentially interfere with an ongoing legal process. In December 2018 one member of SKD pleaded guilty in court to two counts of encouraging terrorism, while another member was charged with five counts of encouraging terrorism and three counts of disseminating terrorist publications – related to the documents and posts including the titles *'Slaughter Women'* and *'They feed you lies from the tablecloth'*.

On February 19 2019, Mullen and I walked back into London's Old Bailey to finish the job started the night in July 2017 when, above a pub in Warrington, Jack Renshaw revealed his plans to kill an MP.

Michal Trubini, Andrew Clarke and Jack Renshaw had all pleaded not guilty to membership of National Action.

CONCLUSION

On Feb 19th 2019, in court nine of the Old Bailey, Robbie Mullen once more took the stand. Jack Renshaw, Michal Trubini and Andrew Clarke sat in the dock looking impassive. Renshaw had already pleaded guilty the year before to preparing acts of terrorism in relation to threats to life against Rosie Cooper MP and the police officer Victoria Henderson. Now it was the supposedly simple matter of whether they had been members of the proscribed organisation National Action.

Mullen accounted well of himself. The boy done well. Methodical and softly spoken he went through the cross examination without a hitch. The time between trials may not have been kind to him, but it was clear that any last possible vestige of loyalty to the group or those friends he had once had in it, was gone.

So well was Mullen doing that Nick Lowles and I were not required as witnesses.

Jack Renshaw did not give evidence. Andrew Clarke the barrack-room lawyer, did give evidence. Clarke asserted he was just a loveable rogue and that National Action's humour had somehow been lost on the general public. He claimed HOPE not hate had ruined his life and he just wanted to meet a nice lady. The court was shown a Facebook status by Clarke calling the Jewish MP Luciana Berger a 'Christ killing cunt.' Trubini was almost comical in his own defence.

The prosecution of other alleged NA members had never been our concern, but the convictions were mounting. There was an almost ache that this trial would end and then we could tell the whole story about Renshaw the paedophile and his plans to kill women. But on and on it dragged as the jury could not agree a decision as to whether Renshaw, Trubini and Clarke had actually been members of National Action at the time when Renshaw revealed his plot above a pub in Warrington.

It was during the many hours (over forty-six in fact) whilst waiting for the jury, that Robbie and I decided this book would be the only way to tell the story of the murder plot and the full story about National Action.

It was not until the 2nd April that the jury finally came back with the news they could not reach a verdict. There would be no further convictions in this trial. By then, Mullen was on a plane out of the country and Nick Lowles and

I had exhausted ourselves climbing the stairs at the Old Bailey to listen to the jury being sent home every night.

Lowles and I popped champagne across the road from the court. Trubini and Clarke were free men, but Renshaw was looking at a life sentence to go on top of his other convictions for inciting hatred and child sexual exploitation.

For Robbie Mullen the struggle that is finding a new life is just beginning. An MP and police officer are still alive because of his actions.

For the rest of us the fight goes on.

TERMS OF REFERENCE

ANTIFASCIST

Term for individuals or organisations opposed to the ideas and apparatus of fascist or Nazi groups or individuals and in defence of democratic ideals. A broad based term that applies to people across the political spectrum. In the United Kingdom the antifascist movement is actively embedded within the Labour movement.

ANTIFA

A broad term for people who are active in combatting or challenging fascists and fascism. For the purpose of this book, the term is used to describe specifically the militant, autonomous antifascist groups or individuals.

FASCIST

A person gripped by an irrational fear that society is beyond (their) control. **Fascism** is often difficult to categorise specifically because it has specific cultural traits or tones that may vary in different countries or continents, or indeed, in different individuals or groups.

To characterise however, it is broadly identified as those who violently fear or feel their privilege is being undermined, and in the call for the curtailing of the democratic process which is responsible for or in crisis. There is often a strong dependence or reliance on military and militarism to counter this "crisis". Fascists tend to identify and organise or favour themselves by the wearing of uniforms and by rallying to or behind particular symbols, symbolism or strong willed individuals.

Fascism strongly opposes the organisation of workers or organisations which may seek to challenge by democratic means the health, wealth and conditions of individuals other than themselves or their likeminded social and economic groups. Fascists are often depicted as racists and reliant on a series of falsehoods and conspiracies that have a strong or extreme nationalist flavour in favour of one group to the detriment of others.

Fascists obsess about the creation and the control of capital. To this end, and in the case of fascist and extreme far-right groups that operate in the United Kingdom, these groups often exhibit a strong belief in conspiracies that all wealth is created and held by secret societies and bodies. These tend to form the basis of anti-Semitic/Islamophobic conspiracy theories and beliefs. For the purpose of this book, all of the far-right groups mentioned herein are designated fascist.

MOSLEYITE

An admirer or follower of British Fascist leader Oswald Mosley (1896-1980.)

NEO-NAZI

Used in reference to organisations, activists and individuals post-war that are adherents of the philosophies and aims of the German Nazi Party often forming or joining similar organisations to the Nazi Party or idolising the Nazi regime, in particular Adolf Hitler. As a footnote, neo-Nazis find the term, although correct, somewhat insulting, preferring to be termed National Socialists. For the purpose of this book, some activists or individuals are referred to simply as 'Nazis' or 'Nazi'.

NAZI OR NAZIS

Members or activists of the original German Nazi Party, the National Socialist German Workers' Party 1920-1945. For the purpose of this book, some activists or individuals are referred to simply as 'Nazis' or 'Nazi'.

WHO'S WHO

ATOMWAFFEN DIVISION
US based neo-Nazi terrorist group that modelled itself on National Action. Heavily influenced by Satanism and the occult, the group were the chief exponents of the 'White Jihad' ideal. Thought to be responsible for some four murders.

AZOV BATTALION
Neo-Nazi paramilitary group active in the Ukraine.

BELL, ASHLEY (1991-)
Aka Tommy Johnson. Former English Defence League and National Front activist from Leeds, West Yorkshire. Led National Action temporarily.

BELL, WAYNE (1980-)
Heavily-scarred and violent thug from Wakefield, West Yorkshire. Also known as Wayne Jarvie, Bell was sent to prison in 2018 for posting racist and anti-Semitic material online. Was responsible for the infamous 'Jo Cox tweet' after her murder.

BERGER, LUCIANA
Former Labour MP for Wavertree in Liverpool. Persistent target of anti-Semitic abuse.

BRITAIN FIRST
Confrontational far-right group that made a name for itself by exploiting social media and carrying out confrontational stunts. Formed in 2011 by former BNP members, it predicts a violent and biblical clash between Christians and Muslims.

BRITISH NATIONAL PARTY (BNP)
Formed in 1982 after a split from the National Front. Led by founder John Tyndall (1934-2005) until he was replaced by Nick Griffin in 1999. Under Griffin's leadership the BNP enjoyed considerable growth picking up a number of council seats and two MEPs. The party went into massive electoral and financial decline after the 2010 General Election. Griffin lost his seat as an MEP in 2014 and was dumped by the BNP soon after.

BRONS, ANDREW (1947-)
Former leader of the National Front 1980-1984. Brons was the BNP's MEP for Yorkshire & Humber from 2009-2014. During this period in office he and Nick Griffin fell out leading to Brons unsuccessfully challenging griffin for leadership of the BNP.

BLOOD & HONOUR
Nazi music umbrella group that quit the National Front in the mid 1980's. Closely aligned in some countries with Combat 18.

CALVERT, SHANE
Leader of the North West Infidels.

CLARKE, ANDREW (1984-)
Known as National Action's barrack room lawyer. Vicious anti-Semite.

COLLETT, MARK (1980-)
Former leader of the Young BNP. Controversial character caught in an undercover television sting. Arrested on the eve of the 2010 General Election for allegedly making threats to kill Nick Griffin.

COMBAT 18 (C18)
Formerly the BNP's security wing. Morphed into a separate entity late in 1991, focused on fomenting a race war. Violent and unpredictable, the group turned on itself after a failed letter bomb campaign. In 1997 an intermediary between two factions was murdered in Essex. The group is mainly active on the continent now. Two factions remain in the UK, one loyal to Paul David "Charlie" Sargent, the other to Wilf "the beast" Browning.

COULSON, JACK (1999-)
Troubled teenager who obsessed about and celebrated the murder of Jo Cox MP. Was convicted of building a pipe bomb and later for possession of a document or record for terrorist purposes.

DAVIES, ALEX (1994-)
Former member of the Young BNP. Founding member of National Action.

DEAKIN, ALEXANDER (1994-)
Leader of the Midlands National Action group. Ran much of the terror group's internal communications in the Midlands. Was jailed for eight years and 16 months in 2018.

ENGLISH DEFENCE LEAGUE (EDL)
Formed in Luton by Stephen Lennon (who preferred to be known as Tommy Robinson) in 2009. A large anti-Muslim street movement at its peak, the organisation has splintered and split on a number of occasions. Now tiny, many of its radicalised former activists have gone on to join or form neo-Nazi groups.

FLEMING, RYAN (DOB UNCONFIRMED)
Paedophile and Satanist linked to National Action. Was twice jailed for sexual offences. Prolific author and fan of the Moors Murderers.

FLETCHER, DARREN (1990-)
Aka Stephens, Clifft and Christopher Philips. Former English Defence League and National Front activist. Was known as the infamous 'Klanman' who lynched a golliwog while dressed in Klan robes. Sentenced to five years in prison in 2018 for five breaches of a Criminal Anti-Social Behaviour Order (CRASBO) and for membership of a proscribed organisation.

GRIFFIN, NICK (1959-)

Former leader of the National Front and British National Party. Griffin made his name in the 1980s by exploring the radical concepts of fascism. A Holocaust denier and anti-Semite, Griffin was elected to the European Parliament as an MEP for the North West of England in 2009 while leading the BNP. He was dumped by the party in 2014.

HANKINSON, MATTHEW (1994-)

Known as the "posh one" from Newton-le-Willows in Merseyside. Hankinson made a speech in Newcastle in 2015 predicting there would be victims to come from NA's actions. Was convicted of membership of a proscribed organisation in 2018 and jailed for six years.

HELM, GARRON (1993-)

Gained infamy by being jailed in 2014 for sending obscene tweets to the Jewish MP Luciana Berger. A man of wild claims, Helm was also linked to the Satanist organisation Order of Nine Angles. Members of the group discussed murdering him for passing information to the police. Was acquitted of membership of the group in 2018.

HICKMAN, PAUL (1981-2017)

Early guiding hand to National Action, Hickman was formerly with the National Front and British National Party. He was edged out of position in NA after the group changed leadership. Committed suicide in 2017 only days before he was due in court.

IRON MARCH

Internet forum where National Action did its early recruitment and let the world know of its revolutionary prowess. The site closed not longer after NA was proscribed.

LYTHGOE, CHRISTOPHER (1986-)

Secretive and unknown leader of National Action until exposed by HOPE not hate in 2017. Ran the group's headquarters and gym in his home town of Warrington. Was sentenced to eight years for membership of a proscribed organisation in 2018.

LONDON FORUM

Also operates as the South West and Yorkshire Forum. Talking shop for those trying to reinvigorate British fascism. Principle people are Jeremy Turner and Larry Nunn.

LOWLES, NICK (1968-)

Cricket buff, occasional Leeds United fan and Chief Executive of HOPE not hate. Had the dubious task of reporting the murder plot to the authorities.

MISANTHROPIC DIVISION

Recruiting arm for the Azov Battalion, Ukrainian neo-Nazi militia.

NATIONAL FRONT (NF)

Formed in 1967, the NF is one of the world's longest surviving fascist political parties. Notoriously unstable and violent, the NF has split more than twenty times.

NATIONAL REBIRTH OF POLAND (NOP)

Polish neo-Nazi gang active in the United Kingdom.

NORTH EAST INFIDELS (NEI)

Splinter from the EDL active in Sunderland.

NORTH WEST INFIDELS (NWI)

A violent neo-Nazi splinter from the EDL based around towns in the north west of England. Notorious for its links to the drugs trade, NWI worked closely with the National Front and National Action.

NUNN, LARRY

Aka Max Musson. Former BNP organizer and financial advisor. Has pumped thousands of pounds into trying to rebuild the fascist movement in Britain.

ORDER OF NINE ANGLES

British Satanist group formed in the 1960s and considered one of the most extreme Occult groups in the world.

PATATAS, CLAUDIA (1980-)

Portuguese national and mother of the child known as Adolf. Took a central role in the Midlands group. Sentenced to five years for membership of a proscribed organisation in 2018.

RAYMOND, BENJAMIN (1989-)

Founding member of National Action. Controlled much of the group's publicity until it went underground. Was mistaken by many to be the leader of National Action.

RED ACTION

Extremely militant antifascist group that operated in Britain and Ireland during the 1980's and 1990's.

RENSHAW, JACK (1995-)

Former member of the Young BNP. Expelled from Manchester Metropolitan University, drifted into National Action where he earned a reputation for outrageous speeches. Was convicted in 2017 for two speeches inciting racial hatred and four counts of child sexual exploitation. In 2018 he pleaded guilty to plotting to murder the MP Rosie Cooper. Was convicted in 2019 for National Action membership and sentenced to....

SOUTH EAST ALLIANCE (SEA)

Confrontational splinter group from the EDL led by Essex-based Paul Prodromou aka Paul Pitt. Closely aligned to the National Front and the North West Infidels.

THOMAS, ADAM (1996-)

Former English Defence League and National Front activist who found God and moved to Israel. Thomas returned to the UK and fathered a child known as Adolf. Convicted of possessing information of a kind likely to be useful to a person committing or preparing an act of terrorism and membership of National Action. Sentenced to six years and six months respectfully.

TRUBINI, MICHAL (1982-)

Slovak national domiciled in Warrington. Was the signatory on the lease for National Action's rented property.

TURNER, JEREMY

Former army intelligence officer and National Front candidate. A leading light of the London Forum. Was jailed in 2018.

TYNDALL, JOHN (1934-2005)

Leader of the National Front for much of its heyday of the 1970s. He formed the BNP in 1982 having rejected the NF's insistence on electing its leader.

UNITE AGAINST FASCISM

Antifascist protest group.

WEBSTER, MARTIN (1943-)

Part of the infamous double act that led the National Front in 1970's. An openly gay man, nobody took issue with Webster's sexuality until he and Tyndall split acrimoniously in 1980.

WESTERN SPRING

Website and blog of the London Forum's Larry Nunn.